MASTERING HAWAIIAN SLACK KEY GUITAR

by

Mark Kailana Nelson

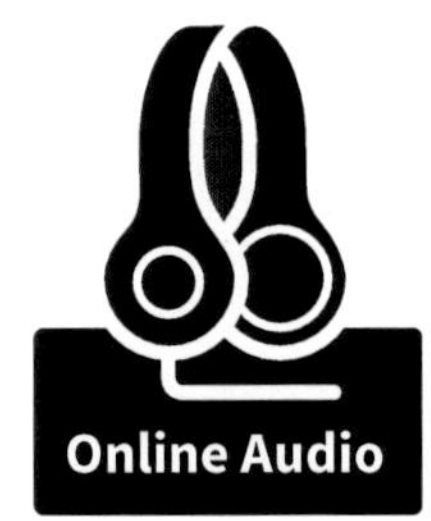

www.melbay.com/30666MEB

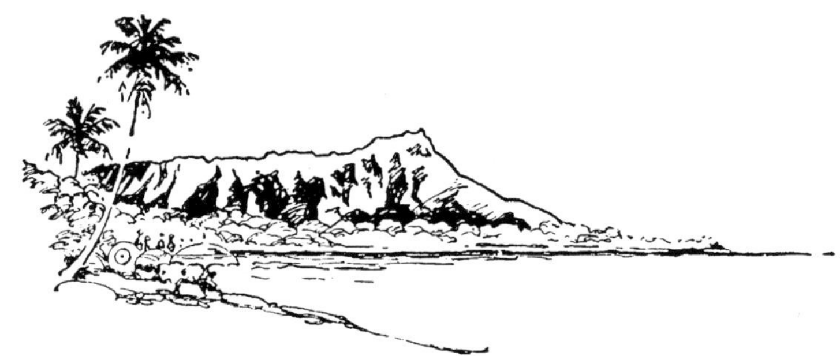

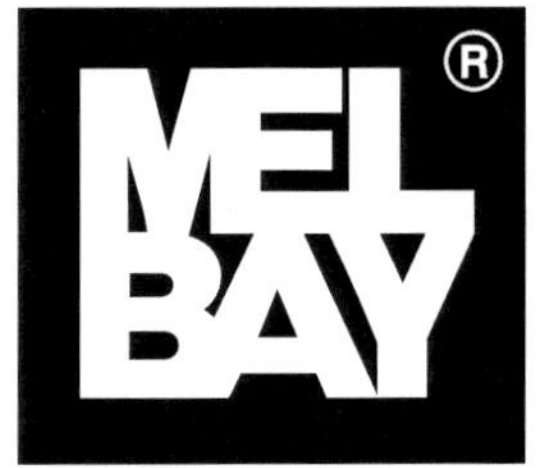

WWW.MELBAY.COM

Table of Contents

Aloha

When Keola Beamer and I sat down to write *Learn to Play Hawaiian Slack Key Guitar* in 1997, few people outside of Hawai'i knew what slack key was, let alone how to play it. So we decided to present a large number of short arrangements in a variety of styles and tunings. Our intention was to give the student a broad overview of the style and a good foundation for further study. In the twenty years since the publication of that book, thousands of guitarists have discovered the pleasures of *kī hō'alu.*

But one thing remains: unless you grew up playing slack key, it's hard to get from the material presented in most books and DVDs to a fluid, play-it-your-own-way style.

In this book I hope to offer some of the insights I have gleaned by playing with and learning from some true giants of the art. How do you go from a simple instrumental tune to a full-blown arrangement? What is the role of improvisation in slack key? How do two slack key guitarists play together? And what exactly does it mean when they say, "Jus' press?"

This book is not for beginning guitarists. If you know how to play some slack key – or other fingerpicked style – and are ready to tackle some fairly challenging material, you have come to the right place.

Kī hō'alu means "loosen the key" – it refers to retuning some of strings to create a harmonious sound. There are hundreds of slack key tunings, though most players stick to a few that define their personal style. Open tunings create a halo of sound around each note, the open strings vibrating in sympathy. Each tuning has its own characteristic sound and mood.

Some tunings include a full major chord, with the bass strings tuned to allow pedal harmonies on the tonic and fifth. "Wahine" tunings employ a major seventh interval, allowing the guitarist to use a hammer-on to move from the dominant chord back to the tonic. "Maunaloa" tunings feature two strings tuned a fifth apart; other tunings might have a sixth or other interval.

Although most players prefer steel-string acoustics, slack key may be played on any guitar. It is a fingerpicking style characterized by a strong bass played with the thumb. In fact, I was once reprimanded in my early attempts at the style by a noted Big Island guitarist: "It's not slack key if I can't hear the bass!"

That is not to say all Hawaiian guitarists play with the same style of bass. Some – notably Ledward Ka'apana and Uncle Ray Kane – favor the kind of steady alternating bass that appear in many of the following arrangements. Big Island guitarists like the late Sonny Chillingworth and Keola Beamer often employ a syncopated bass pattern based on the clave rhythm. And many players use their thumbs to play both bass patterns and melody notes. I have sat next to both Kevin Brown and John Keawe for countless hours and I have *never* figured out how they use their thumbs!

Melodies are often harmonized in sixths or thirds-sometimes played as double stops but more often broken up into single notes that are played out of double stop positions. Players incorporate slides and chimes (harmonics) in highly individualized styles. Another common feature is the use of hammer-ons and pull-offs, often in dizzying combinations.

Like most Hawaiian songs, slack key songs are concerned with love – love of the land, love of family and romantic love. Even when playing an instrumental, the guitarist brings forth the feelings inherent in the lyrics. Generally speaking, slack key is played at a languid pace with a slight swing – what the Hawaiians call *nahenahe*. Think about lying in the shade at the ocean enjoying the tropical breeze and you'll get the idea. But don't be fooled – some songs are best at a blistering tempo.

I would like to thank the many great Hawaiian musicians who have graciously shared their *mana'o*: Kevin Brown, John and Hope Keawe, Bradda Matt, Sonny Lim, Ozzie Kotani, Cindy Combs, George Kahumoku, Jr; Owana Salazar, Keoki Kahumoku, Jeff Peterson, Uncle Raymond Kane, Cyril Pahinui, Leilehua Yuen, Ke'ala Kwan, and the Beamer *'ohana*, among many others.

Even though I'm not from the tradition, shortly before she passed Aunty Nona Beamer said to me, "Please keep teaching Hawaiian music to everyone who wants to learn." I'm doing my best, dear.

Applegate Valley, Oregon
Winter 2018

How to Read Tablature

All of the music is written in standard notation and tablature for guitar. Tunings are given twice, once as the common name for the tuning, for example Taro Patch, and again as pitches immediately to the left of the first line.

In tablature, or TAB, the lines represent the instrument's strings, starting with the highest string on top. Fingering positions are indicated by numbers. TAB doesn't give any indication of how long to hold each note; for that refer to the staff above the TAB.

For example:

Taro Patch tuning

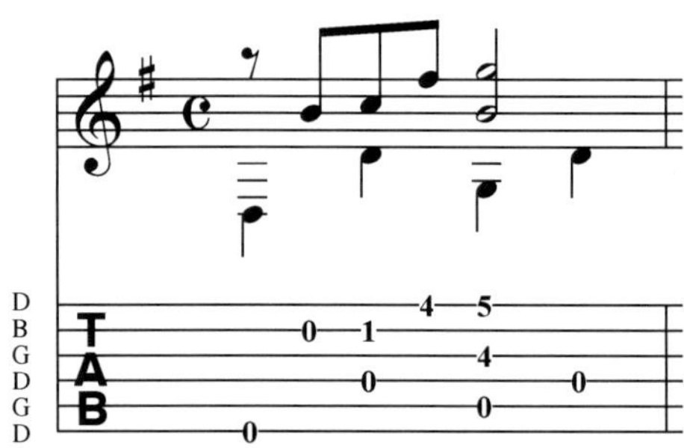

In this example you would play the open sixth string with your thumb before plucking the open second string. Then you'd play a pinch with the open fourth string and the second string at fret one, and so on. Pay attention to the direction of the note stems. Downward pointing stems are played with your thumb; upward pointing stems are sounded with your fingers.

Fingerings have not been indicated to allow each player to develop a personal style. Experiment with different fingerings to see what works best for you. Although some old-style slack key players use only one or two fingers to pick the strings, there is nothing wrong with using all three. Let your experience be your guide.

For the most part, I play with my first two fingers. For chords on three strings, I'll either use three fingers to execute a rapid arpeggio or brush up or down with one finger. The best way to approach these passages (and there are lots of them) is to listen to the recording and see what you come up with. Slack key isn't supposed to be played the same way twice – so feel free to experiment.

Here are some additional symbols you will encounter. The following examples are all in Taro Patch tuning.

Slide: Play the first note, and slide up or down to the next. Try to sound each note cleanly. As with all slurs, be sure to give each note its full value.

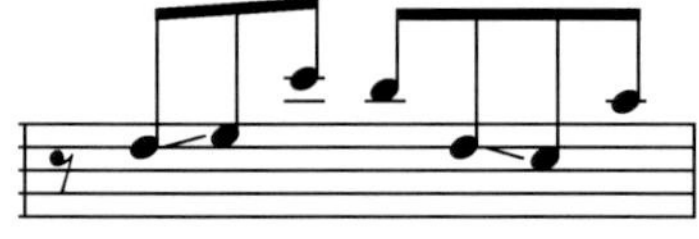

To ensure a smooth flow, play this example from these double-stop positions:

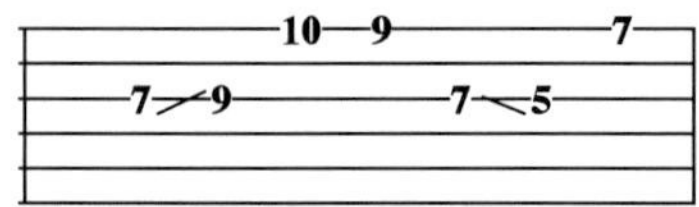

Hammer-on: Play the first note, then rapidly press your finger down to the fretboard to sound the second note. You can use a hammer-on to move to any higher note on the same string.

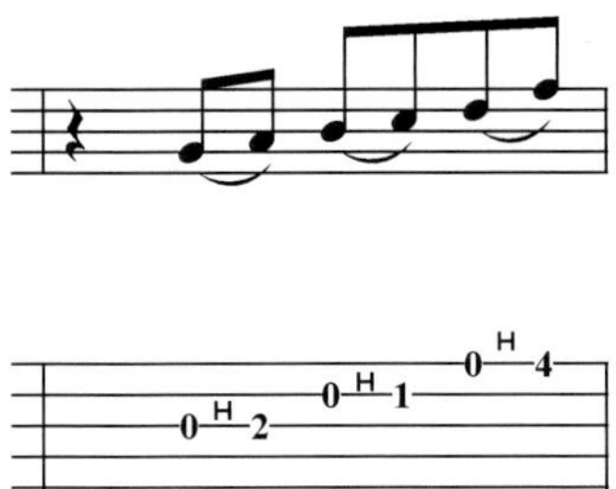

Pull-off: Play the first note, then quickly pull off your finger to sound the lower note. Use pull-offs to move down on any string.

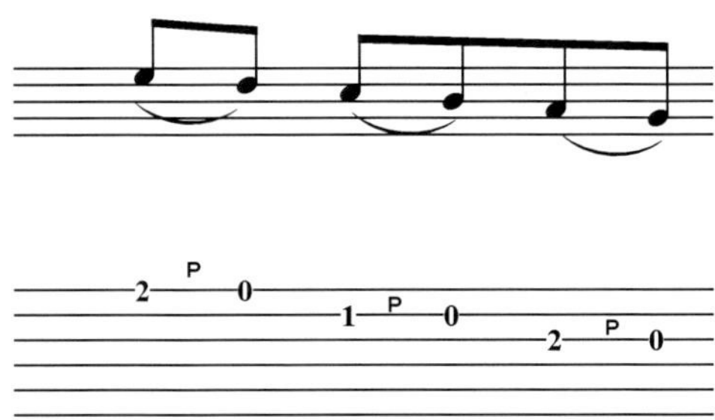

Hammer/pull combination: A common feature of slack key, this is a rapid combination of a hammer-on and pull-off executed as a quick flick of the finger. Slack key artists may combine hammers, pulls and slides (all technically called slurs in the music world) in bewildering variety. Mastery of these techniques is something so personal that an individual player can often be identified just from listening to their slurs.

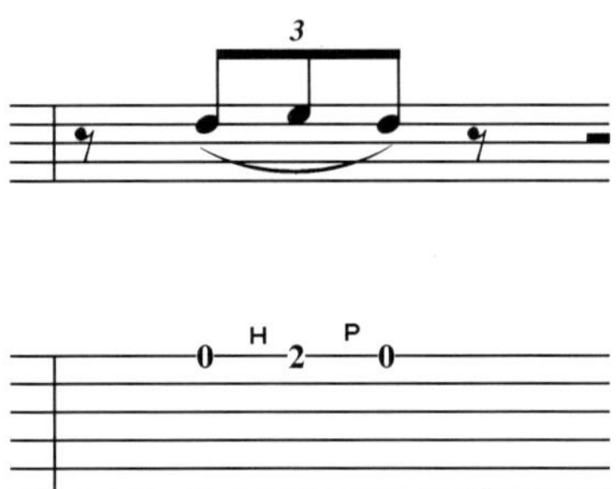

Harmonics: Also called *chimes* in Hawaiian music. Lightly touch the string directly over the fret to produce a ringing tone. Try moving your plucking hand back towards the bridge slightly to better define the harmonic.

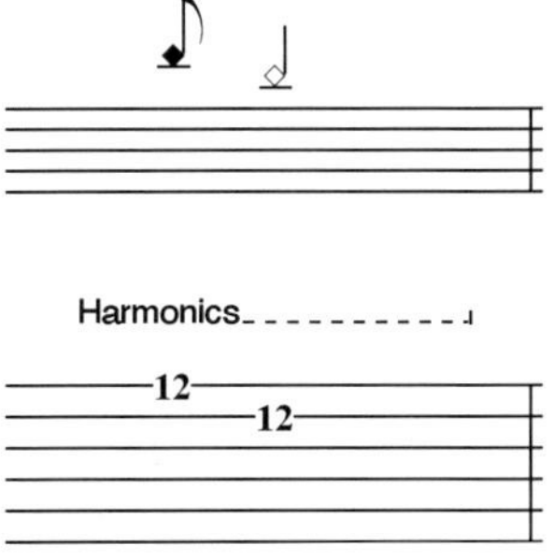

As you work through these songs, take note of how these various techniques are combined in different ways, often in the same measure!

I have provided detailed explanation where necessary. To facilitate page turns, sometimes these notes precede the TAB.

Tunings Used in This Book

There are literally hundreds of tunings used for slack key. No one plays them all; most stick to a few that they learned through their familes or friends. Of course, everyone has at least one special tuning that may only be used for a single song!

These are the tunings that I use the most. You will notice that a number are related in some way: you only need to drop one string to change keys from G – Taro Patch – to Drop C; handy when you are onstage. Likewise going from C Wahine to F Wahine requires a couple quick twists of the tuning keys.

All tunings are given from low to high.

Taro Patch D-G-D-G-B-D (also called "Spanish" among blues players.)
Taro Patch is probably the most common slack key tuning. Most people learning slack begin with this tuning, but don't think it is just for beginners. Uncle Ray Kane, Sonny Chillingworth, Led Ka'apana, and Kevin Brown all use this tuning extensively.

Double Slack D-G-D-F♯-B-D ("G Wahine," "Alice Namakelua's Tuning")
A wonderful tuning with a real old style sound. Tunings with a major seventh interval are called *wahine* after the Hawaiian word for *woman*. It's very easy to get to from Taro Patch; just lower the third string a half step.

Drop C C-G-D-G-B-D ("Leonard's C," after Leonard Kwan)
One of my favorite tunings. Also easy to get to from Taro Patch, yet it has its own unique sound.

C Wahine C-G-D-G-B-E ("Keola's C" after Keola Beamer)
The top four strings are the same as standard guitar tuning, which makes C Wahine a good entry point for many guitarists.

F Wahine C-F-C-G-C-E ("Leonard's F" after Leonard Kwan)
Dropping the three lowest strings really makes your guitar sing. Notice that you raise one string from standard pitch for this tuning.

B♭ Major F-B♭-D-F-B♭-D
Sonny Lim taught me this tuning a few years back; it offers some really interesting possibilities.

D Major Add9 D-A-E-F♯-A-D
I stumbled across this tuning when I was fooling around with the more common D Major tuning (D-A-D-F♯-A-D). Tuning the fourth string up a step from D to E allows you to play alternating bass notes in both the tonic and dominant chords.

C Mauna Loa C-G-E-G-A-E ("Gabby's C" after Gabby Pahinui)
In Mauna Loa tunings the two highest strings are tuned a fifth apart. The numerous different tunings in this large family are well worth exploring.

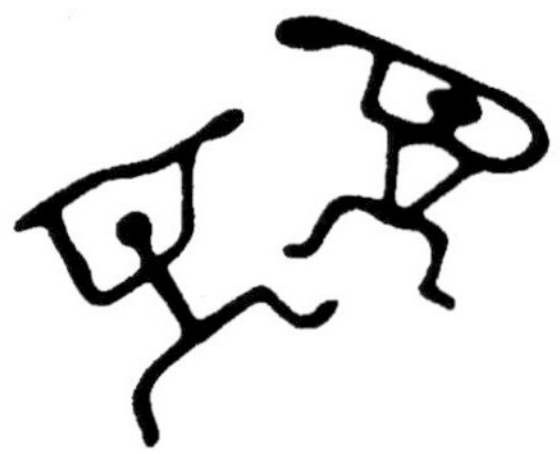

I recorded slightly different arrangements of "The Road to Duke's," "Sanoe," "Annie's Slack Key Lullabye," "Pua Sadinia," "Las Blancas Flores," and "Aunty's Christmas Goose"– along with a decidedly non-traditional setting of "Opihi Moemoe"– on my CD "The Water is Wide." Alternate arrangements of many other songs in this book may be found in *Old Time Hawaiian Slack Key Guitar*.

Part One: *Kani Kī Hōʻalu*
Taro Patch Tuning
D-G-D-G-B-D

These seven songs are designed to answer several age-old questions: How do you make a slack key arrangement sound like *you*? How do you take a melody from the page and turn it into something beautiful? How do you improvise? How do you create an original slack key piece? And how *do* you play well with others?

To begin, here are two common tunes often played at a *kani kapila* – jam session. Each is fun to play on its own and each has features that you might wish to add to your bag of tricks.

Gabby's Hula Medley

Years ago, just about everyone I knew played some version of this tune. This setting is the way I learned the piece; it is not a transcription of any particular recording. The arrangement is made up of three short unnamed tunes; after each new tune, go back and repeat the first one. Stringing together a number of short pieces into a medley is a time-honored slack key arrangement style.

Notice the flashy ending lick: I heard someone play this onstage and knew I had to steal it. I hope you do likewise.

Kolomona Slack Key

I got this great jam tune from Maui's Kevin Brown.

The following songs are presented as a series of lessons intended to demonstrate different approaches to finding your own style of slack key.

Lesson One: From Melody to Arrangement

Pua Sadinia

"Pua Sadinia" (The Gardenia Blossom) is a deceptively simple melody that can express great emotional depth. I present it in two versions. The first, a very simple statement of the melody and harmony, will give you the building blocks to create your own setting. The second arrangement shows one way to approach that goal.

Lesson Two: Creating Your Own Take on a Classic

Opihi Moemoe

When I was first learning slack key, the one thing everyone asked to hear was Leonard Kwan's tour de force "Opihi Moemoe." Sadly, it was beyond my ability at the time. So I studied his recordings til I could play it note for note. The next time someone asked, I was ready. After hearing me play, my teacher said, "Yeah, that's the way Uncle Leonard plays it, but how do *you* play it???"

To help you find your own way, I first offer a road map to the song. Next, I'll show you some variations you can plug in here and there, and discuss how subtle changes can have a large impact. Finally, I present a transcription from a spontaneous live recording I made some years back so you can see how to put some of those ideas into play.

Mahalos to Keʻala Kwan, Leonard's son, who gave me permission to teach this great song.

Lesson Three: Playing Together

Hawaiian slack key guitarists have a unique approach to playing together. Rather than strum chords, the backup guitarist will often play complimentary melody and harmony parts. Here are two arrangements that look into that style.

Kealoha

What a spontaneous accompaniment might look like.

Kimo's Slack Key

A duet-style arrangement with interlocking parts and role switching.

The Road to Duke's

The answer to the musical question: Why drive the Road to Hana?

Lesson Four: Some Thoughts on Composing

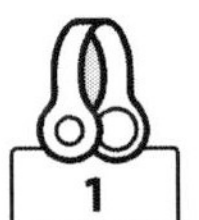

Gabby's Hula Medley

Taro Patch tuning

Traditional

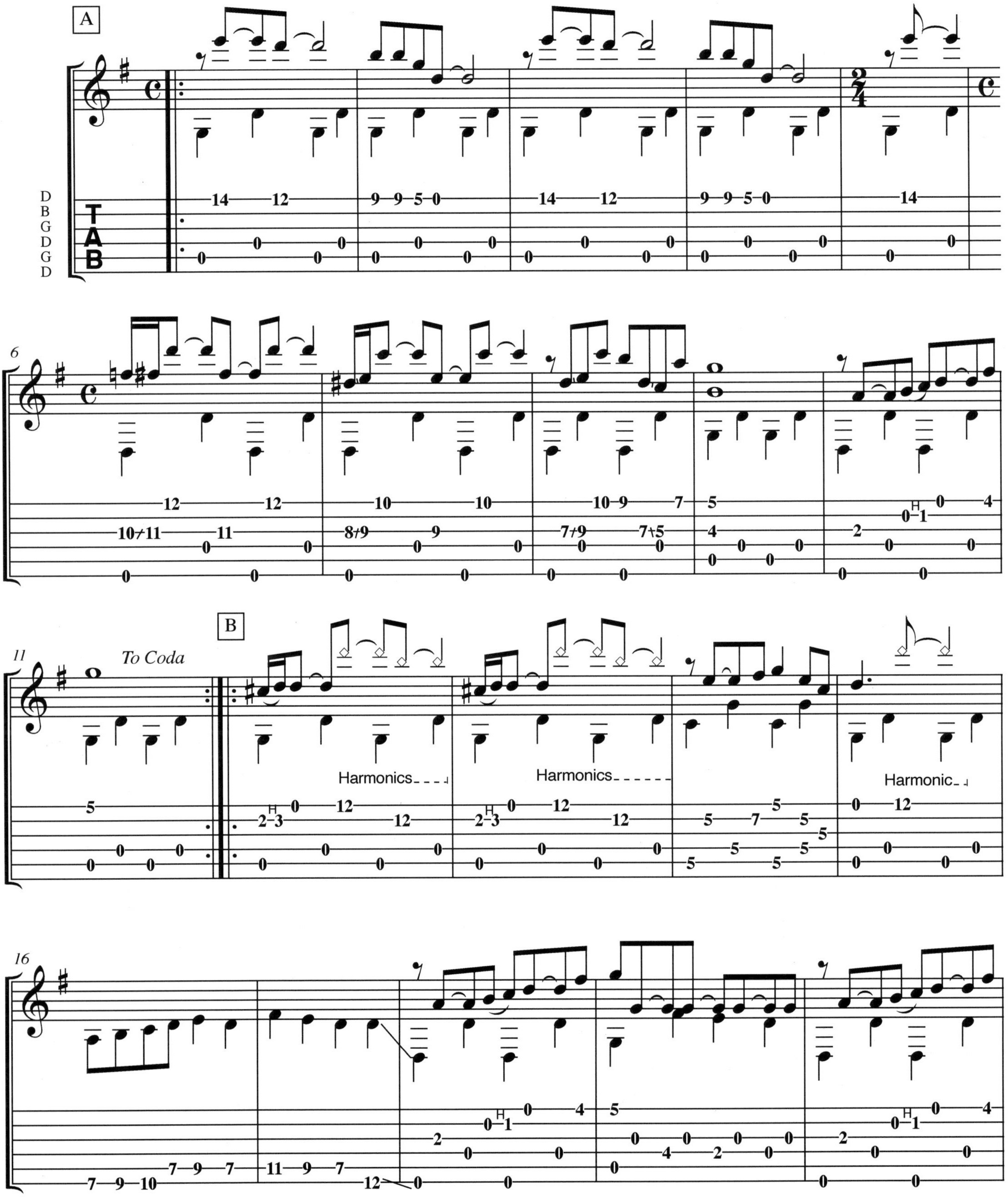

A

D B G D G D

6

11 *To Coda*

B

Harmonics

Harmonics

Harmonic

16

Go back to A, then jump to C

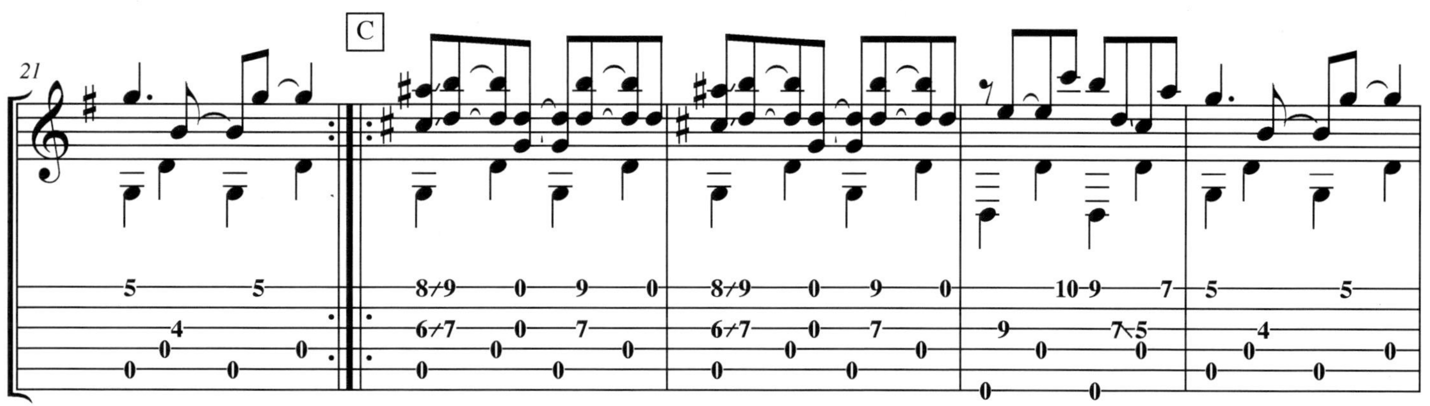

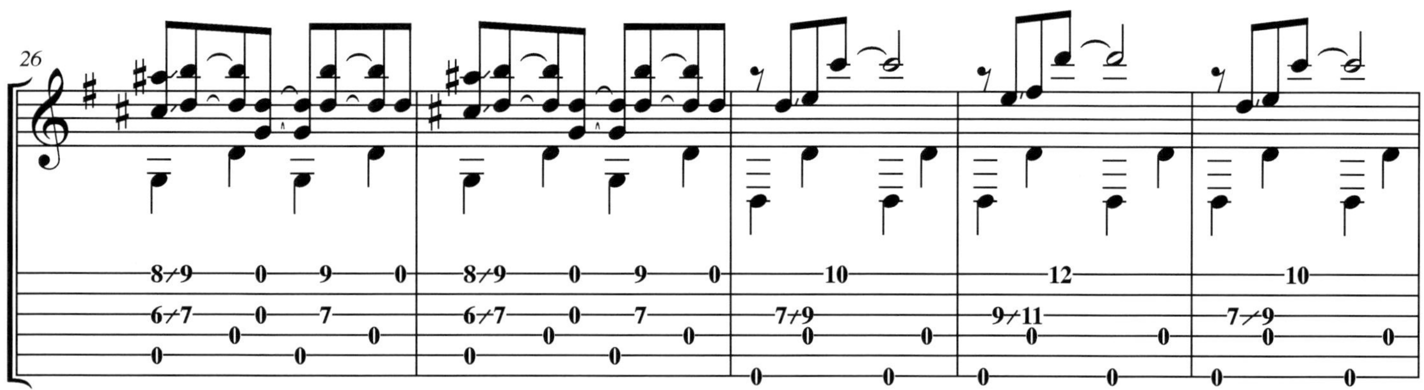

D.C. al Coda

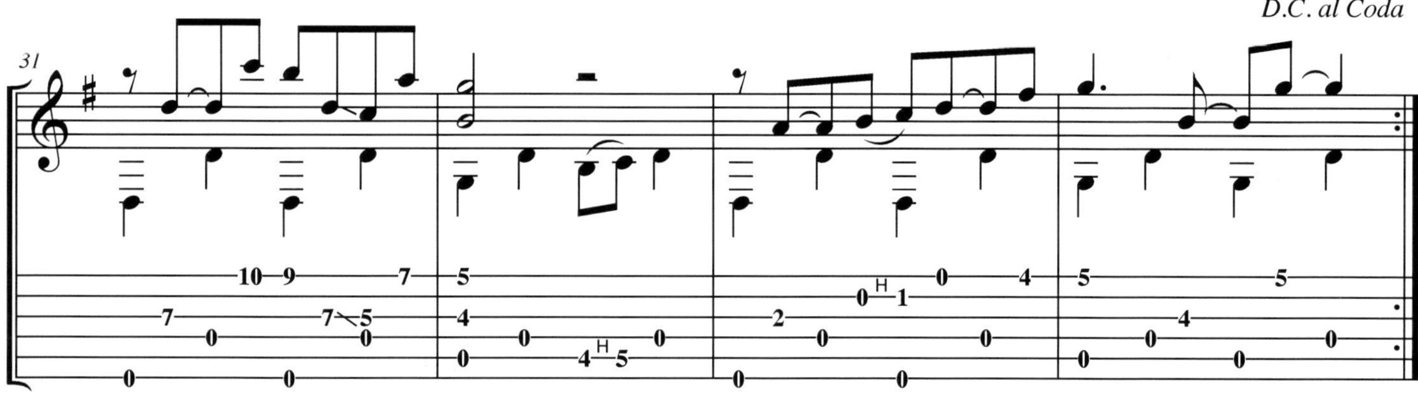

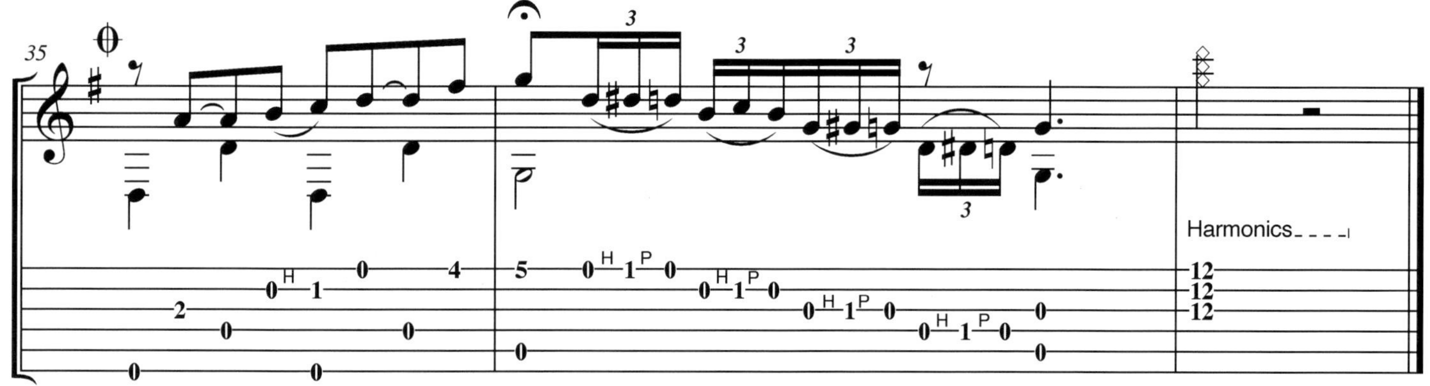

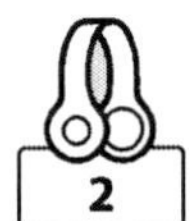

Kolomona Slack Key

Taro Patch tuning

To Coda

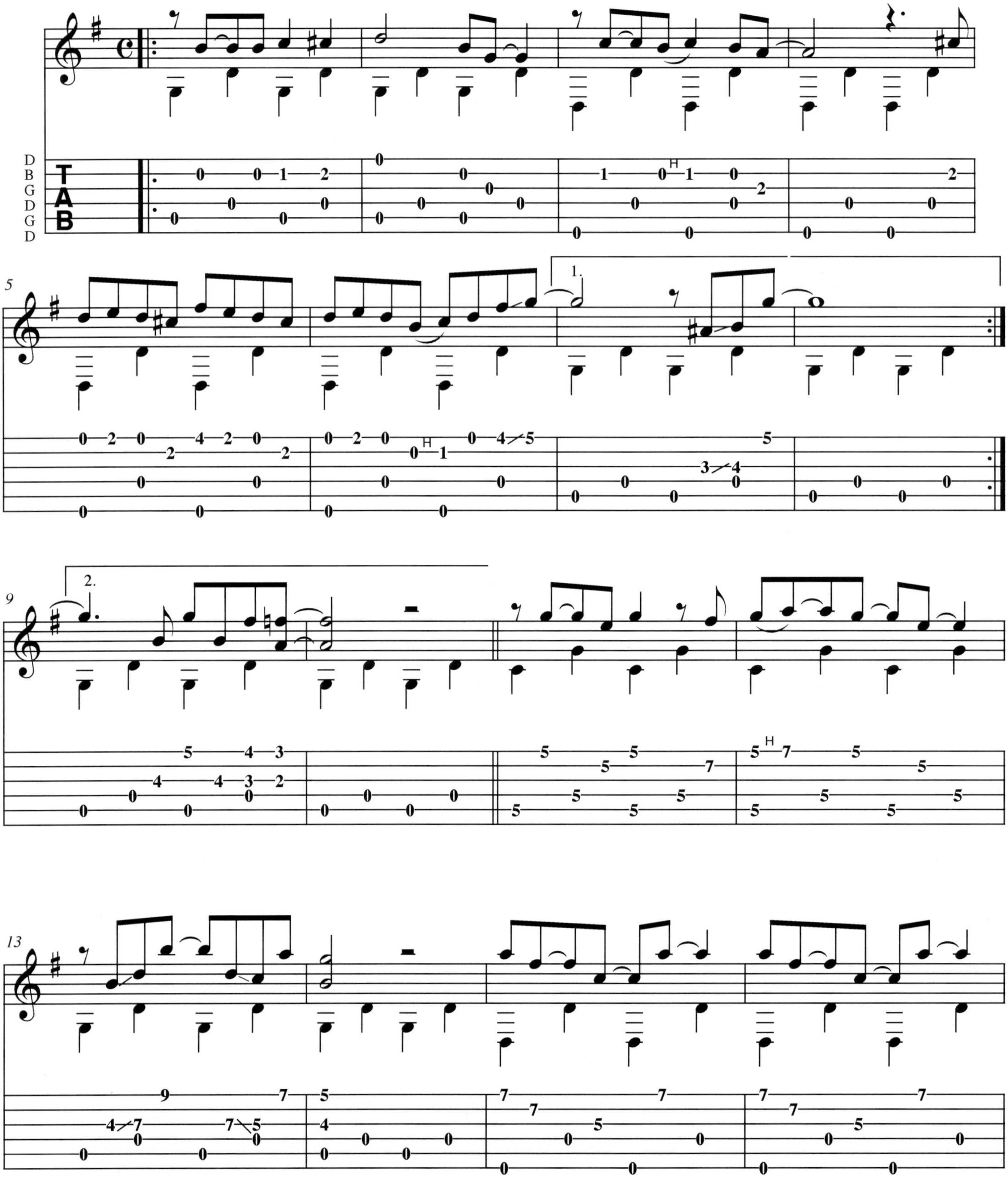

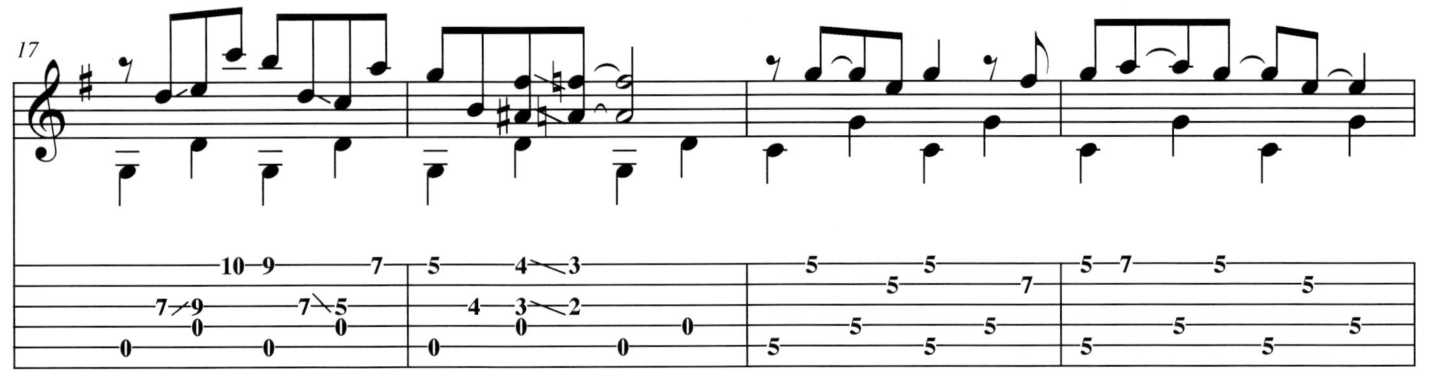
17
10 9 7 5 4 3
7 9 7 5 4 3 2
0 0 0 0 0 0 0
5 5 5 5 7 5 7 5 5
5 5 5 5 5 5 5

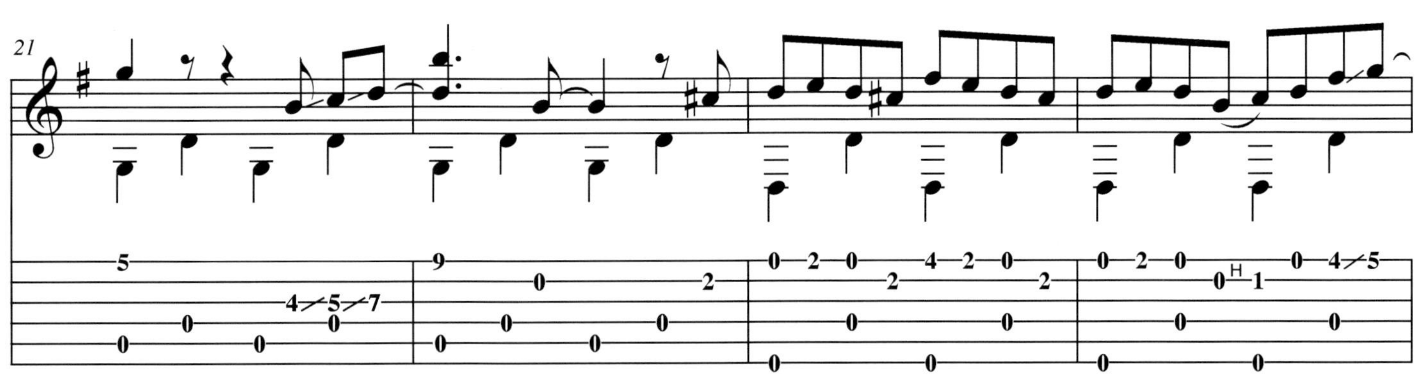
21
5 9
4 5 7 0 2
0 2 0 2 4 2 0 2 0 2 0 0 1 0 4 5
H

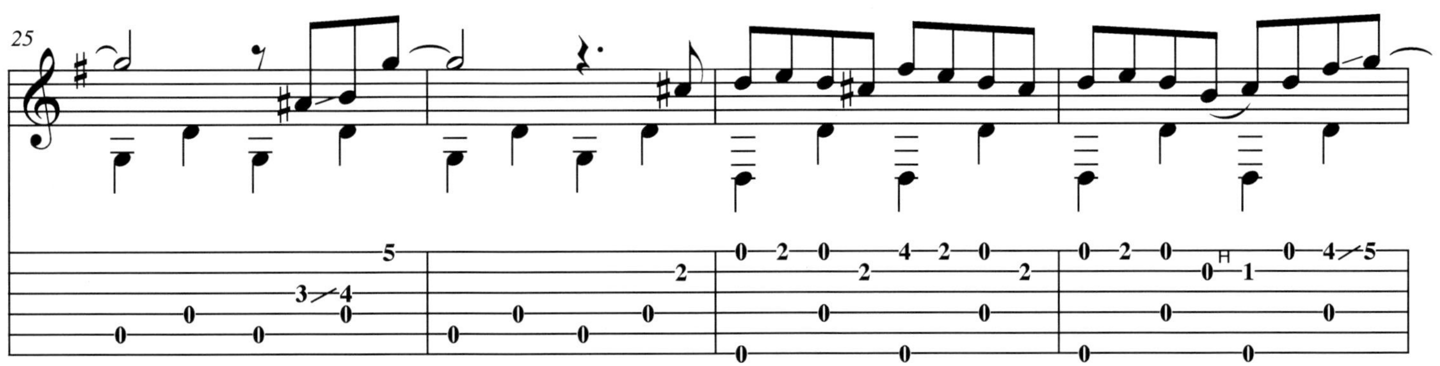
25
5
3 4 2
0 2 0 2 4 2 0 2 0 2 0 0 1 0 4 5
H

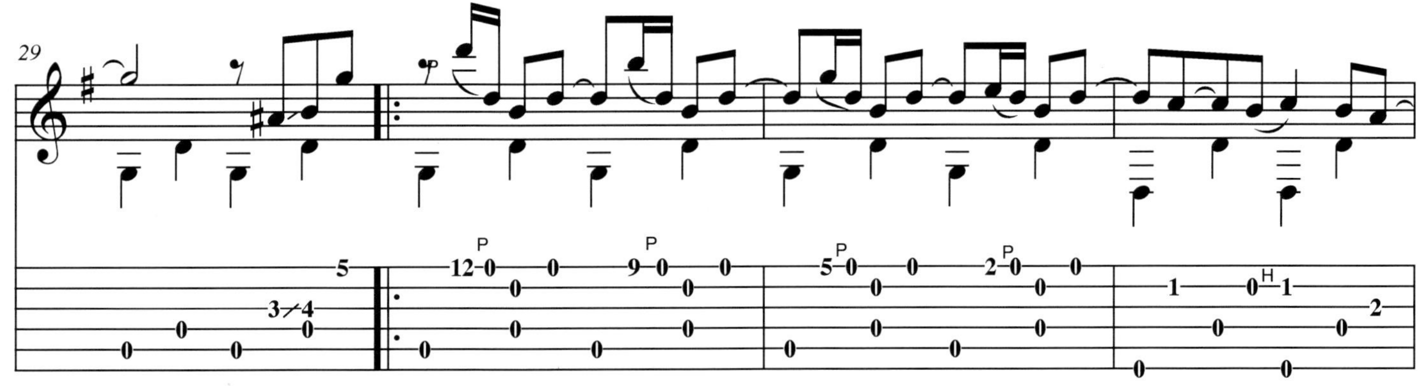
29
5
3 4
P P P P H
12 0 0 9 0 0 5 0 0 2 0 0
1 0 1 2

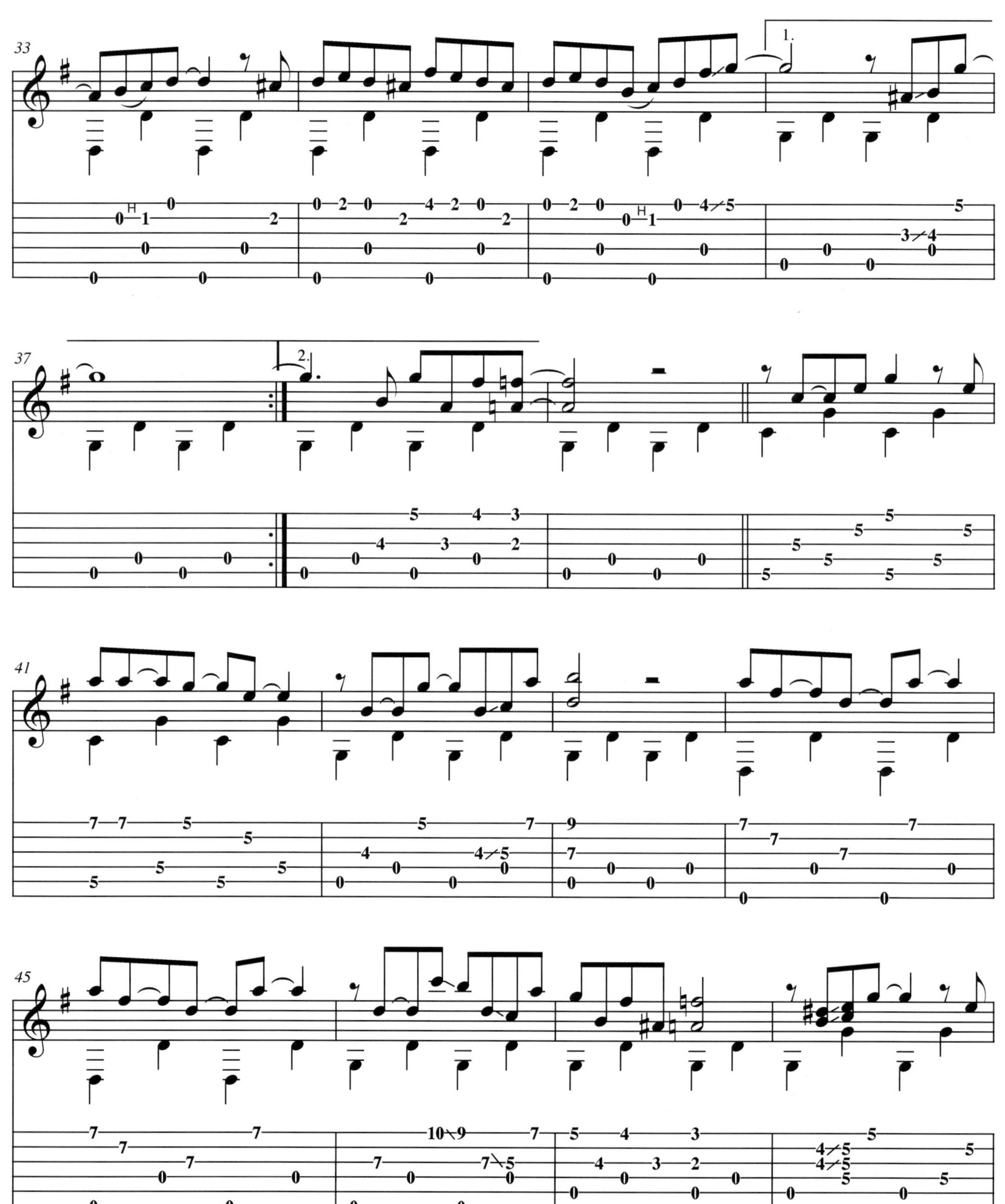

33
1.
37
2.
41
45

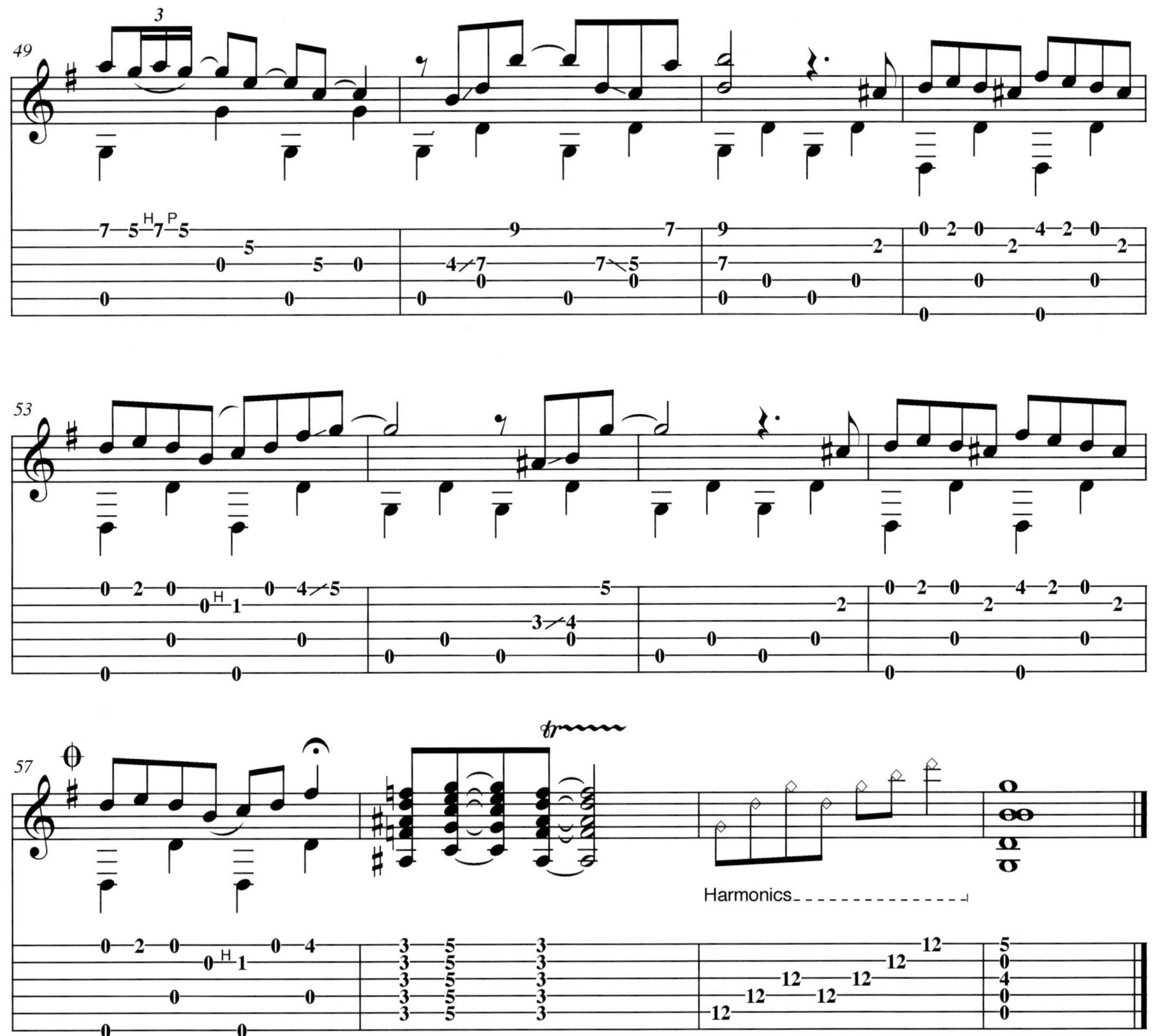

Kolomona Slack Key
Notes

Measures 1-8: Although built on the same formula as countless slack key instrumentals, there is no second turnaround in the first part of "Kolomona Slack Key."

Measures 11-29: The second strain follows another typical slack key pattern and uses just about every trick in the book.

Measures 30-37: A nice way to break up the tune. I've heard similar variations in any number of slack key instrumentals.

Measures 57-60: Hold the last note under the fermata, then quickly slide a barré from the 3rd to the 5th fret and back. Trill the final chord with a rapid tremolo strum; let the tension build before finally resolving back to the tonic. The harmonics riff can be used in just about any Taro Patch tune as an intro or, as here, a coda.

Lesson One: From Melody to Arrangement

Over the course of the book we'll be looking at a number of songs as tools to teach important slack key techniques. The next few arrangements are intended to give you some ideas for finding your own style. I'll walk you through how I approach turning a basic outline of a song into a complete slack key performance.

To begin, here is a very simple setting of a classic slack key song, "Pua Sadinia."

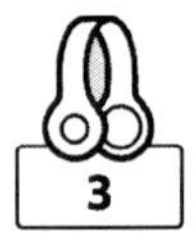

Pua Sadinia
Basic Arrangement

Taro Patch tuning

David Nape

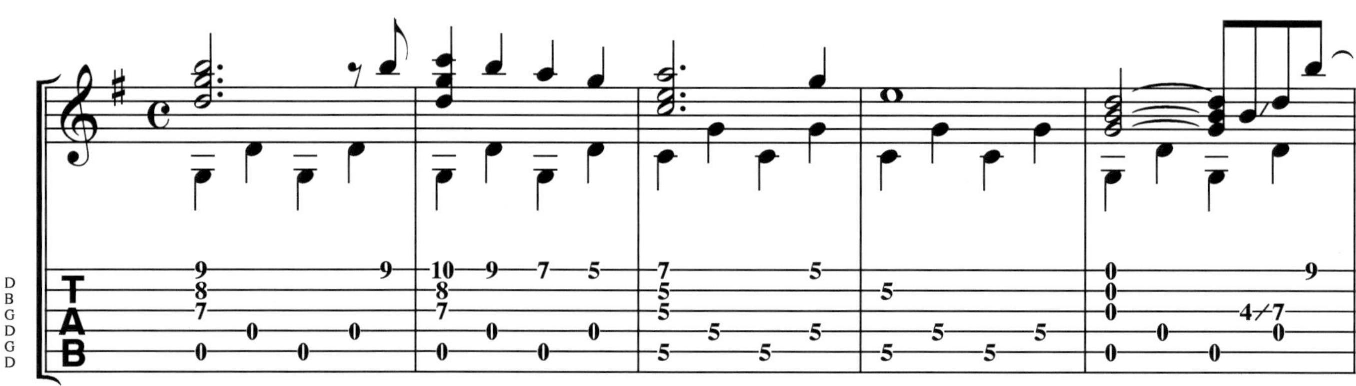

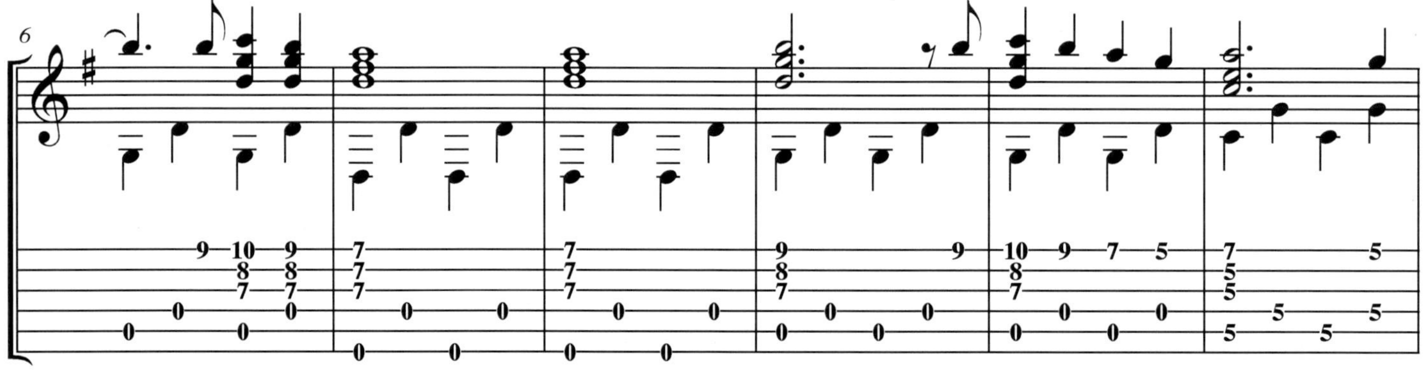

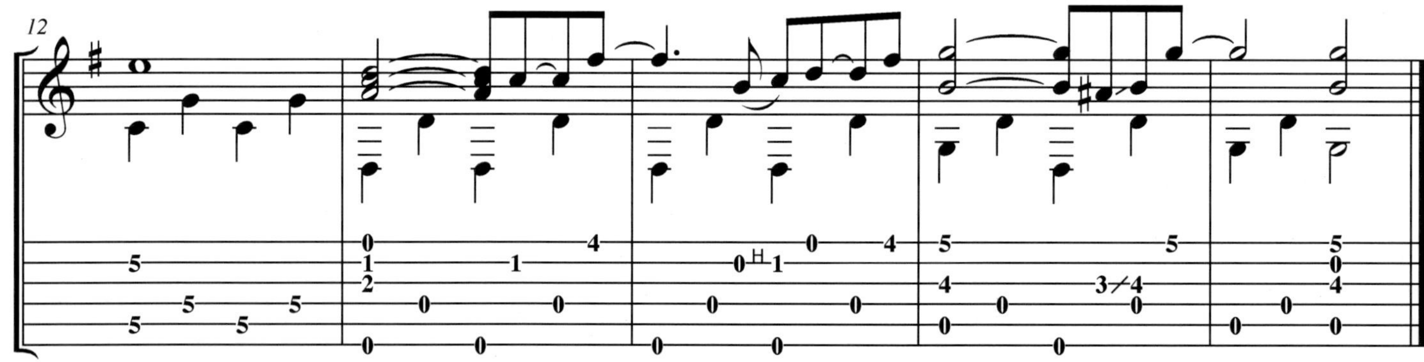

Pua Sadinia - Basic Style
Notes

There isn't anything too difficult here. After you have played it a few times, see if you can come up with your own way of playing it. Think about how you might set things up.

Do you want to give listeners a chance to settle into the mood by creating a short introduction? Or maybe you'll want to let the beauty of the melody stand on its own.

How many times are you going to play the melody? How will you keep your listeners - and yourself - engaged?

What classic *kī hōʻalu* techniques such as slides, triplets or syncopations can you work into the arrangement?

After you've played through this a few times, take a look at the next page where I have written out a complete arrangement based on the way I approach the song.

Of course, I never play it exactly the same way every time, and neither should you. The essence of slack key is spontaneity and personal expression.

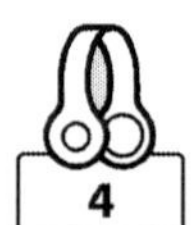

Pua Sadinia

Taro Patch tuning

David Nape

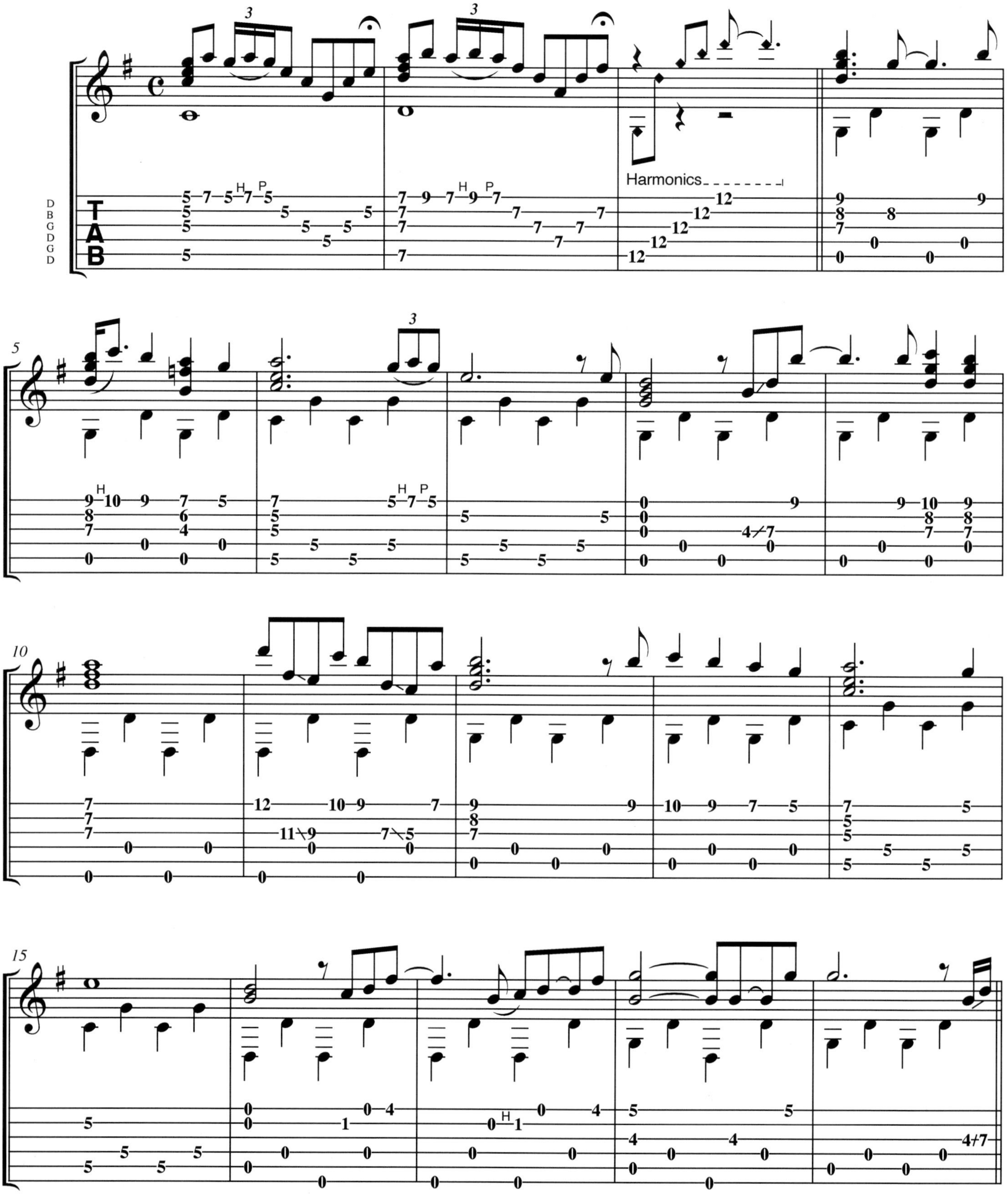

D
B
G
D
G
D

TAB

Harmonics

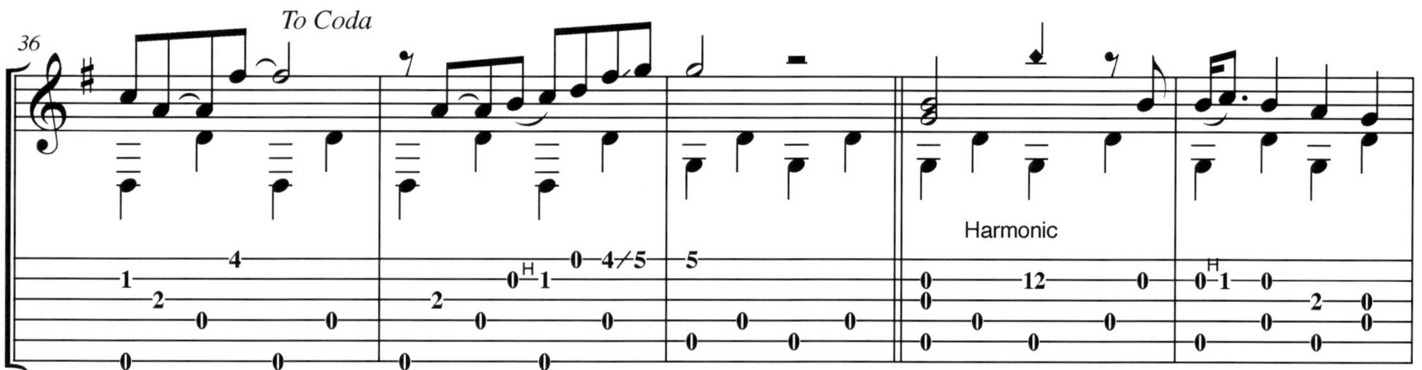
To Coda
Harmonic

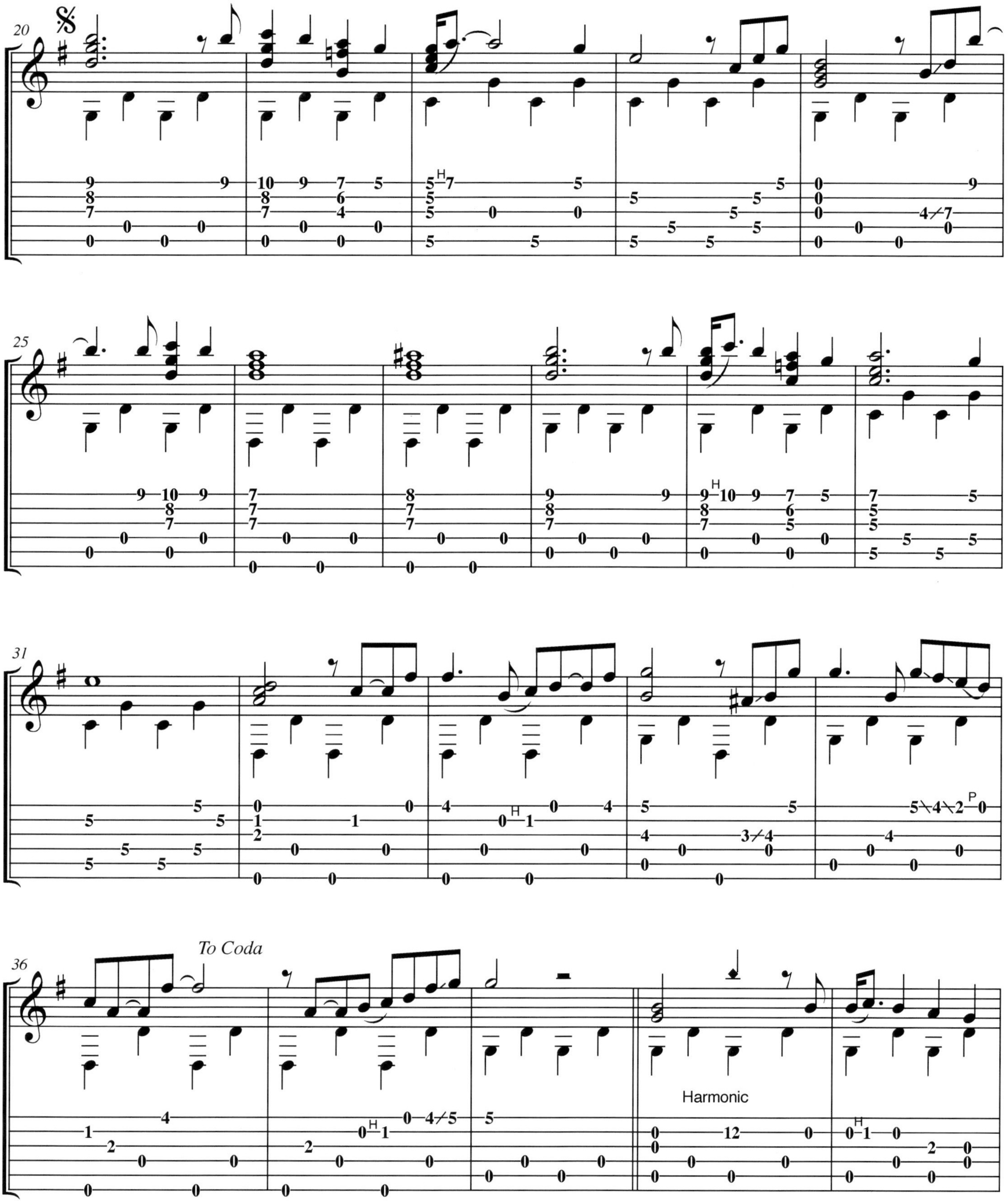

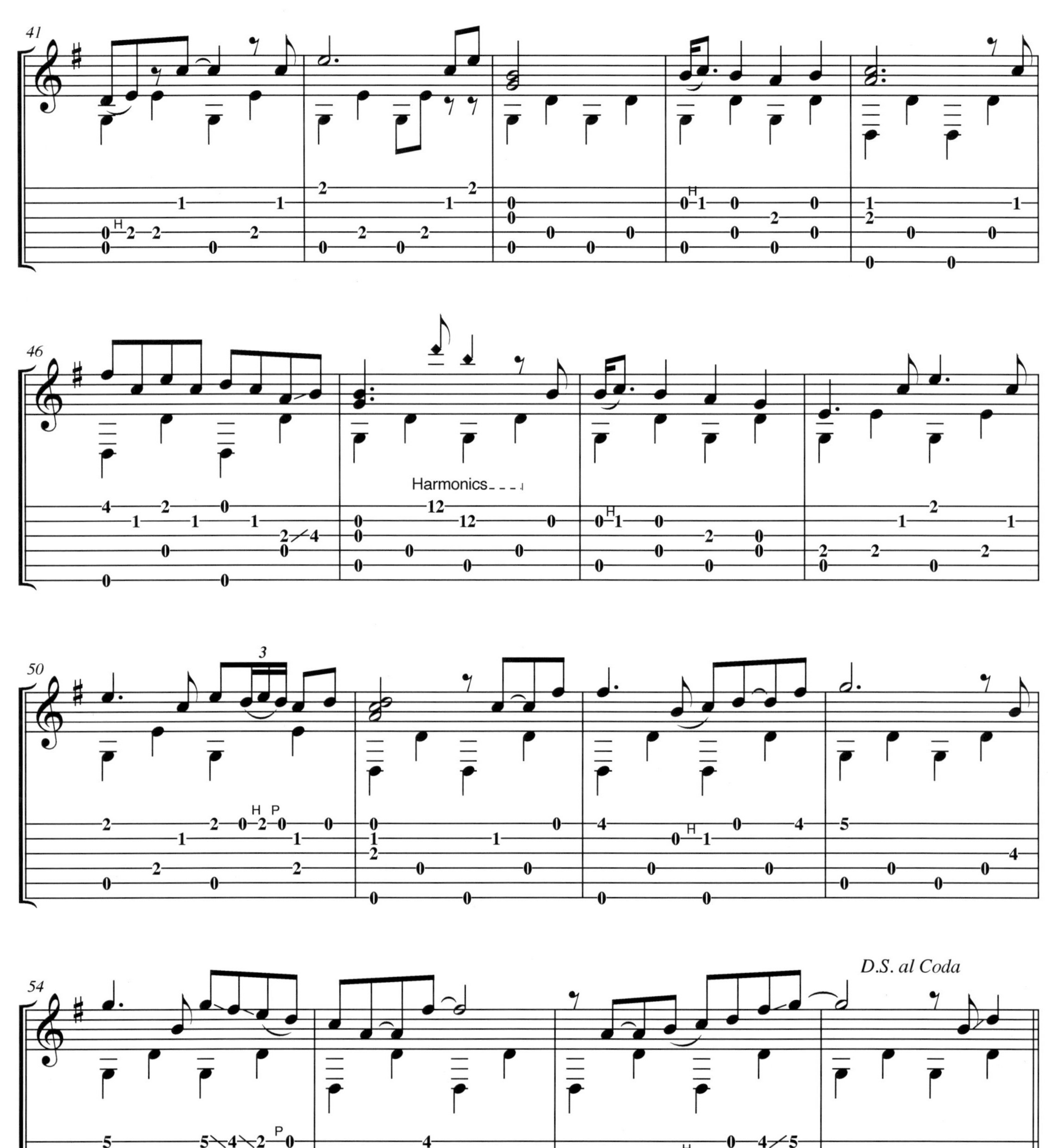
41
46
Harmonics
50
54
D.S. al Coda

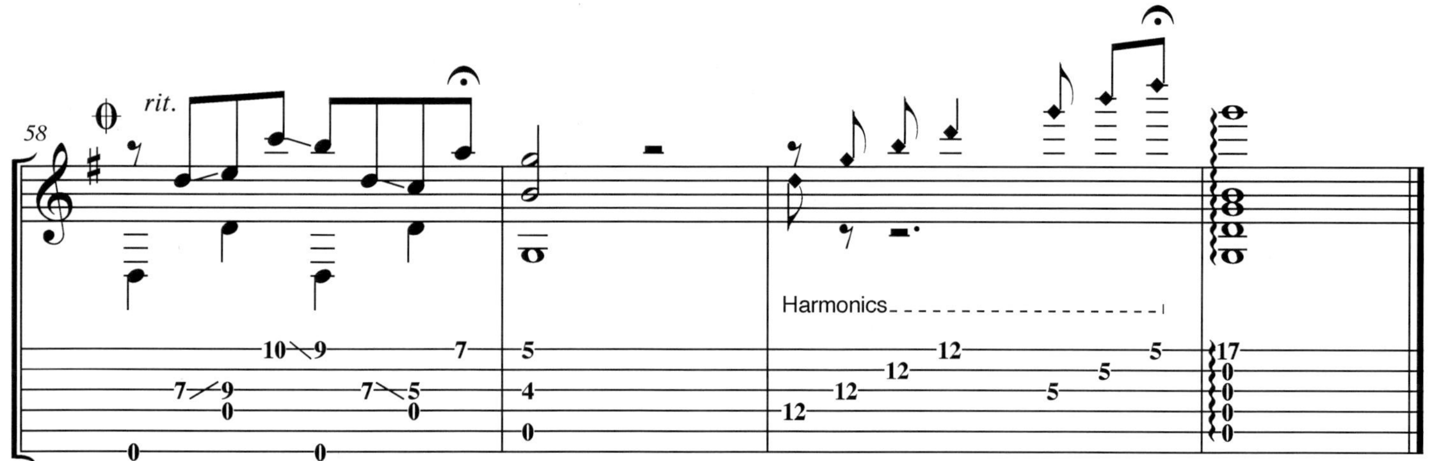

Pua Sadinia
Notes

Measures 1-3: This simple introduction may be extended by adding harmonics on the 7th and 5th frets. Play it freely.

Measures 4-9: For the first time through, I stick fairly close to the original melody. Pay attention to how adding slurs, syncopations and grace notes can make a simple tune come alive.

Measures 20-34: Again, the arrangement sticks close to the basic melody. The main difference is the addition of some more sophisticated harmony, such as the D+ chord in measure 27. I borrowed this idea from Uncle Ray Kane, by the way. Notice the sign at measure 20; when I reprise this section after measure 57, I would not play it exactly the same way as written. Listen to the audio for some ideas on how you can vary the arrangement.

Measures 35-38: Measure 35 is an example of what I call "the turnaround to the turnaround," a lick to walk you back to the dominant chord. This little four-bar section makes an effective bridge before restating the melody. As you work through this book, pay attention to some of the other ways a short bridge can help create an effective arrangement.

Measures 39-53: The melody drops down an octave. That allows you to have some fun with harmonics, among other tricks. This variation also makes an effective accompaniment to a vocalist or second guitarist, as we shall see in a few pages.

Measures 54-57: Simply a slightly different version of the bridge.

After measure 57, go back to measure 20 and play through to measure 26. From there, jump to the coda. Try to come up with some of your own variations here. This could be something as simple as swapping measure 11 for measure 27, or perhaps you can find some new triplet slurs.

Measures 58-61: Another typical slack key coda. Even better, you could swap the intro and the coda for a slightly different take on the song!

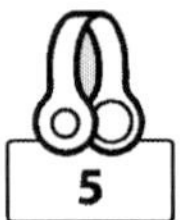

Opihi Moemoe
Structural Outline

Leonard Kwan

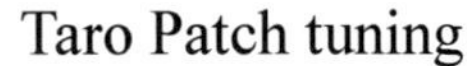

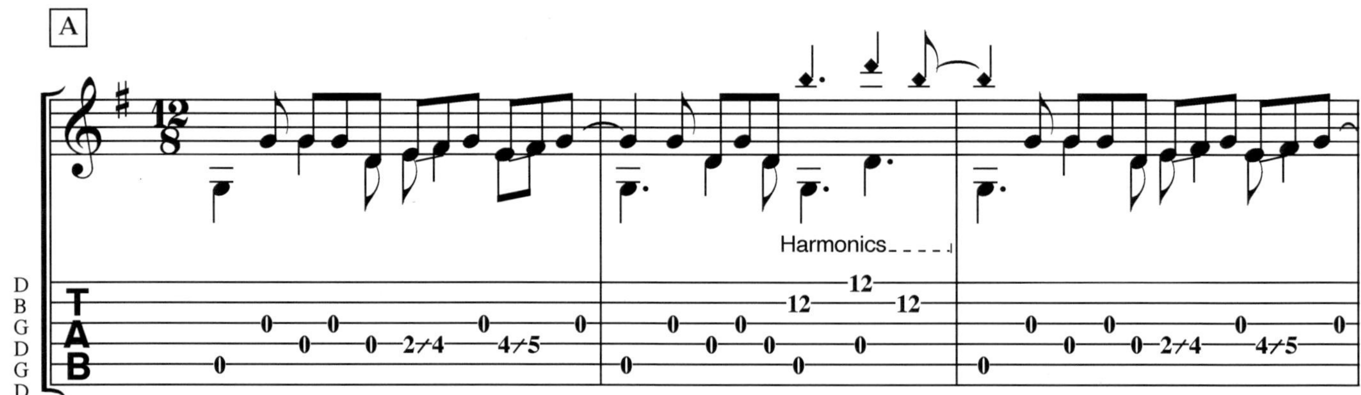

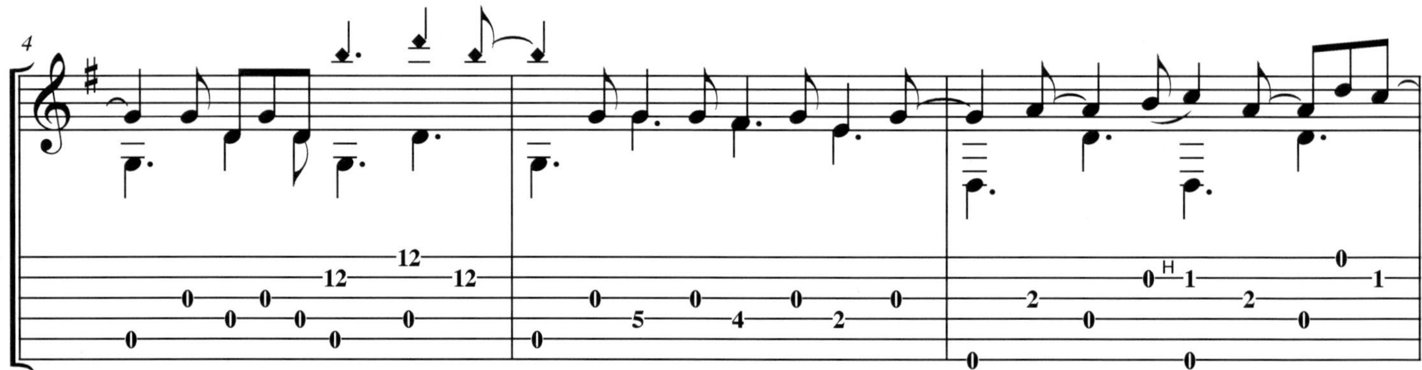

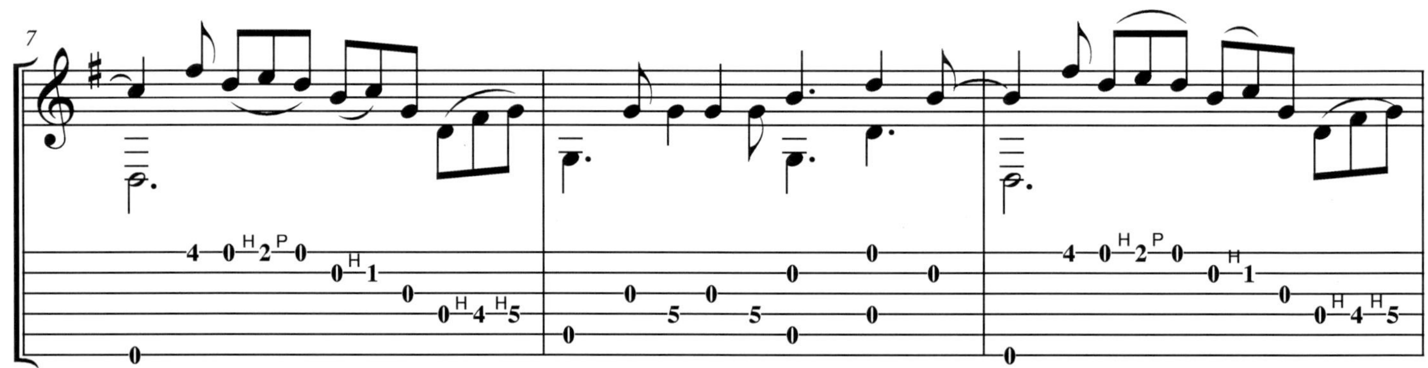

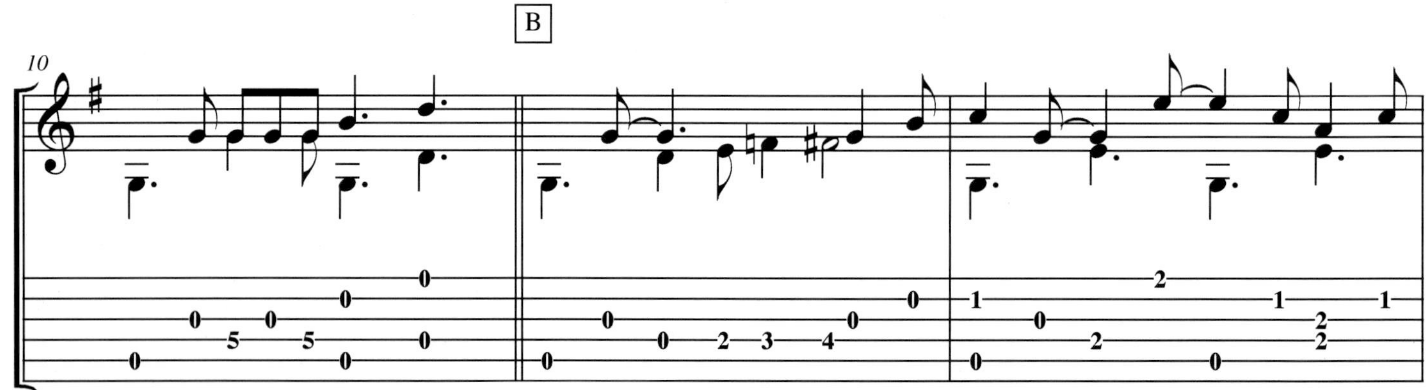

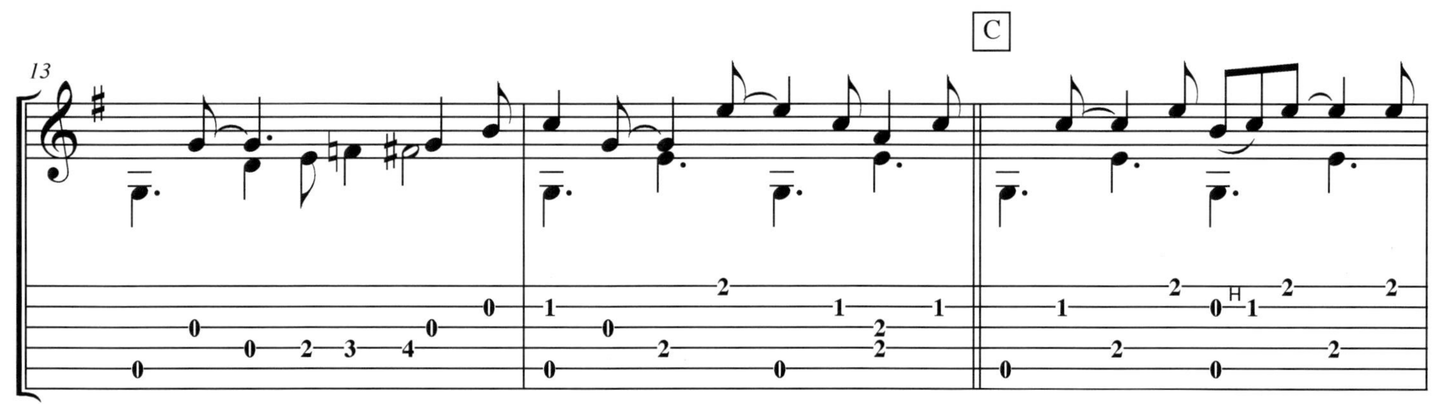
13
C

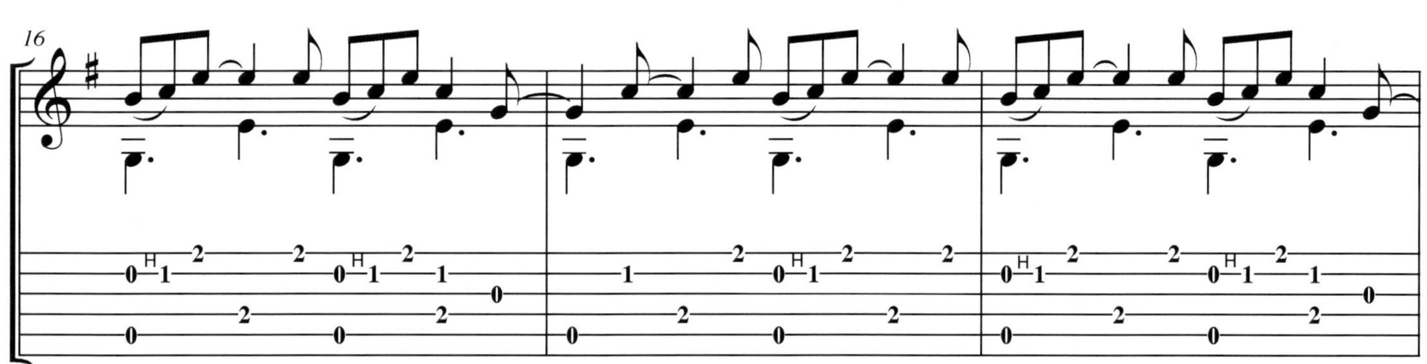
16

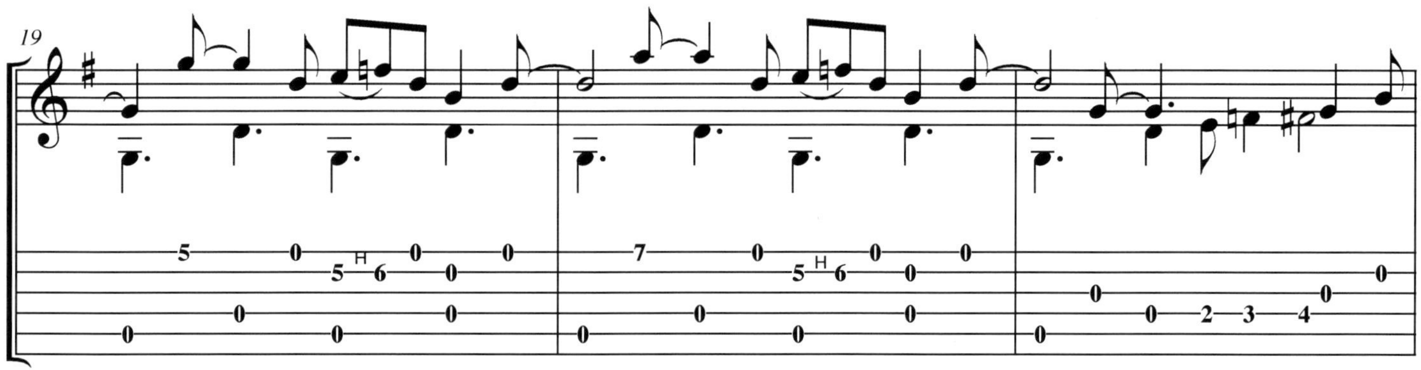
19

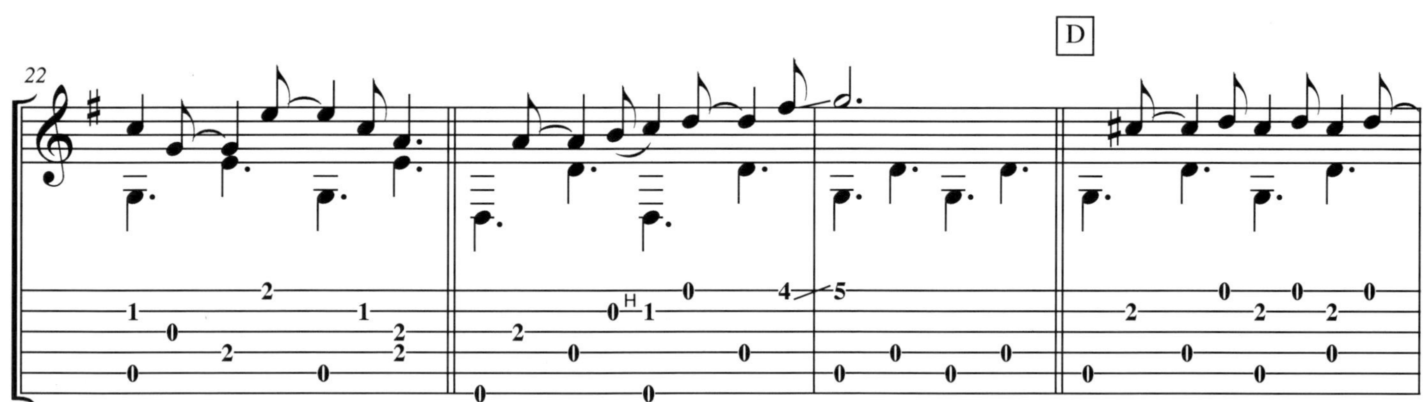
22
D

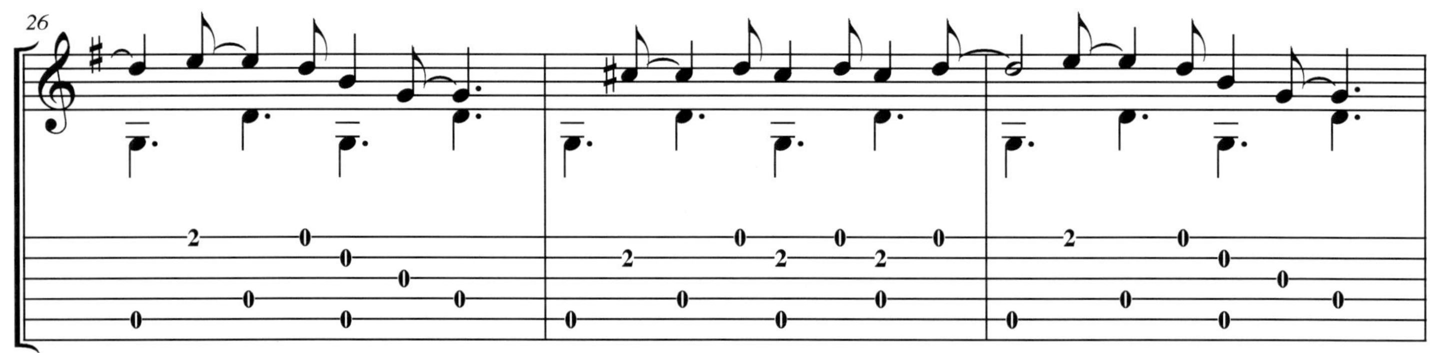
26

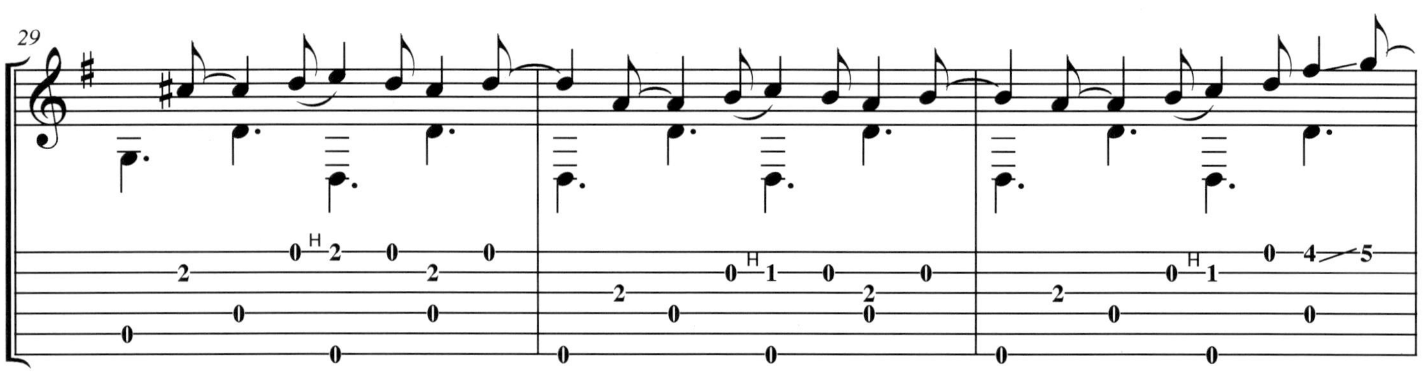
29

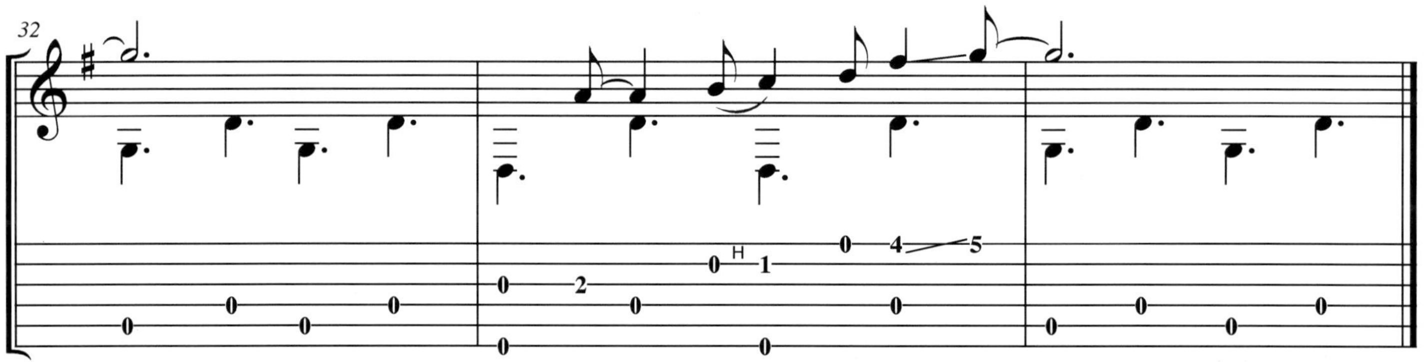
32

Opihi Moemoe: Structural Outline
Notes

Leonard Kwan's wonderfully complex "Opihi Moemoe" (The Sleepy Limpet) is based on a typical slack key structure of theme and variation. When each part of the song is repeated, you have the option to plug in a variation– anything from a simple slur to a dazzling triplet figure – at certain points.

Compare this with similar theme-and-variation tunes like Ray Kane's "Punahele" or Sonny Chillingworth's "Moe 'Uhane Slack Key." "Po Mahina Slack Key" and "Aunty's Christmas Goose," which appear later in this book, also follow this idea.

To begin, here are the four essential themes the make up "Opihi Moemoe."

[A] Measures 1-10: These ten measures are the heart of the tune. Notice the 12/8 time signature; "Opihi Moemoe" has a triplet swing feel! Pay careful attention to which notes are played with your thumb – those with downward flags – and those played with your fingers. In general, the thumb plays all the notes on the bottom three strings; the fingers stay on the top three.

Before you dig in, practice playing just the first few notes in measure 1 – up to the slides – to get the proper rolling rhythm between your thumb and index finger. Once you are comfortable with that, add the slides. Note that you end each slide at the same time as plucking a note on the open G string with your finger.

The turnarounds in measures 7 & 9 are a wonder! Drop in a bass note, then grab the note at fret 4. Immediately follow that with a series of slurs and single notes, eventually ending up on the fifth fret of the D string. Strive for an effortless flow of notes. Believe it or not, it is easier than it looks.

Play through the A section a few times before moving on.

[B] Measures 11-14: The second strain is basically just a modulation up to the key of C by way of a G7 chord. You will find variations of this all over the slack key universe.

[C] Measures 15-24: We are now firmly in the key of C, so our melody will be moving between the tonic on C and the dominant chord of G7. Note that the bass has a more familiar "four-on-the-floor" feel. The turnaround at measures 23 & 24 brings us back to G. From here you would either go back to the A section and then repeat B & C; or, having done that once or twice, move directly on to the last bit.

[D] Measures 25-34: Now we have a series of moves between the tonic and dominant chords played out on the high strings. Again, the whole feel of the song has shifted from the triplets of the A section to something much more familiar. Most people play this section two or three times – with variations, of course – before finally bringing the whole thing to a close.

Once you are comfortable playing through these parts, turn the page and I'll introduce you to some ways you can spice things up.

Opihi Moemoe Variations

The previous structural outline presents the essential four sections of the tune. Each part is whole in itself, yet each represents the base upon which you can build something new. Rather than creating an entirely new melody each time the section repeats, the slack key guitarist will often keep the structure intact, changing only one or two measures. The next repeat may feature slight new changes to the same measures. The overall effect is to develop an increasingly complex arrangement without losing the listener.

Here is a typical way to organize the song. I'm using a superscript numeral to denote a repeat with a variation.

A-A^{1}-A^{2}-B-C-A^{3} -B^{1}-C^{1}-D-D^{1}-D^{2}

Here are some ideas you can try.

A Section:
This section defines the song, so slight changes will have a huge impact.

Example 1:
Try substituting this example for measures 2 & 4 on the repeat.

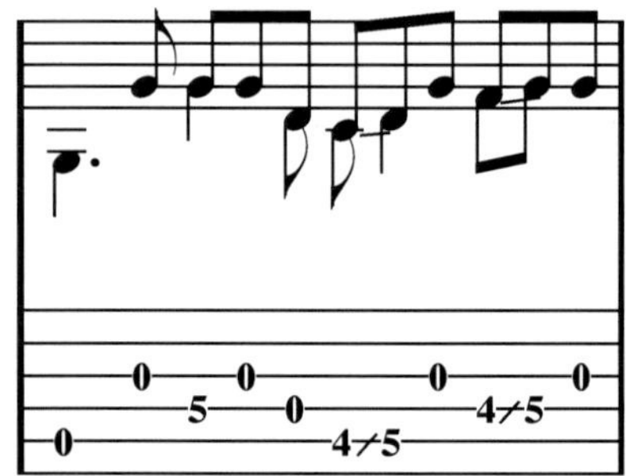

Example 2:
This bluesy lick fits those same two measures.

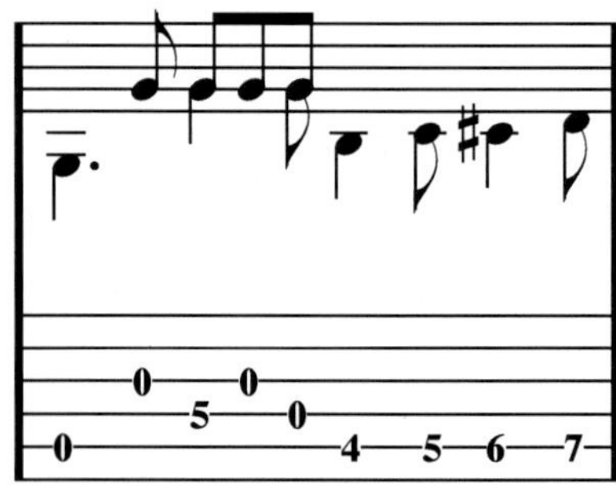

Alternately, use Example 1 for measure 2 and Example 2 for measure 4, or vice versa; you get the idea.

Here is another way to set up the modulation in section B.

Example 3:

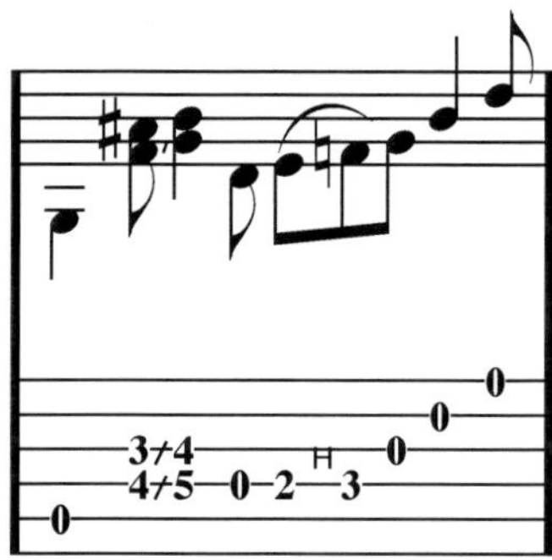

Section C offers a few options. For instance you can use this to replace the licks in C in measures 15-16 or 17 & 18.

Example 4:

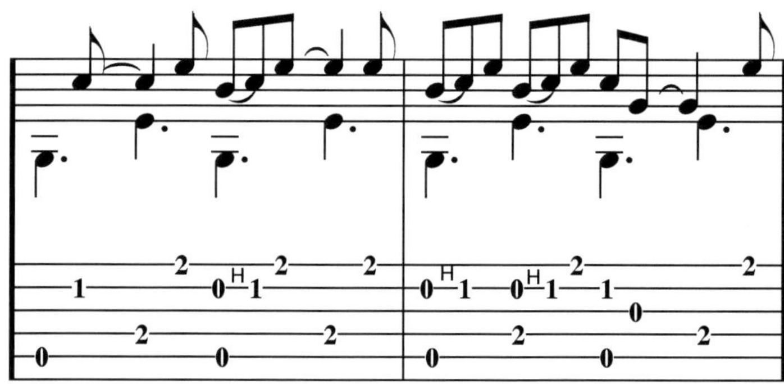

If you used Example 3 to set up the modulation, you might want to use it again in measure 21.

And you can always substitute any turnaround you know for measures 23 & 24, including the cascading figure from the top of the tune.

As I mentioned, the final section offers the most room for creativity. You can do pretty much anything you want, as long as you follow the chord structure. Or not; I will sometimes play a completely different tune here, such as "Kolomona Slack Key," thereby creating an instant medley.

Here is one typical variation you can drop in for the first measures of the D section. I'm sure you will discover more.

Example 5:

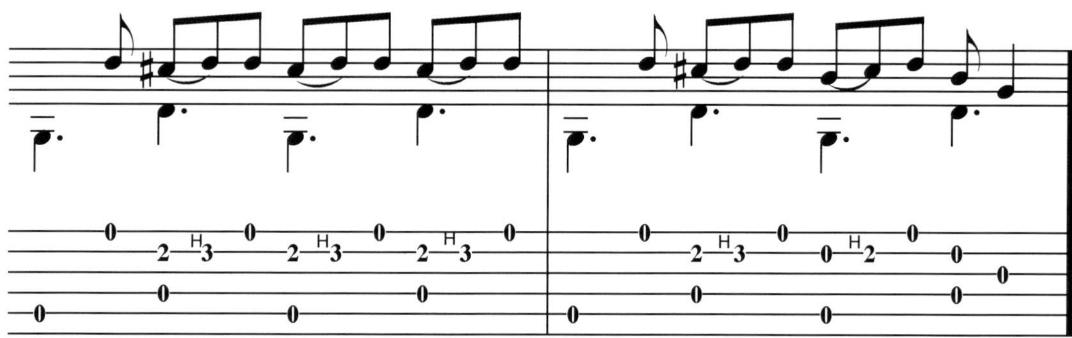

To see how substitutions/variations work in real time, turn the page, where I offer a transcription of a spontaneous live performance by the elusive Uji Oma'oma'o.

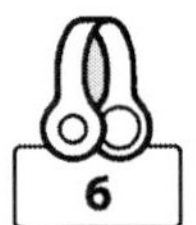

Opihi Moemoe

Transcription from a Live Performance

Taro Patch tuning

Leonard Kwan

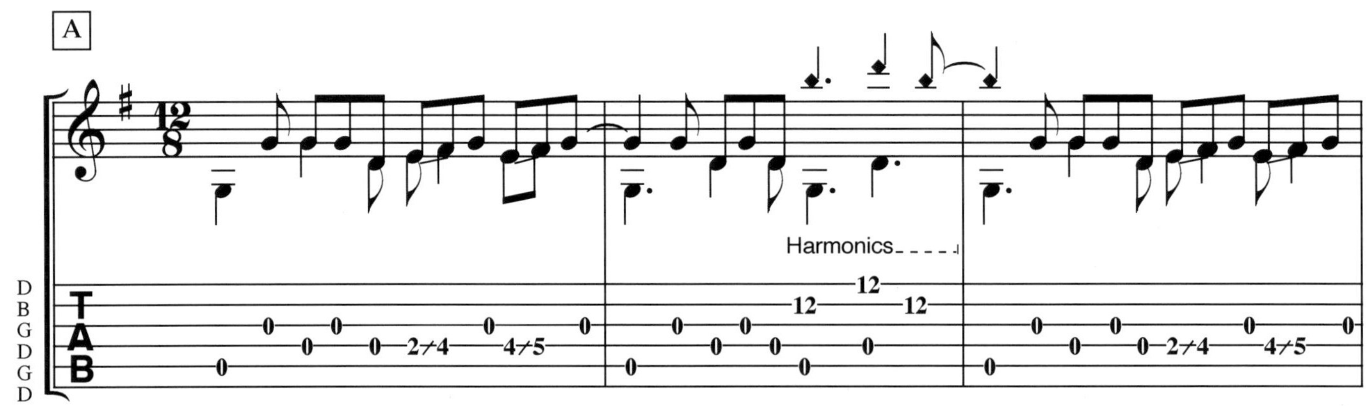

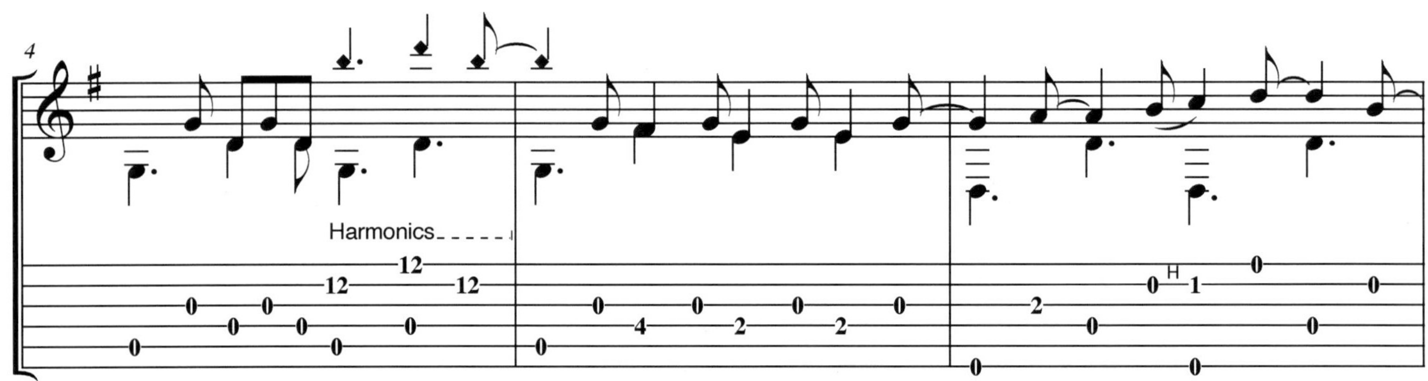

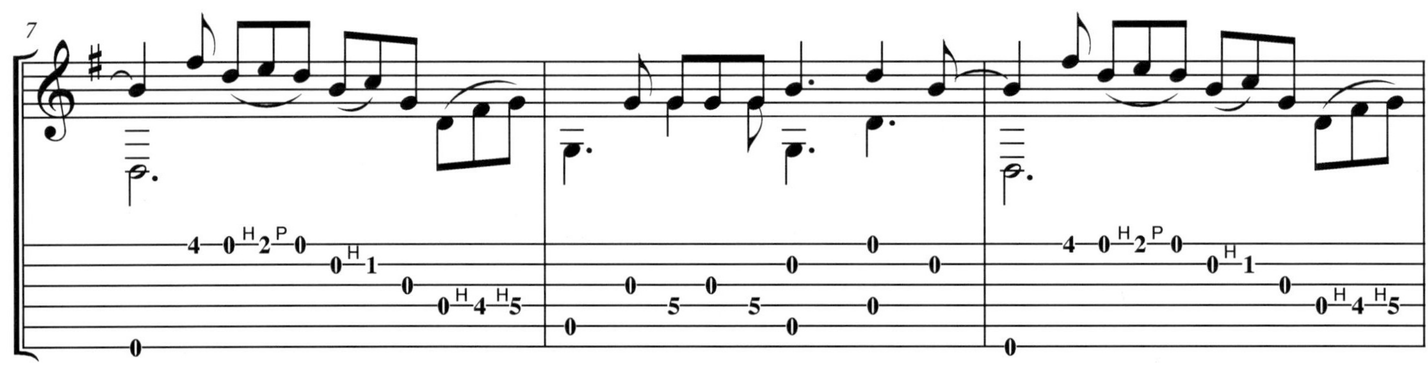

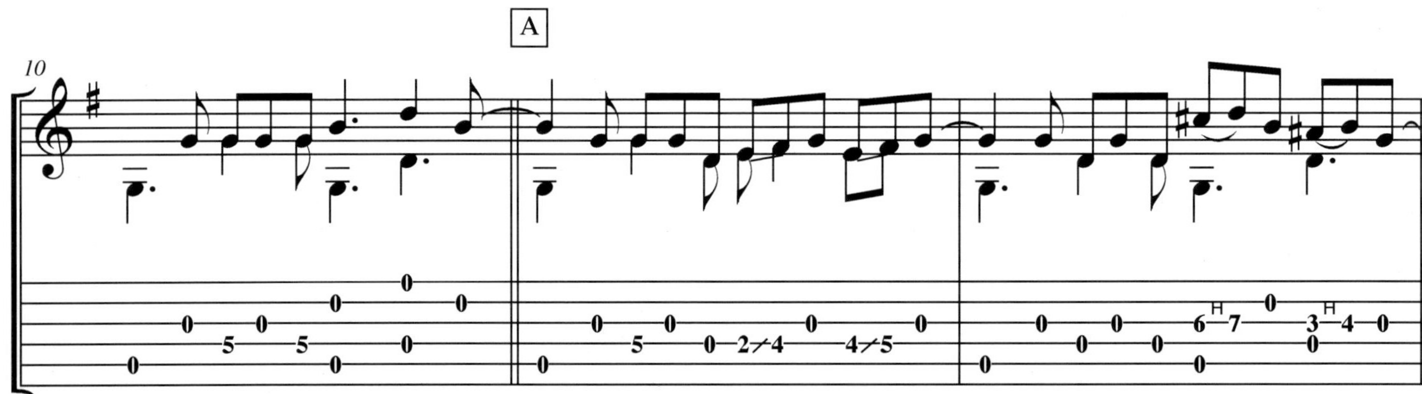

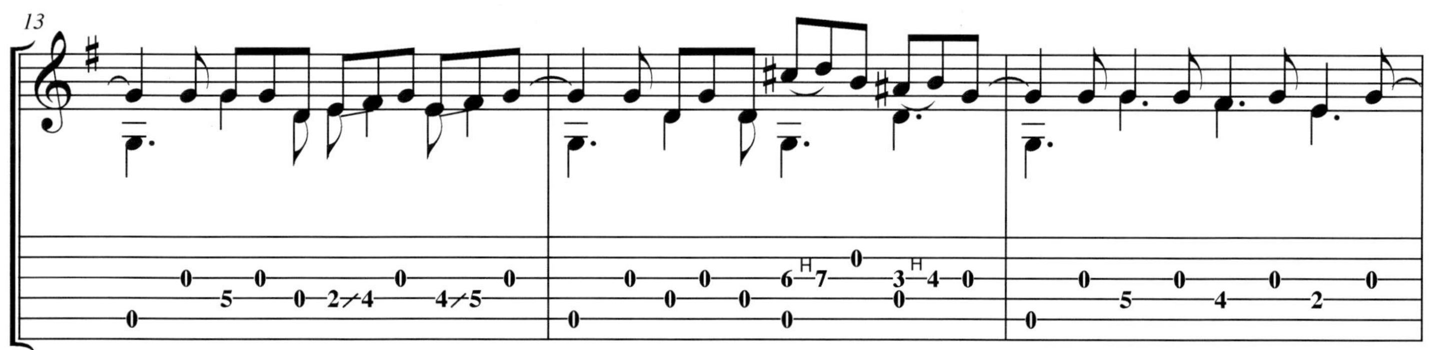

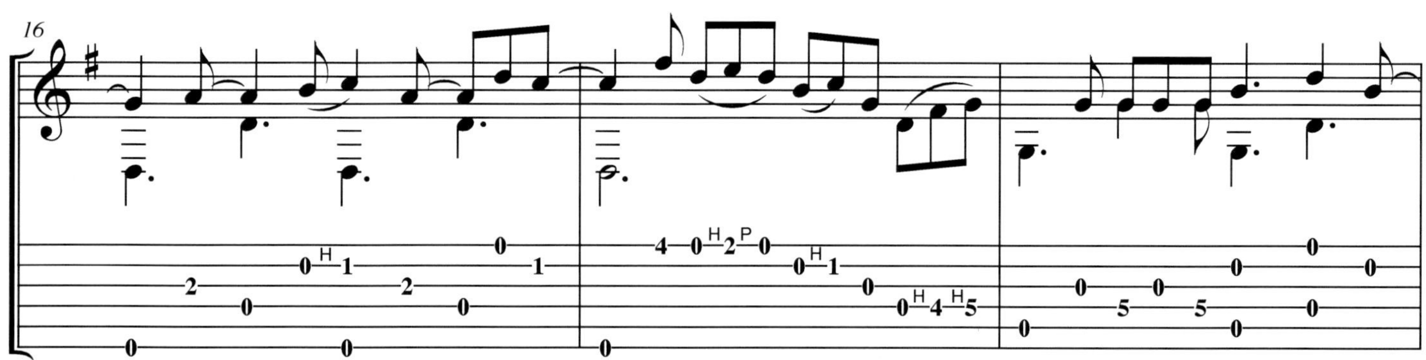

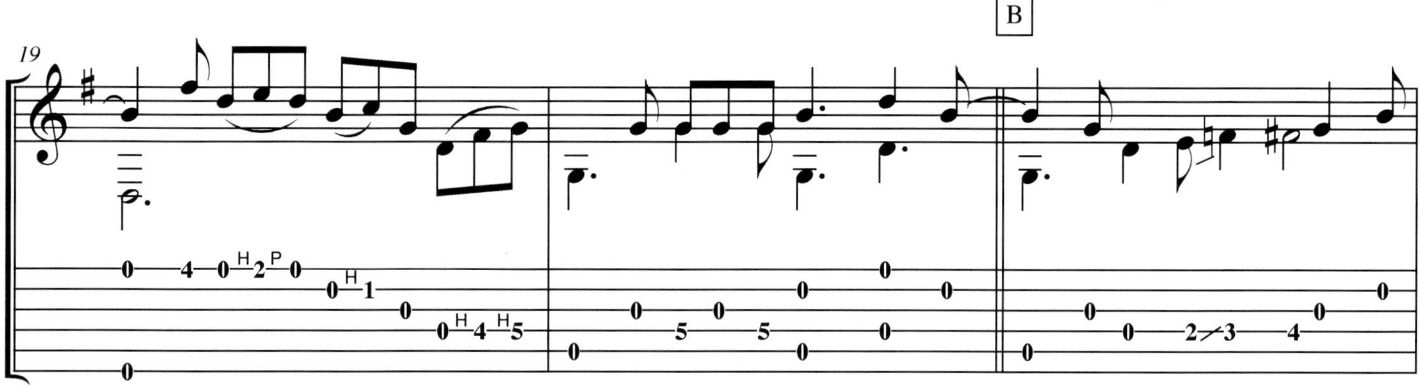

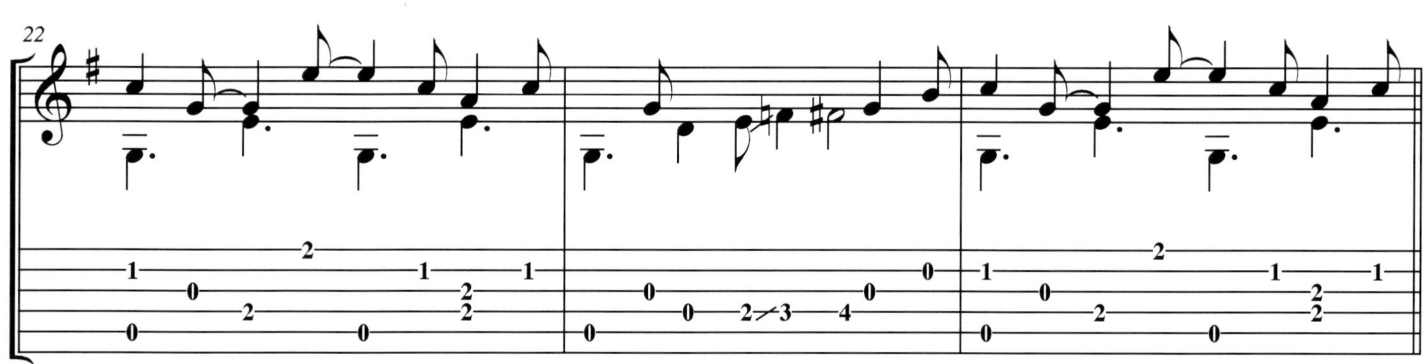

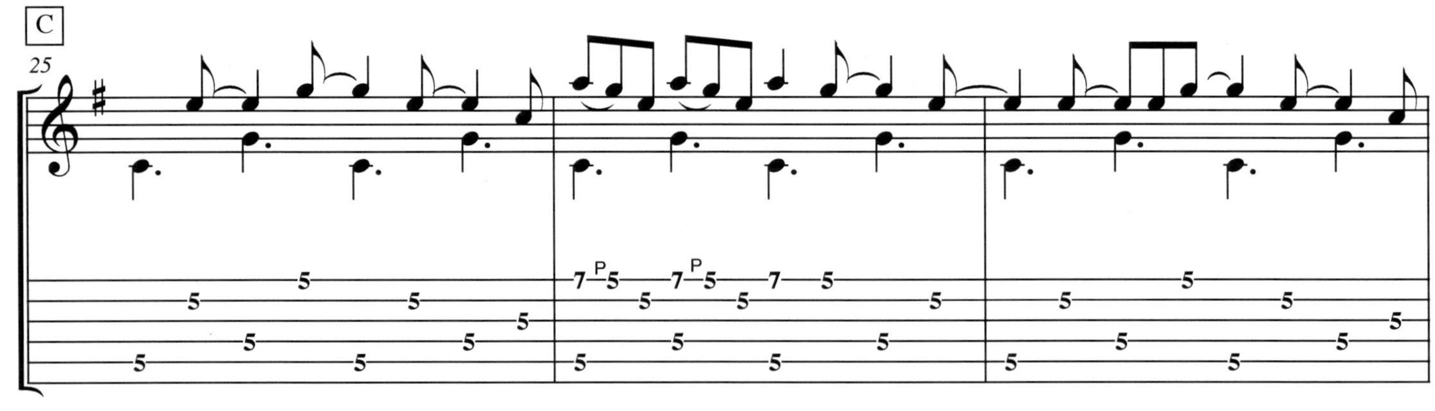
C
25

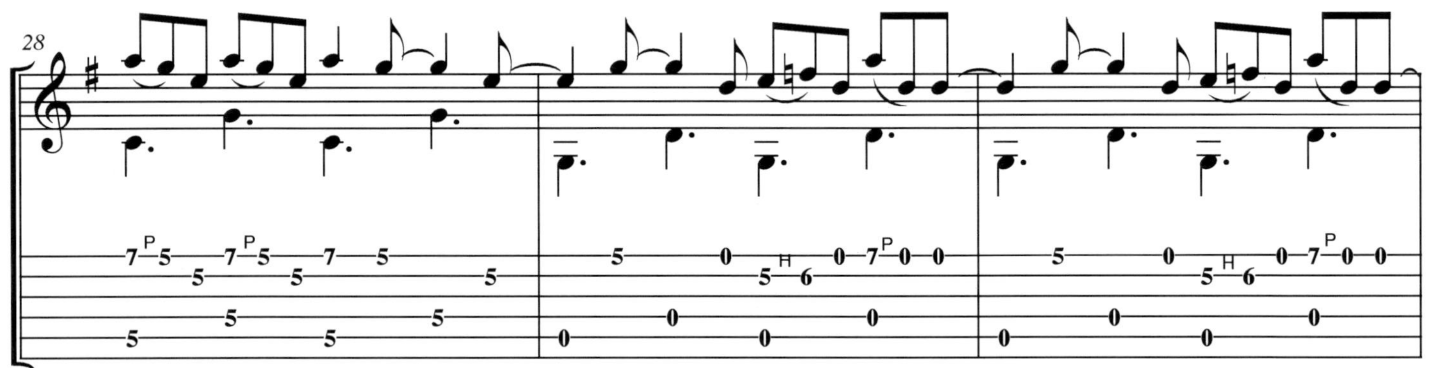
28

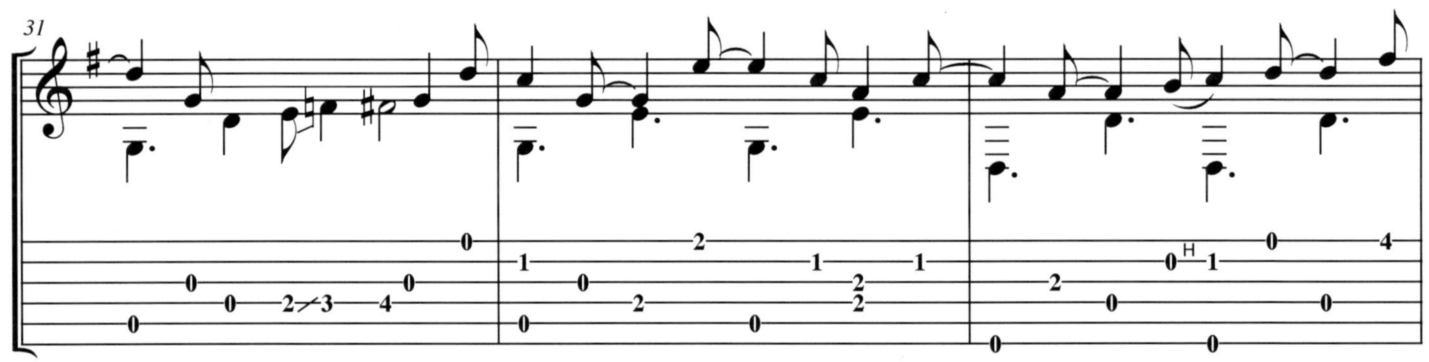
31

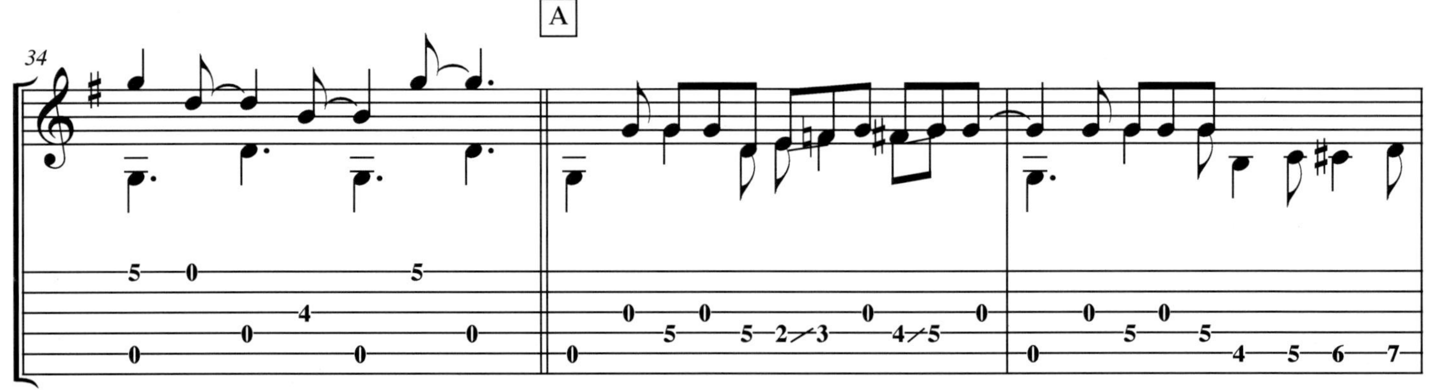
34
A

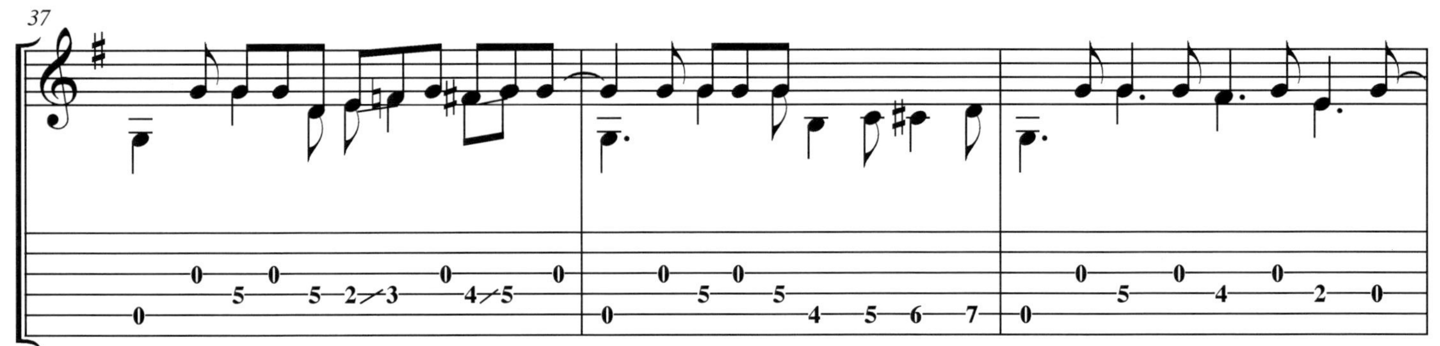
37

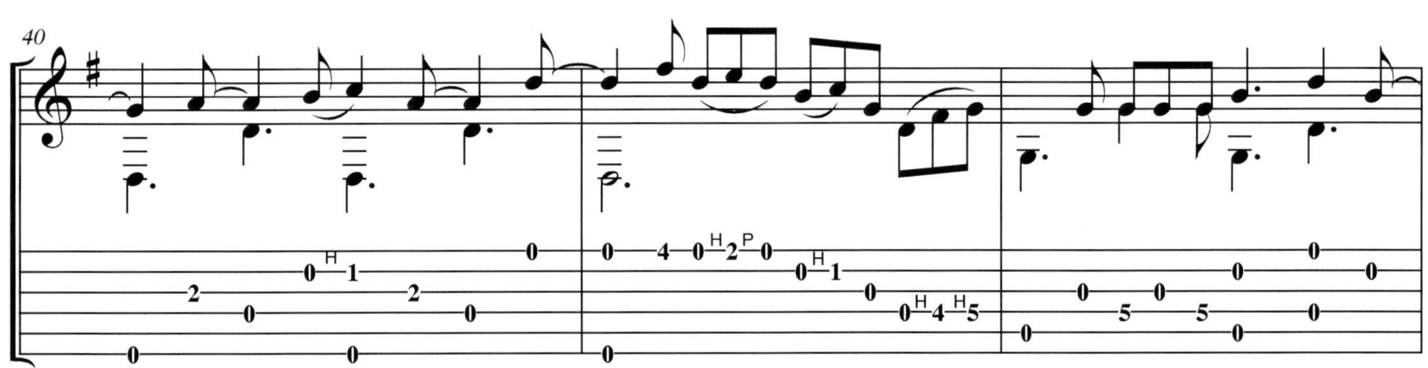
40

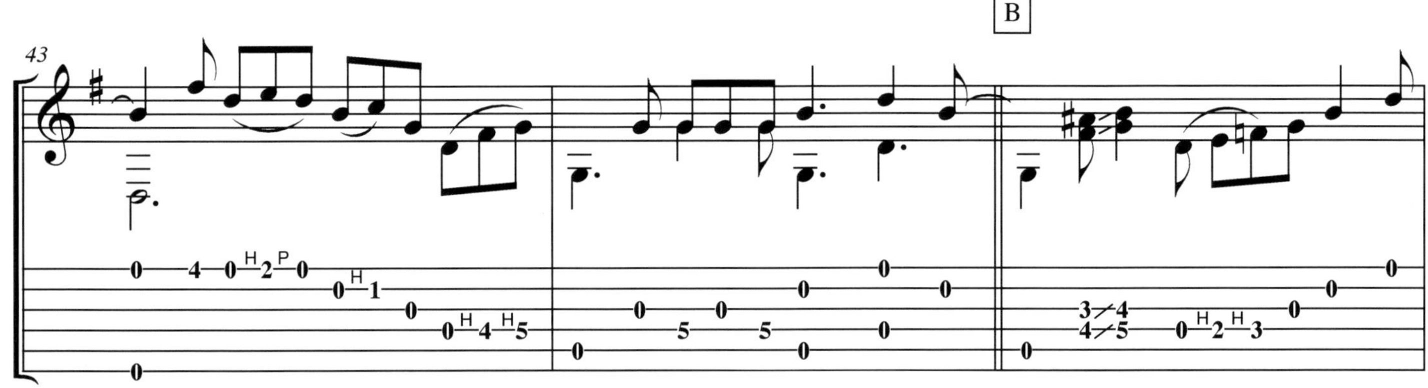
B
43

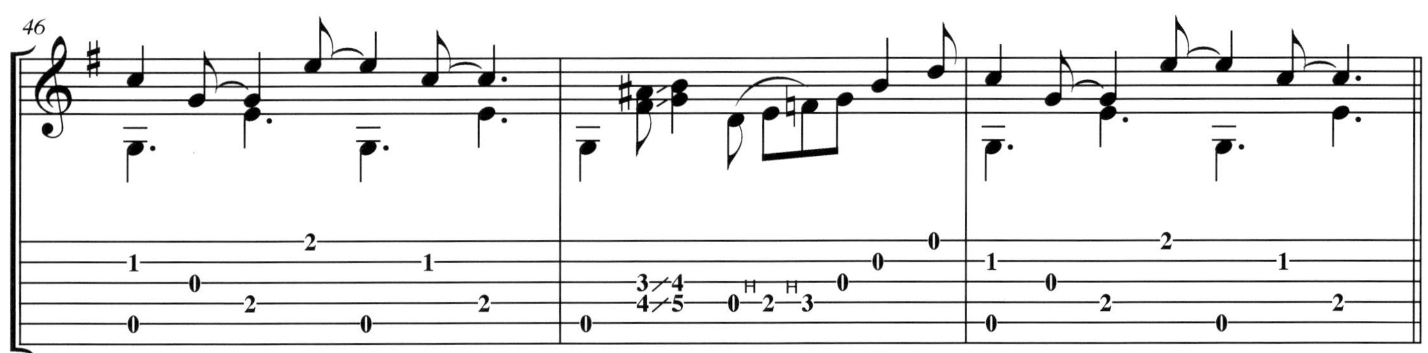
46

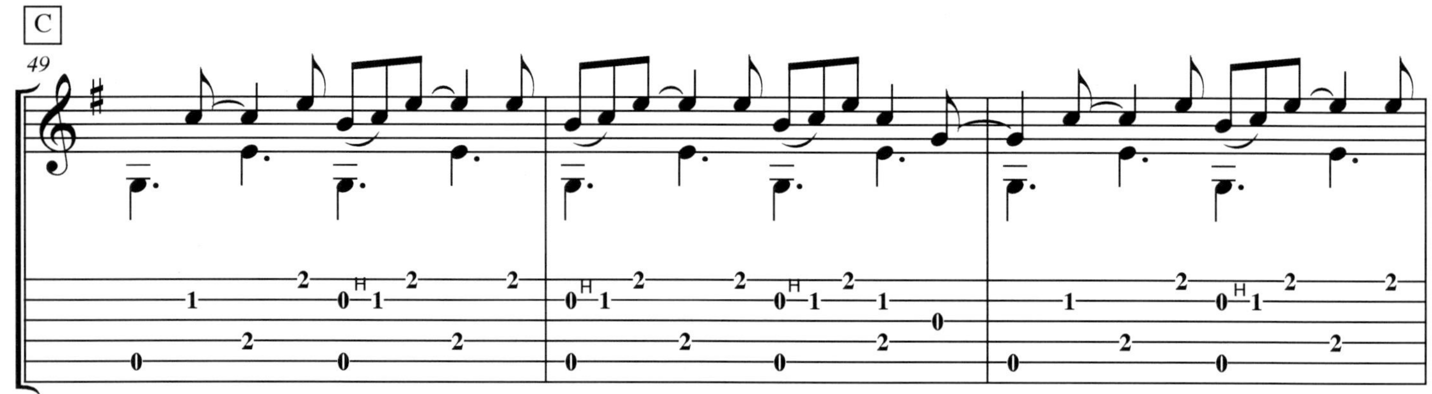
C
49

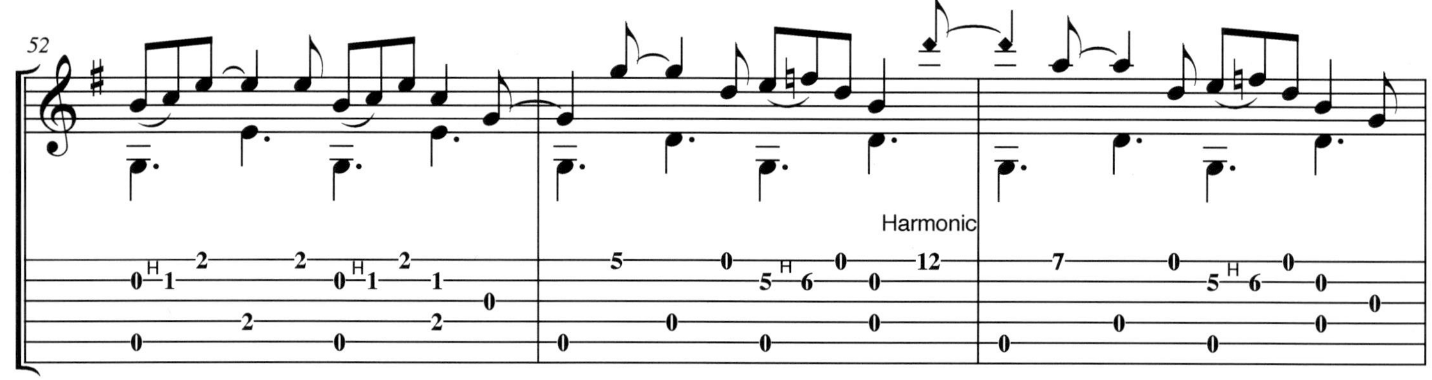
52
Harmonic

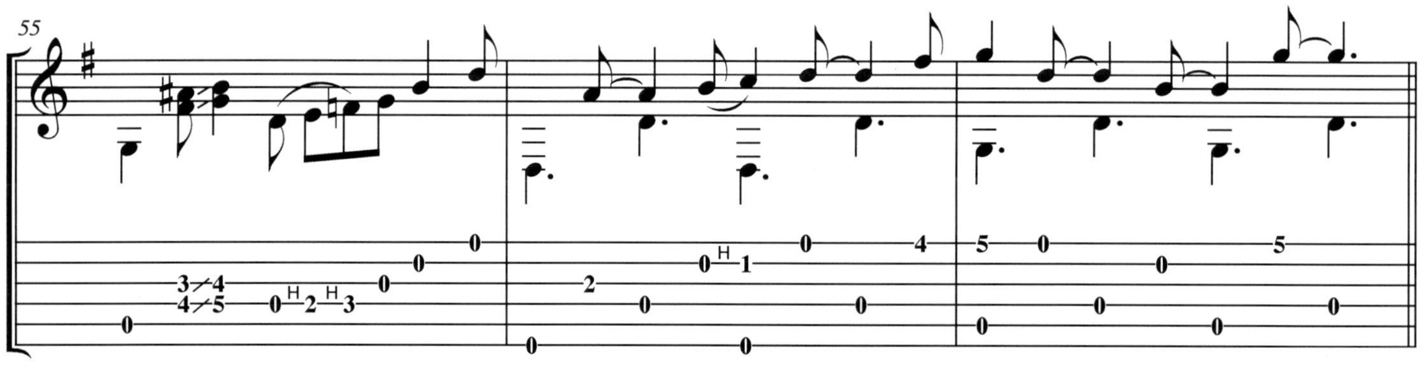
55

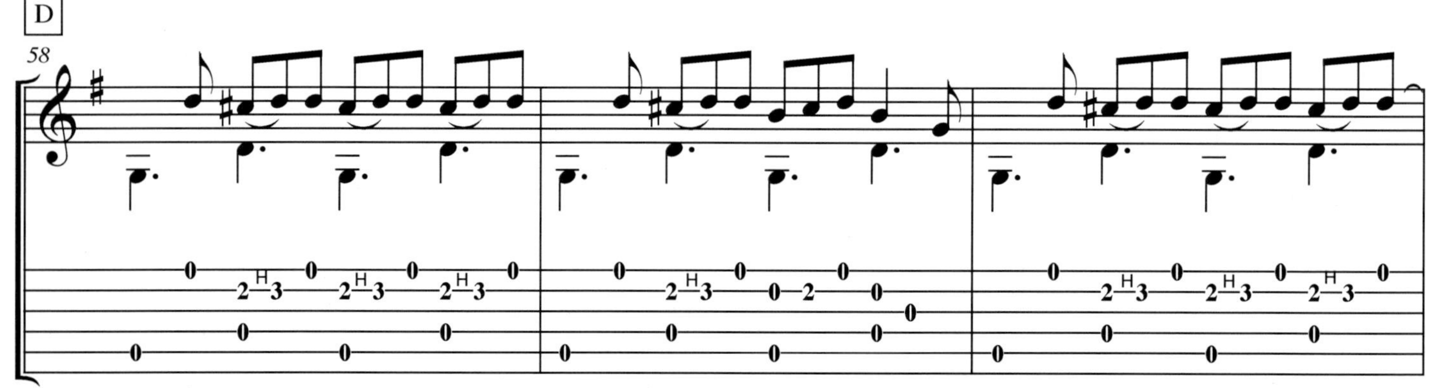
D
58

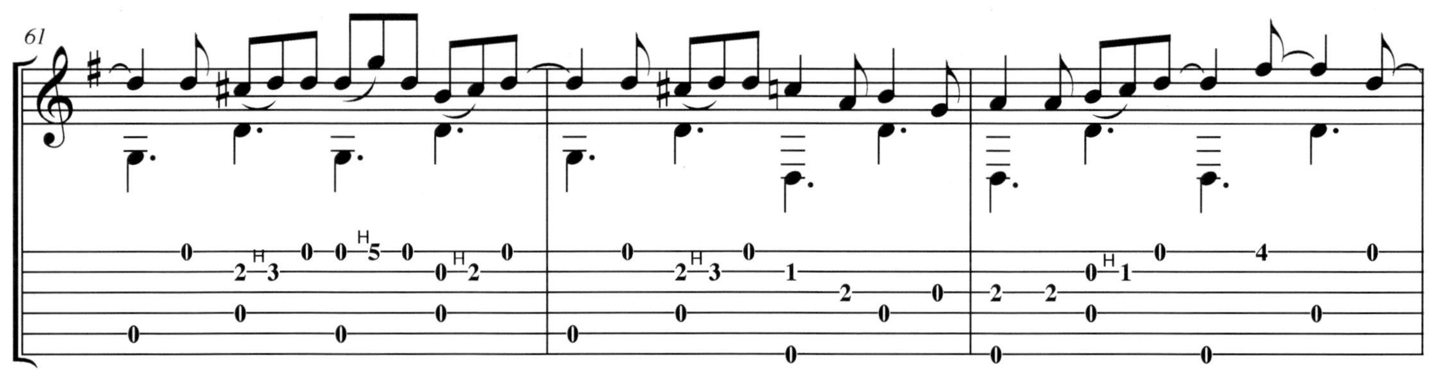
61

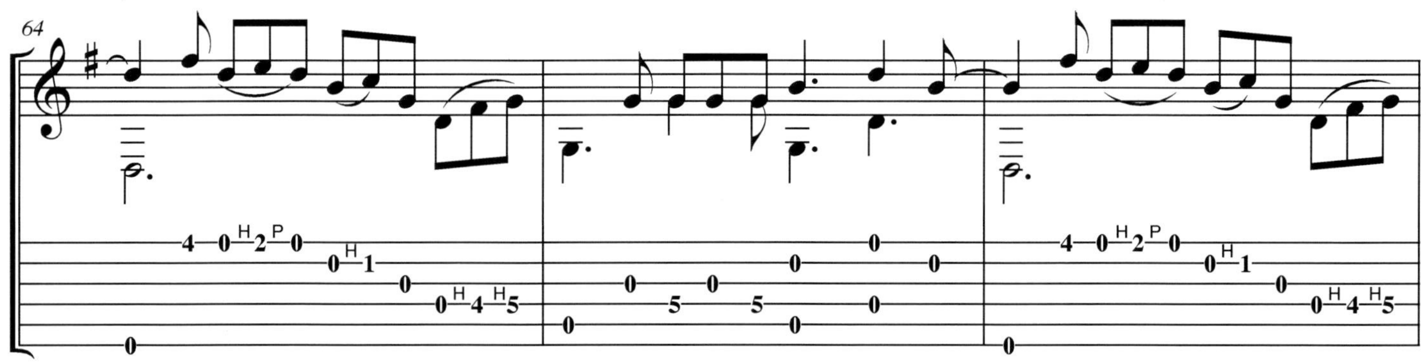
64

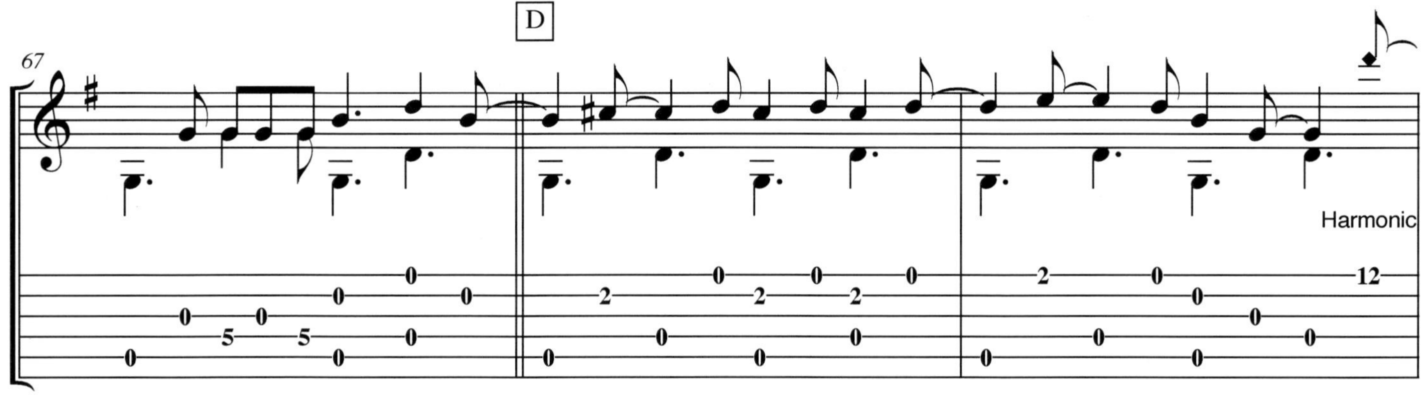
D
67
Harmonic

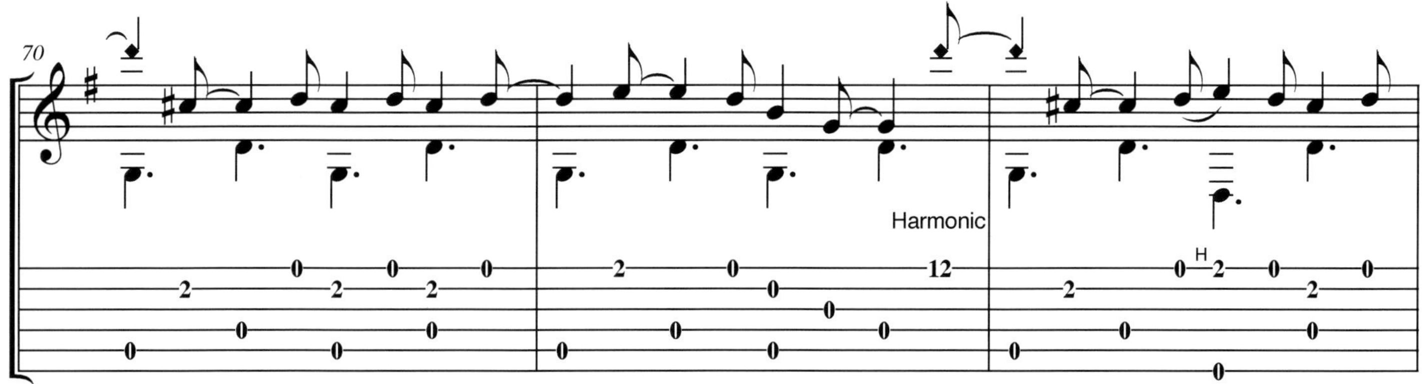
70
Harmonic

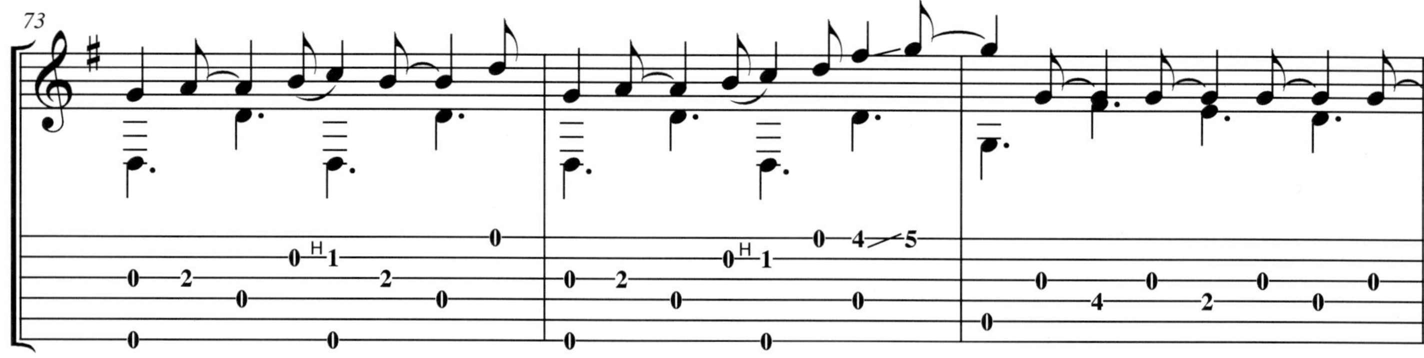

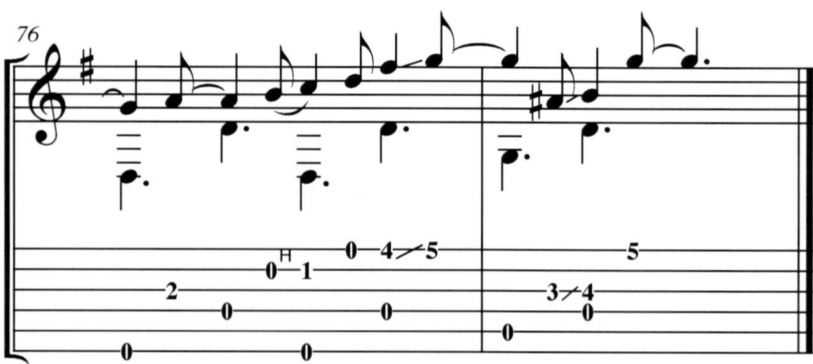

Opihi Moemoe – Live Transcription
Notes

In 2006, I recorded a double CD's worth of slack key instrumentals as a work-for-hire project. Due to a number of factors I wasn't satisfied with the recordings and so insisted they be released under a pseudonym, Uji Oma'oma'o. So now you know the answer to *that* mystery. I later took a handful of the best takes and released them as a CD and book set called "Old Time Hawaiian Slack Key Guitar."

In the final minutes of the sessions – with the clock ticking, the producer distracted and yours truly feeling a great deal of pressure – I decided to have a go at "Opihi Moemoe." I'm not sure why; it isn't a song I'd prepared – in fact I hadn't played it in years. This transcription comes from that completely spontaneous first take.

I've labeled the various sections so you can compare my version with those on the previous few pages.

A Section: I stick pretty close to the basic melody the first time through, with a couple subtle changes. For the first repeat I jump up to the treble strings instead of the more usual variations on the lower strings. Notice how changing the slides to include an F natural in the repeat beginning at measure 35 emphasizes the bluesy nature of the tune.

B Sections: No surprises here, simply the two variations I've already shown you.

C Section: On the first time through, I play out of a barré at the fifth fret – note the variation in measures 29 & 30 – bringing it back to familiar territory on the repeat.

D Section: Nothing really new here, just a few slight deviations from what I've already shown you. I guess I was just happy to be back on firm ground.

I hope you are able to take some of these ideas and create your own take on this classic song.

Lesson Three: Playing Together

Hawaiian slack key guitarists have a unique approach to playing together. Rather than strum chords, the backup guitarist will often play complimentary moving parts based loosely on the song's harmony. The effect is a twisting flow of simultaneous melodic notes – what musicologists call heterophony. It is a difficult technique to pick up if you came up in the "lead guitar rhythm guitar" school.

There are as many ways to *second* as there are slack key guitarists, but I think I can offer a few generalizations.

In the first place, the role of the second guitar is to support the lead. The accompanist will generally play with a lighter touch to allow the main guitarist – or other instrumentalist – to shine. Guitarist number two may use many of the same techniques employed by the lead, including movable two-note "chords," slides, hammer-ons and pull-offs, etc.

The second guitar part may be played at a different register as the lead. For example, if the main guitar is playing a figure that begins at the 9th fret, the accompanist may play down at the bottom of the fretboard. The two parts may move in the same general direction – if the melody moves up the scale, so does the backup. Or the accompanist might choose to move counter to the melodic part. Often the parts will cross, or even come together on the same notes for a brief moment.

Although Hawaiian music does not have the strong call and response tradition found in blues, gospel or other African-American-based musical forms, there is a place for it. When backing up a singer, the guitarist might punctuate the end of a vocal phrase with a chime (harmonic) or insert a short lick as an accent. The goal is to stay out of the way, let the melody shine – and then throw in a bit of punctuation.

Some other things to listen for: When it comes to the turnarounds, each guitarist will often play different vamps. When playing full chords, the accompanist is likely to play arpeggios or broken chords. In certain instances, the second guitarist may play a part based on a repeated figure, or even play bass notes only.

One final note: often slack key guitarists will tune their guitars differently when playing together. The built-in idiosyncrasies of each tuning bring a great deal of variety to the two parts.

The next two arrangements just begin to scratch the surface of how to play slack key with more than one guitarist.

Kealoha

This short arrangement has guitar number one playing a melodic part that stands on its own. The accompaniment is typical of an improvised second part.

Kimo's Slack Key

It is no secret that slack key guitarists like to challenge each other to playful musical duels. I've arranged this great instrumental as if a couple of friends were swapping licks in the back yard.

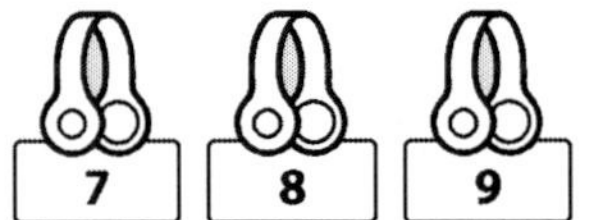

Kealoha
Duet

Maddy Lam & Lei Collins

Taro Patch tuning

Guitar 1

Guitar 2

5

Gtr. 1

5

Gtr. 2

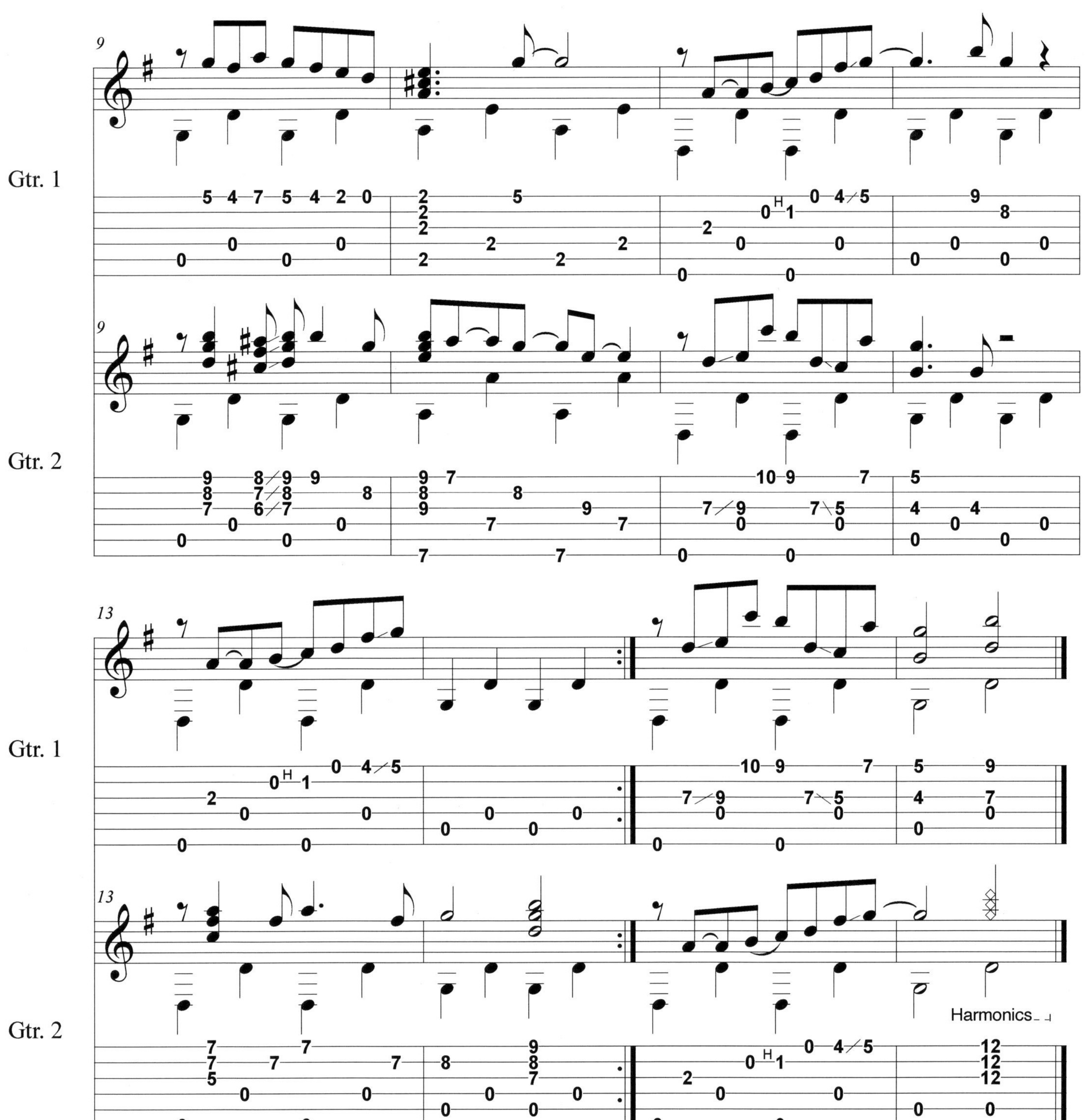
Gtr. 1
Gtr. 2
Harmonics

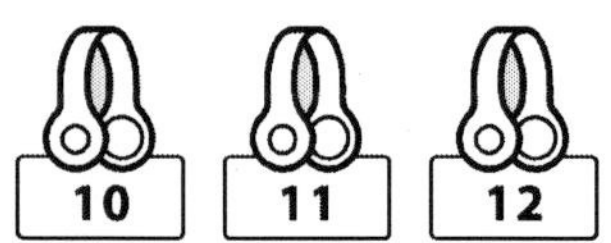

Kimo's Slack Key
Duet

Taro Patch tuning

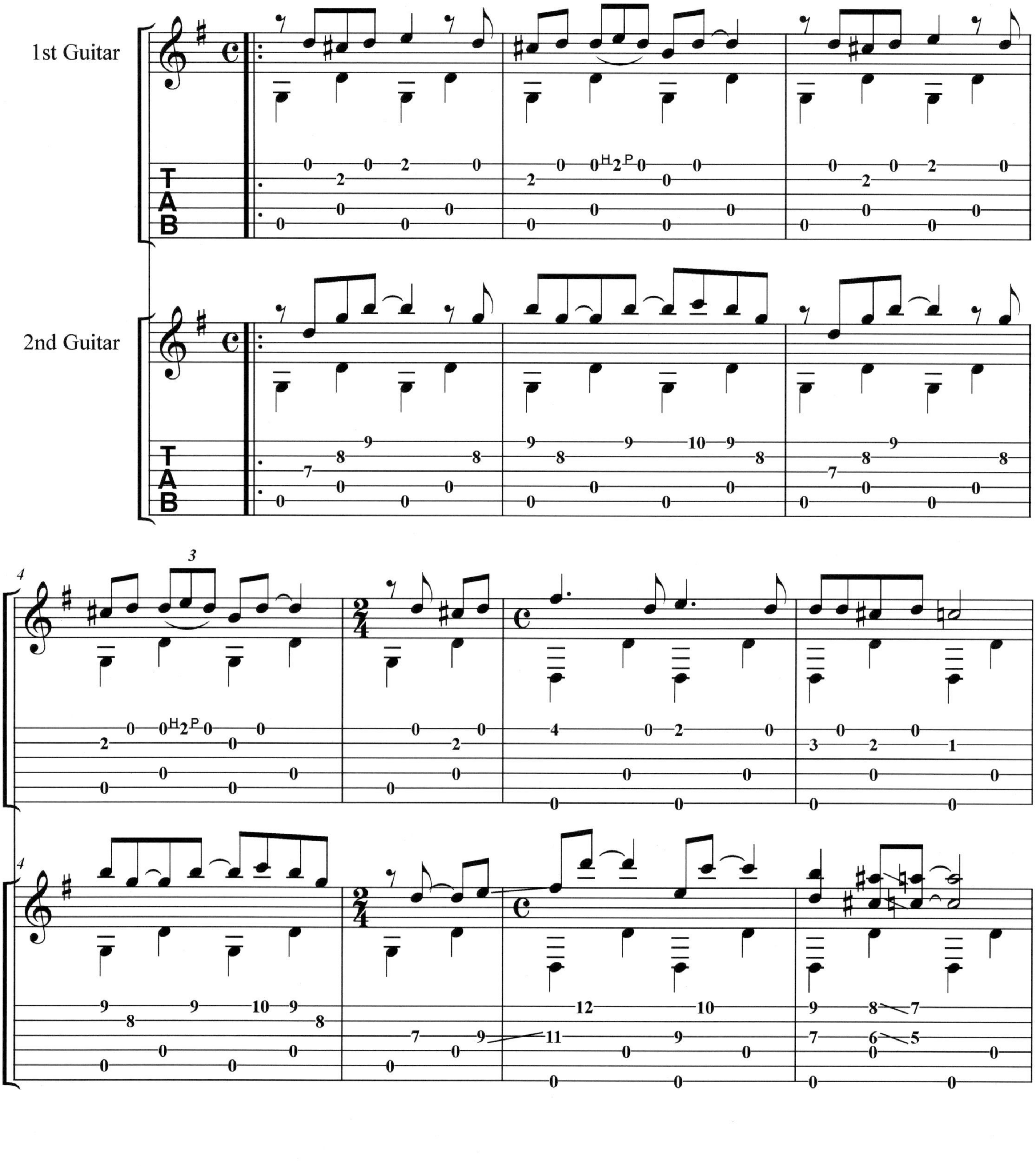

1st Guitar

2nd Guitar

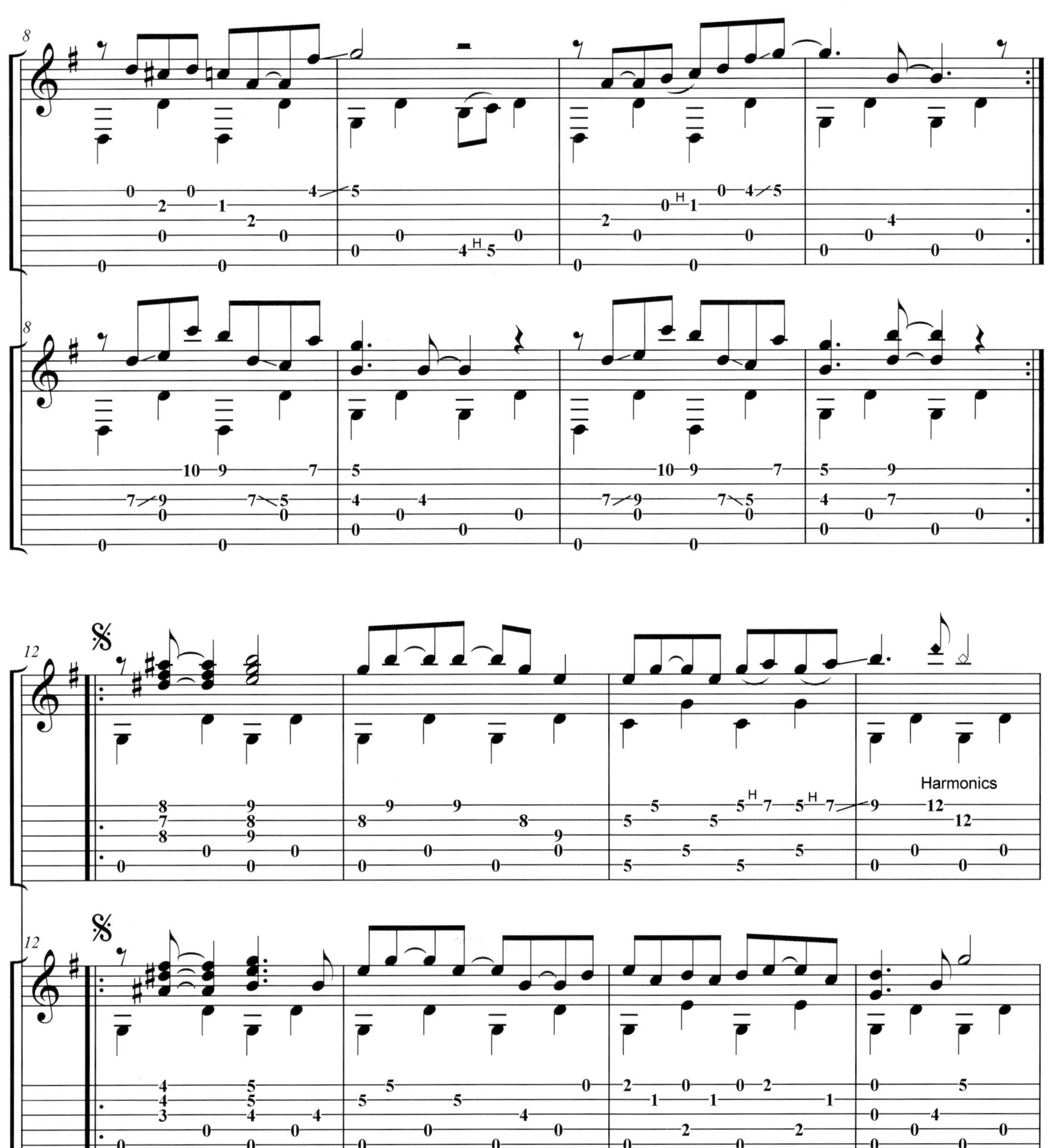
Harmonics

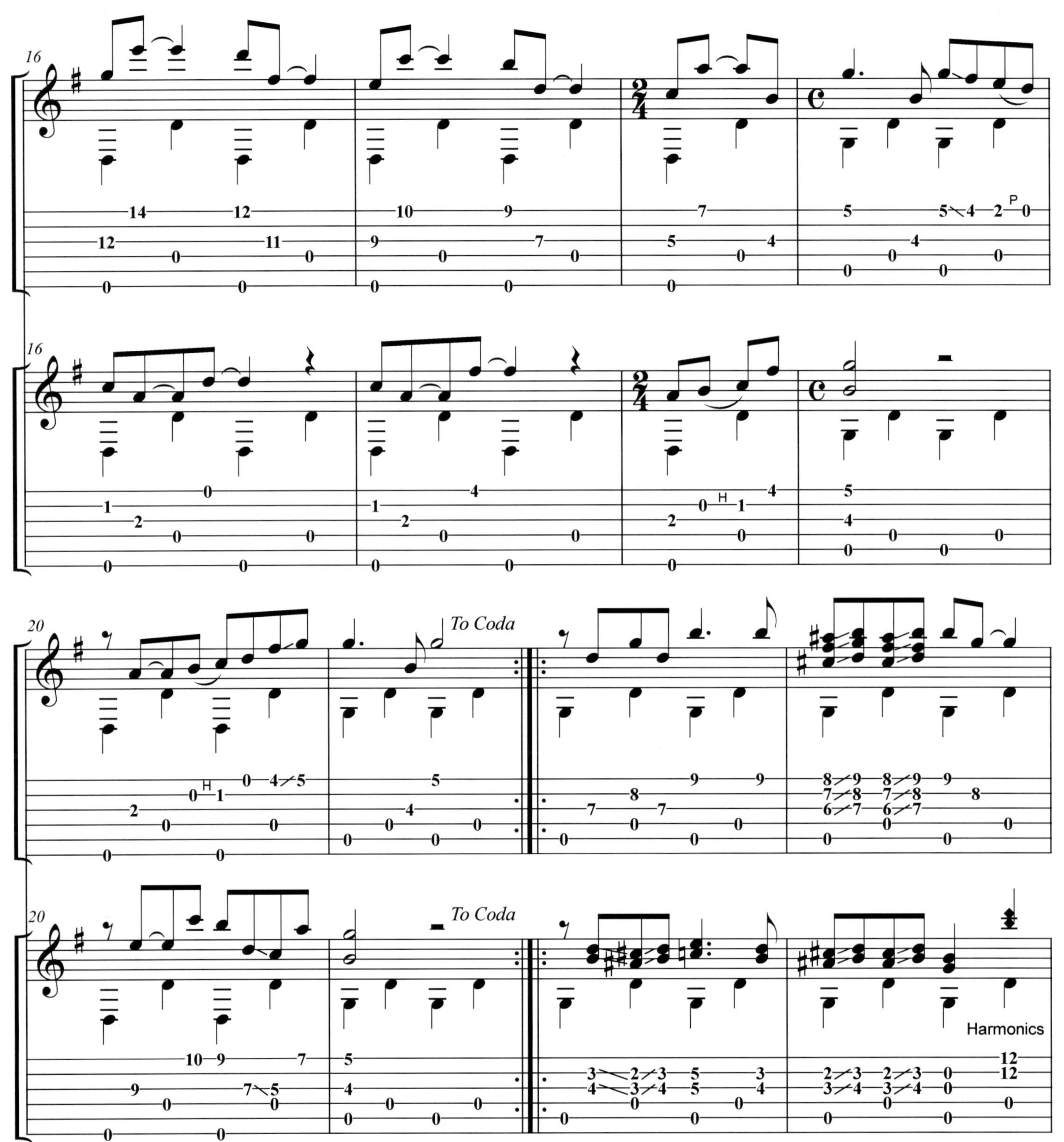
To Coda
To Coda
Harmonics

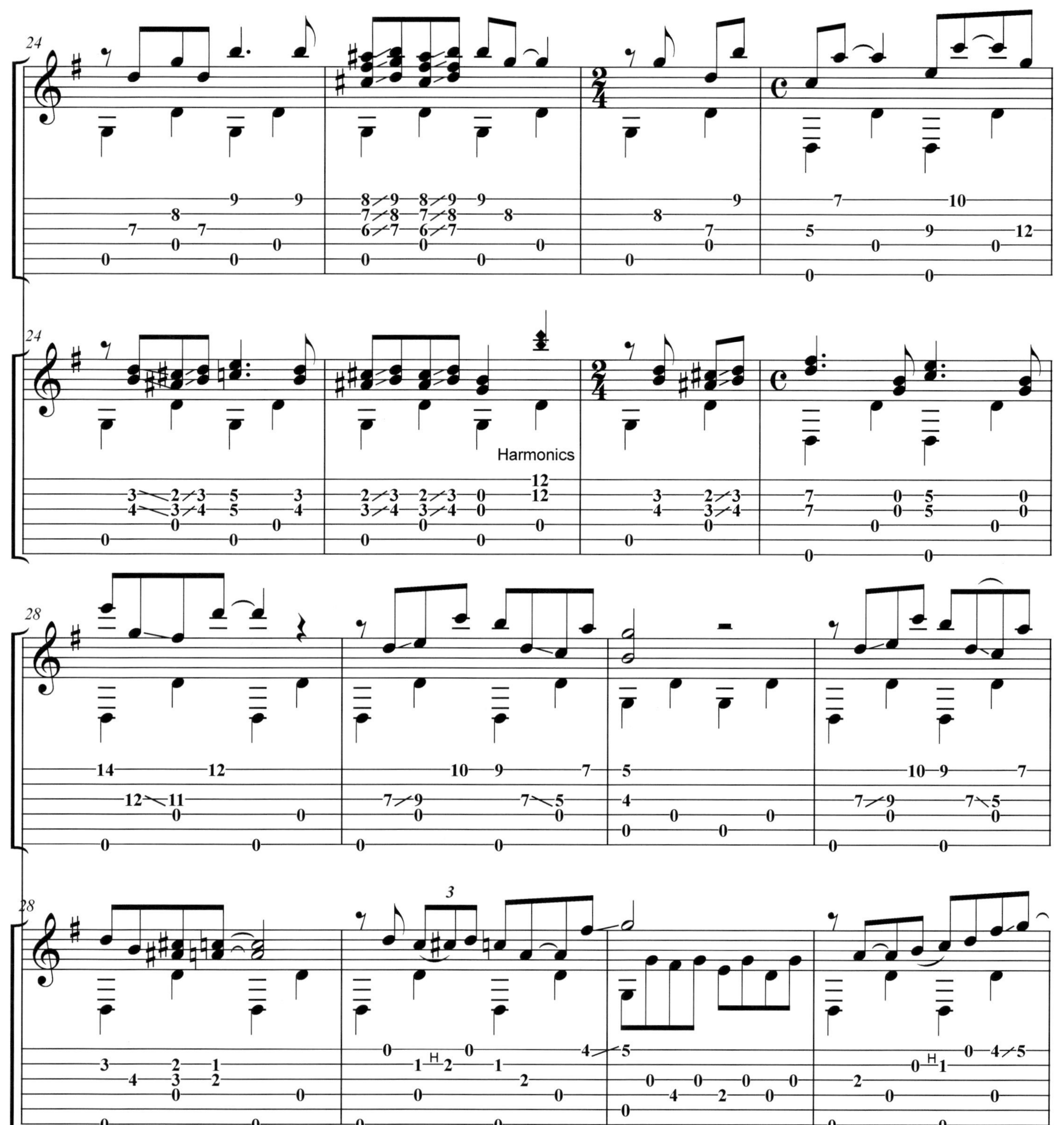
Harmonics

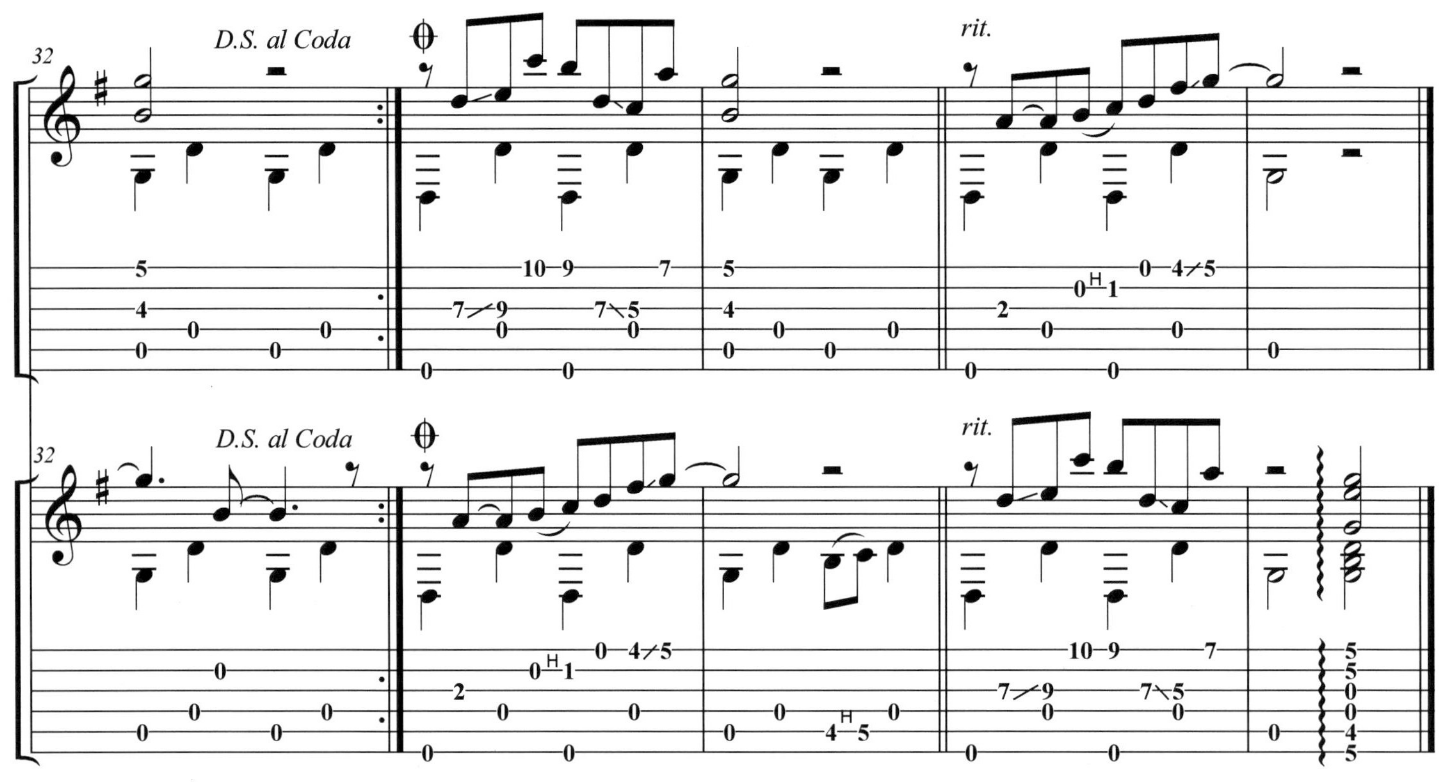
32
D.S. al Coda
rit.
32
D.S. al Coda
rit.

Kealoha
Notes

This duet is structured as if two guitarists were playing in an informal jam. The first guitarist plays the melody and the second creates a simple accompaniment based on the chords.

Measures 1-4: When you are playing together, you need some way to begin. Rather than count things out, a slack key guitarist might play a couple of turnarounds. By the second one the tempo is established and the accompanist can jump in.

Measures 5-8: The melody begins at the 5th fret, so the second part moves higher. Compared to the busy melody, the second part is fairly simple: chords punctuated by a slide. Note the contrasting turnarounds; one low, one high.

Measures 9-12: The melody repeats in the first bar, so the accompaniment does as well. Then each part plays a different inversion of the A major chord before dropping back into a pair of turnarounds.

Measures 13-14: Rather than repeat the vamp again, the second part softens things up with a simple chord. Notice that the two parts do not resolve back to the tonic on the same beat.

Kimo's Slack Key
Notes

The two closely interlocked parts in this arrangement make for a fun duet.

Measures 1-4: Pay attention to how the rhythmic emphasis shifts between the two parts. The second guitar plays a simple arpeggio pattern behind the melody, adding a pull-off as a response figure in measures 2 & 4.

Measures 5-7: Another example of the second part moving to a different part of the neck. Here is a good trick to know: You can usually play a descending series of double-stops whenever the song goes to a dominant chord. Don't worry about the time signature change in measure 5; just keep a steady quarter-note pulse in the bass.

Measures 12-15: The accompanist plays a part that closely follows the rhythm of the melody. The dissonance in measure 14 is intentional; it is inspired by similar dissonance in the first part of the melody. You will find that not all Hawaiian music is sweet and smooth; there is a little volcanic grit in there too.

Measures 16-21: The two parts move parallel in different registers. It isn't exactly a harmony, more like the synchronized swimming of a couple of dolphins moving through the surf together.

Measures 22-25: For the next time through the melody, the two guitars trade roles. The second guitar now has the lead and guitar 1 plays backup. Wanting to show off a bit, Guitar 2 lets loose with a variation of the first section that uses double stops and slides to play the twisty bits. Guitar 1 answers with arpeggios and slides to punctuate the rhythm.

Measure 26-32: Since the melody moves down, the accompaniment moves up.

At measure 32, go back and repeat the second part of the tune. Rather than write a complete new arrangement for the repeat, I left it up to you. Try switching the two parts, or see what else you can come up with. Listen to the recording for some ideas.

For an extended solo arrangement of this song, see *Old Time Hawaiian Slack Key Guitar.*

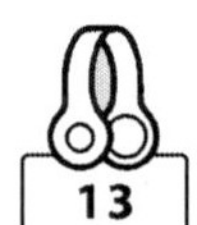

The Road to Duke's

Mark Nelson

Taro Patch tuning

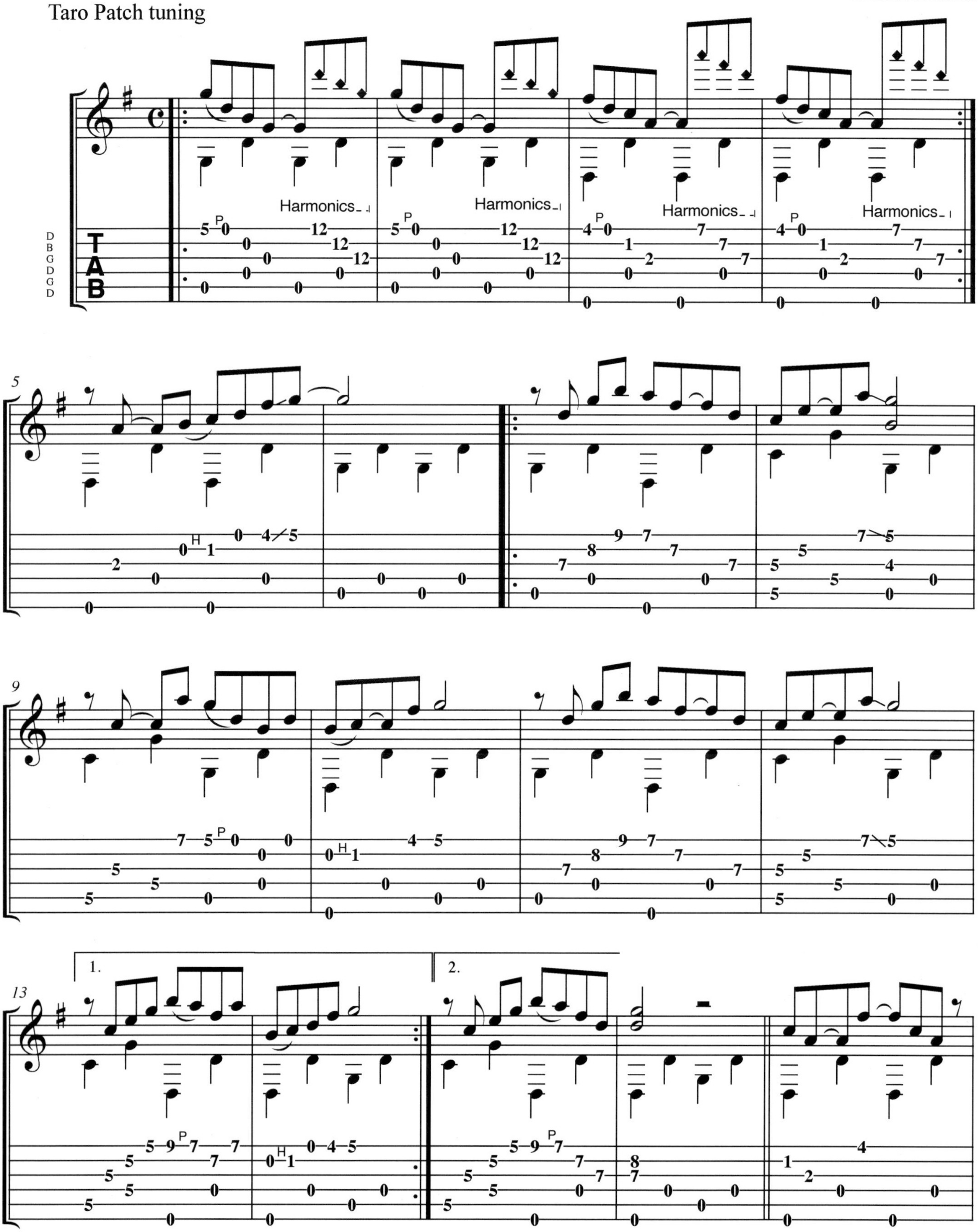

D B G D G D

Harmonics

5

9

13

1.

2.

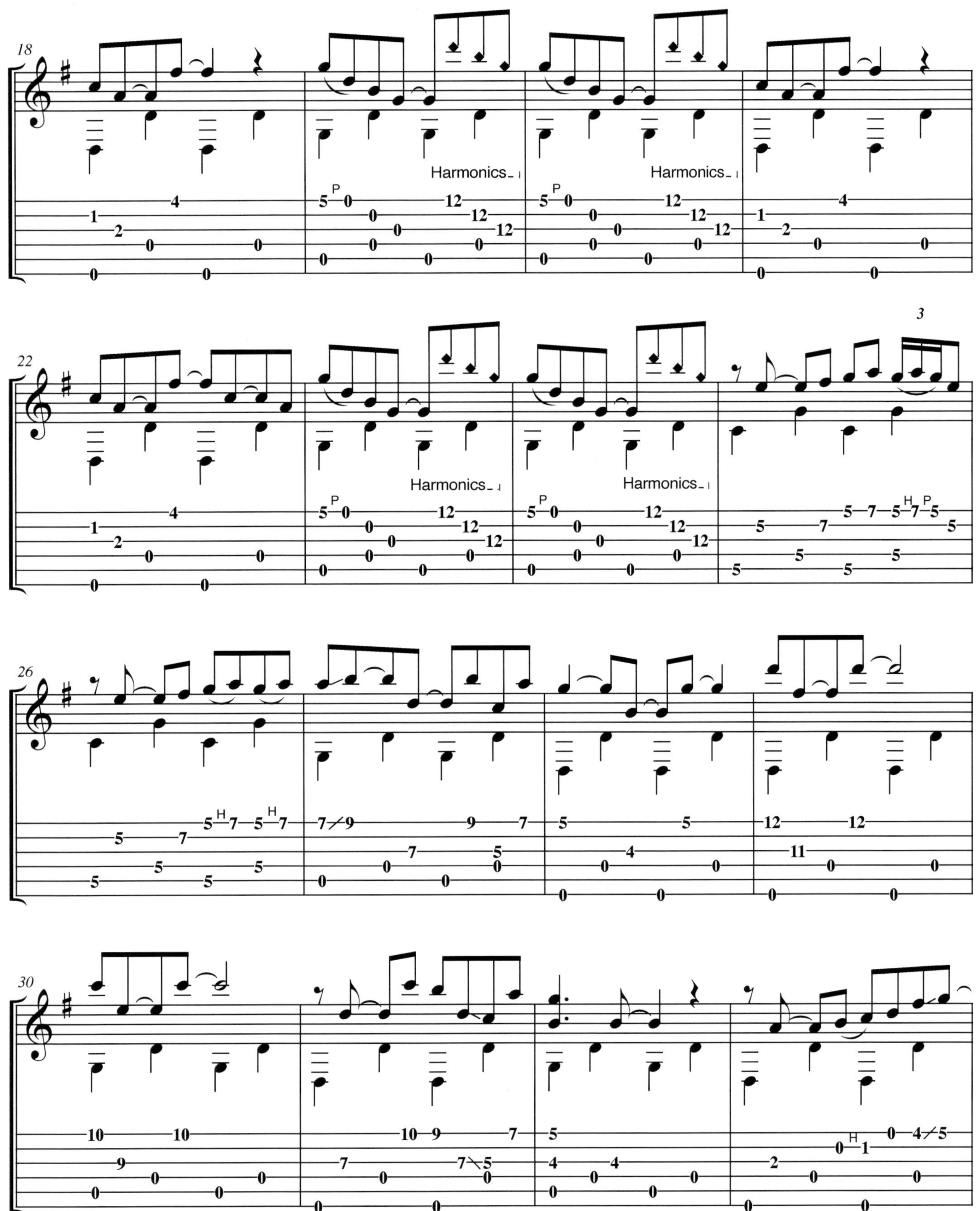
Harmonics
Harmonics
Harmonics
Harmonics

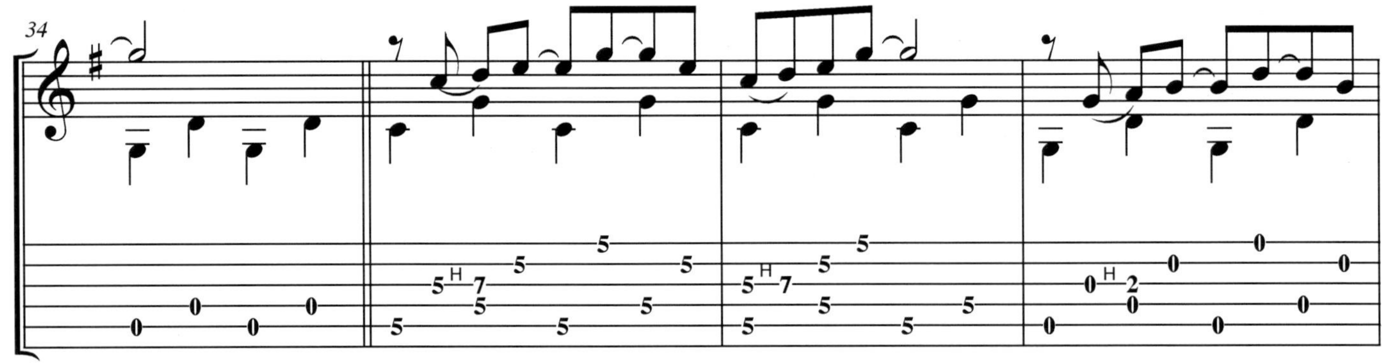
34
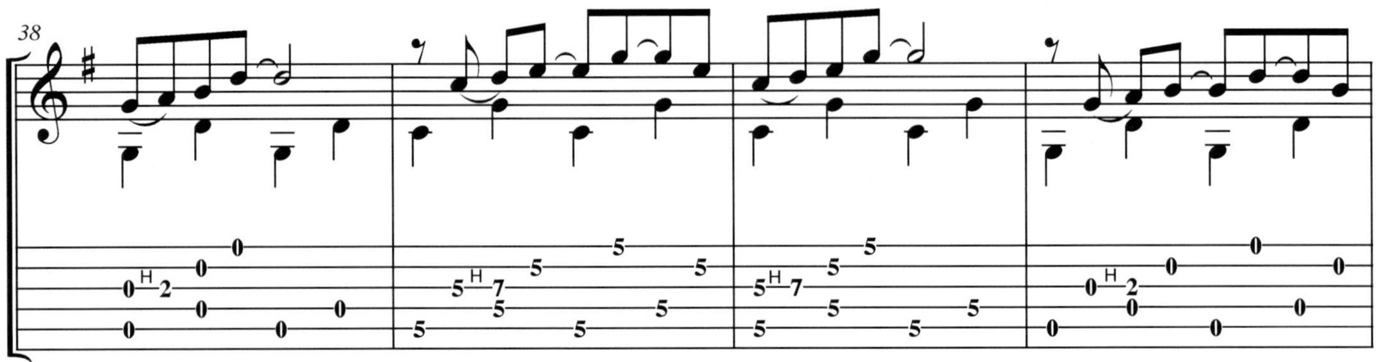
38
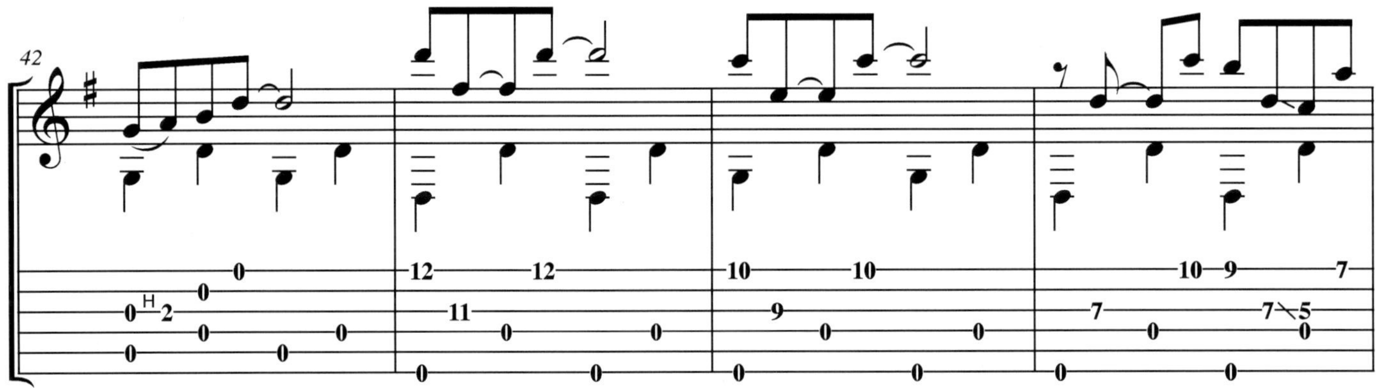
42
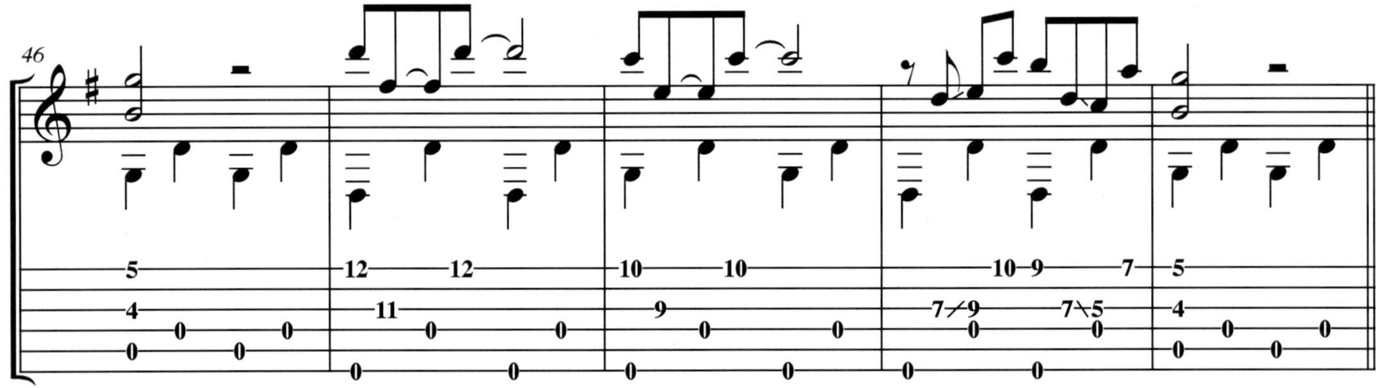
46

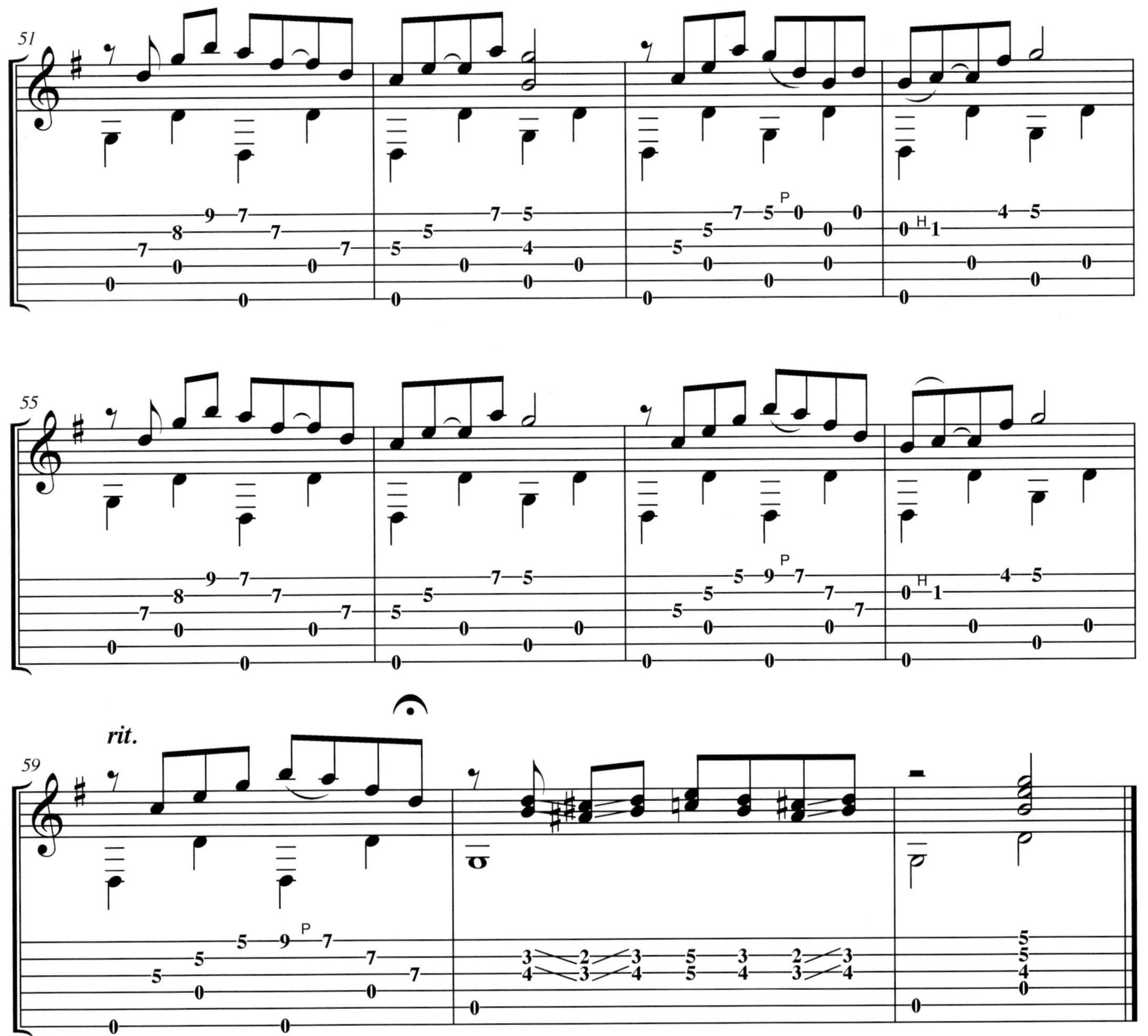

The Road to Duke's
Notes

Measures 1-4: The intro moves between the tonic and 5th chords with harmonics tossed in. It might take some practice to be able to get the chimes to sound while keeping in time.

Measures 7-15: The main melody moves quickly between the I, V & IV chords in just the first two measures. Pay attention to which notes are played out of barré positions. You'll be shifting in and out of barres often.

Measures 17-34: The second part of the tune begins with a figure based on the introduction. It then moves through the C and G chords before the descending broken double-stop figures played over the D7 chord.

Measures 35-50: To emphasize the contrast, play the interlude at a greatly reduced volume. Gradually increase the volume as you play through the descending figures beginning at measure 43.

Measure 60: You can use this ending figure in many different Taro Patch songs.

Lesson Four – Some Thoughts on Composing a New Slack Key Song – “The Road to Duke’s”

Sooner or later, everyone who plays slack key wants to compose an original tune. You might want to capture the feeling of watching the moonlight play on a calm ocean – the inspiration for Uncle Ray Kane’s “Punahele.” Or perhaps you want to challenge other guitarists to up their game, as with Sonny Chillingworth’s “Wee Haw Swing.”

Occasionally a melody just comes out of nowhere and you have to get to your guitar and play it. That was the genesis of “The Road to Duke’s.” My wife and I were on our way to Hana, Maui, to visit a friend. As we wound our way down that supremely twisty road, a tune popped into my head that would not go away. When we reached Duke’s home, I waved away the proffered Martini, grabbed my guitar, and played the entire tune just as it appears here.

But, is “The Road to Duke’s” slack key, or is it just another guitar instrumental? That is a very good question.

Not everything played out of an open tuning is slack key. I have heard countless student compositions that, while pretty and well crafted, bear no resemblance to slack key style. The music might be harmonically complex – moving between lush chords in slowly revolving arpeggios – the tempos as languid as a Moloka‘i morning. But there is nothing to distinguish the music from any other fingerpicked guitar genre.

So what is it that makes slack key *sound* like slack key?

Here are my thoughts on the subject:

Slack key is primarily melodic – most slack key pieces originated as songs. Techniques such as sliding two-note figures based on thirds and sixths, syncopation, triplets and other slurs, and chimes are employed to give life to the melody. Most slack key songs employ repeated turnarounds – the “Hawaiian Vamp.” The bass strings are always prominent. You have encountered all of these elements as you have worked through this book.

Instrumental slack key pieces often consist of one or two themes that are then subjected to countless variations. Slack key songs may be played slowly, or they may run at a blistering pace. Most players play with a subtle swing that is almost impossible to define.

You may also have noticed that the music favors major keys and is relatively uncomplicated harmonically. The majority of slack key songs are built around the tonic and dominant – I and V – chords, often with an implied II7 chord – an A7 in the key of G – for the turnaround. That is not to say Hawaiian music cannot be harmonically sophisticated; take a look at some of the passing chords in “Pua Sadinia” or “Pua Lilia.”

“The Road to Duke’s” meets all of those criteria for slack key save one. It wasn’t written by a Hawaiian – or at least by someone from the Islands – an argument that I respect. Of course, neither were “La Paloma,” recorded by Raymond Kane, “Bali Hai” recorded by Keola Beamer, or “Silver Threads Among the Gold,” recorded by Leonard Kwan.

Some say that to be slack key, the composition must be based on an existing Hawaiian song style or traditional slack key instrumental form. But that would leave out many newer slack key compositions by noted Hawaiian musicians.

I offer “The Road to Duke’s” as a example of how to compose something new using elements of the slack key style. As you play through this – and “Po Mahina Slack Key,” “Annie’s Slack Key Lullabye,” and “Aunty’s Christmas Goose,” – take note of how the tunes make use of melody and harmony, vamps, and other features common to the traditional slack key pieces. And take note, too, on how they differ.

“The Road to Duke’s” begins with pull-offs, chimes, and typical slack key vamps. It then moves into the main theme, a melodic figure based around quick shifts between G, C, and D chord positions. The long middle section is based around the intro lick, and then moves up to a passage beginning on the C chord that is similar to the second strain of “Kolomona Slack Key.” So far, everything is right out of the slack key playbook.

The only non-standard bit is the bridge beginning at measure 35, with the repeated C $^{add\,2}$ – G $^{add\,2}$ chords. Of course, I’ve heard any number of modern slack key players do something similar.

Is it slack key? That is up to you. Duke liked it, and, yes, he makes a great Martini.

Part 2: A Voyage Through *Kī Hōʻalu* Tunings

Here are a number of classic slack key songs – and a couple of my own – arranged to give you a taste of how a different tuning can radically change the sound of your guitar. Each tuning suggests a new approach and a new sonic palette.

As you play through these new tunings, pay attention to how familiar licks like turnarounds and two note "chords" fall in different parts of the guitar. Take note, too, of the changes in the way you use the bass. Some tunings have open bass strings for the tonic and dominant chords, others do not.

As I said, these are but a few of the hundreds of tunings slack key guitarists employ. Think of this section as a quick sail around the Islands – a glimpse into the vast ocean that is *kī hōʻalu.*

Double Slack Tuning: D-G-D-F♯-B-D

Po Mahina Slack Key

My take on a quintessential slack key instrumental style. Dedicated to Dennis Lake, luthier extraordinaire, and his wife Nancy.

Drop C Tuning: C-G-D-G-B-D

Sanoe

Queen Liliʻuokalani's immortal love song, in an arrangement that shifts from C to F and back again.

Annie's Slack Key Lullabye

Once upon a time I asked my wife what she wanted for her birthday. She said, "Write me a song."

Aunty's Christmas Goose

Aunty Nona Beamer called me one day to chat. When she told me she was cooking a goose for Christmas dinner, an image popped into my head of Aunty chasing the poor fowl while clutching an axe.

Lesson Five: Jus' Press – Improvisation in Slack Key

C Wahine Tuning: C-G-D-G-B-E

Kawohikukapulani

An elegant classic from the Golden Age of Hawaiian music.

Las Blancas Flores

The melody comes from a folio of early Californio music. The vaqueros who brought the first guitars to Hawaiʻi may have played this song.

F Wahine Tuning: C-F-C-G-C-E

He Aloha Noʻo Honolulu

A celebration of Hawaii's capitol city.

Makee Ailana

The song is named after a popular spot for courting in the early days of Waikiki.

B♭ Major Tuning: F-B♭-D-F-B♭-D

Green Rose Hula

A hula classic that shows off some of the finer points of this tuning.

Pua Lilia

One of the most beautiful melodies I've ever heard.

D Major Add 9 Tuning: D-A-E-F♯-A-D

Kuʻu Lei Awapuhi Melemele

The title translates as "My Yellow Ginger Lei."

C Mauna Loa Tuning: C-G-E-G-A-E

Aloha Medley

Two lovely songs of parting: "Isa Lei" and "Aloha ʻOe." A fitting closing for your slack key journey.

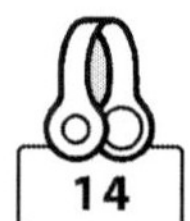

Po Mahina Slack Key

Double Slack tuning

Mark Nelson

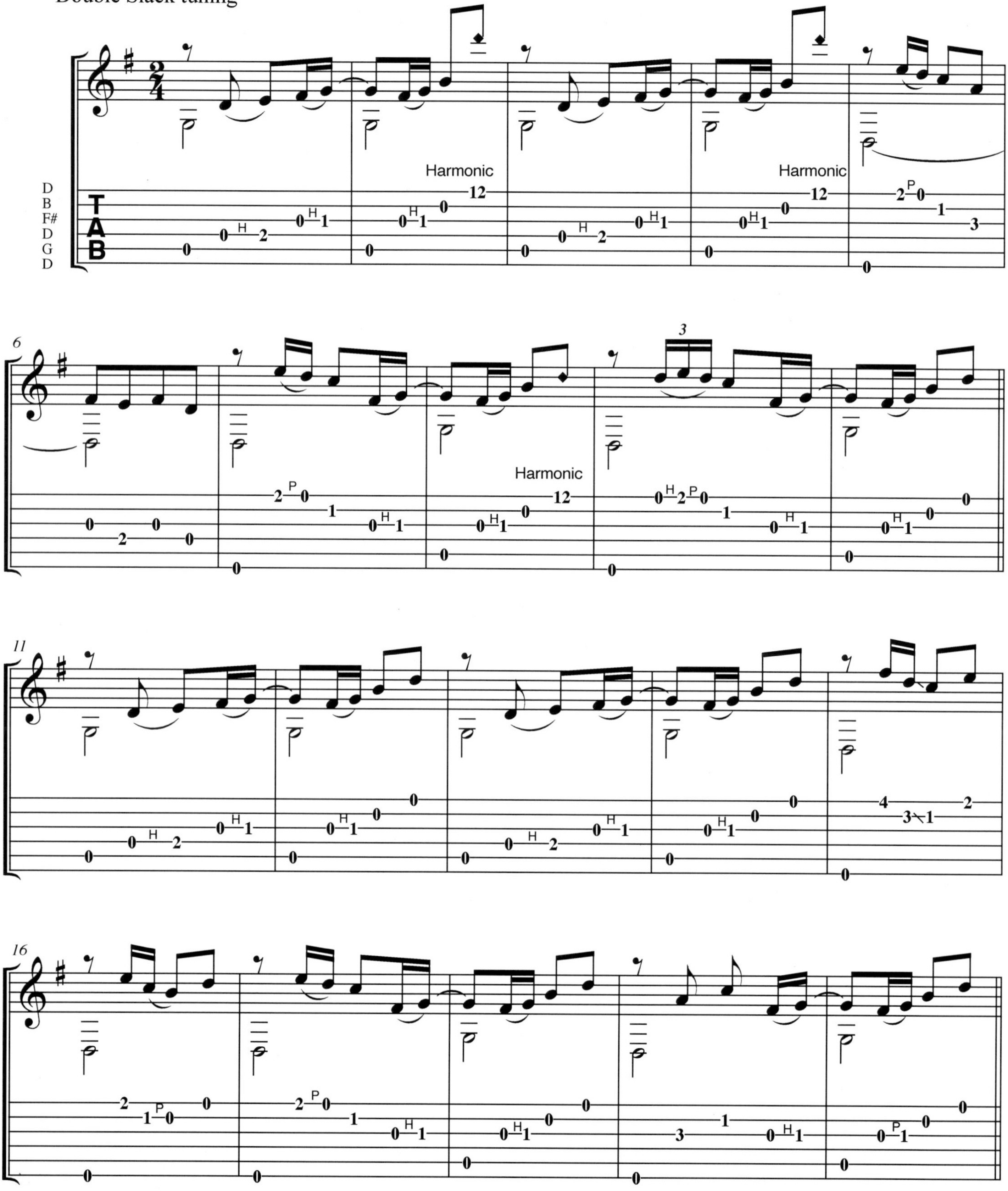

Harmonic

Harmonic

D B F# D G D

TAB

6

Harmonic

11

16

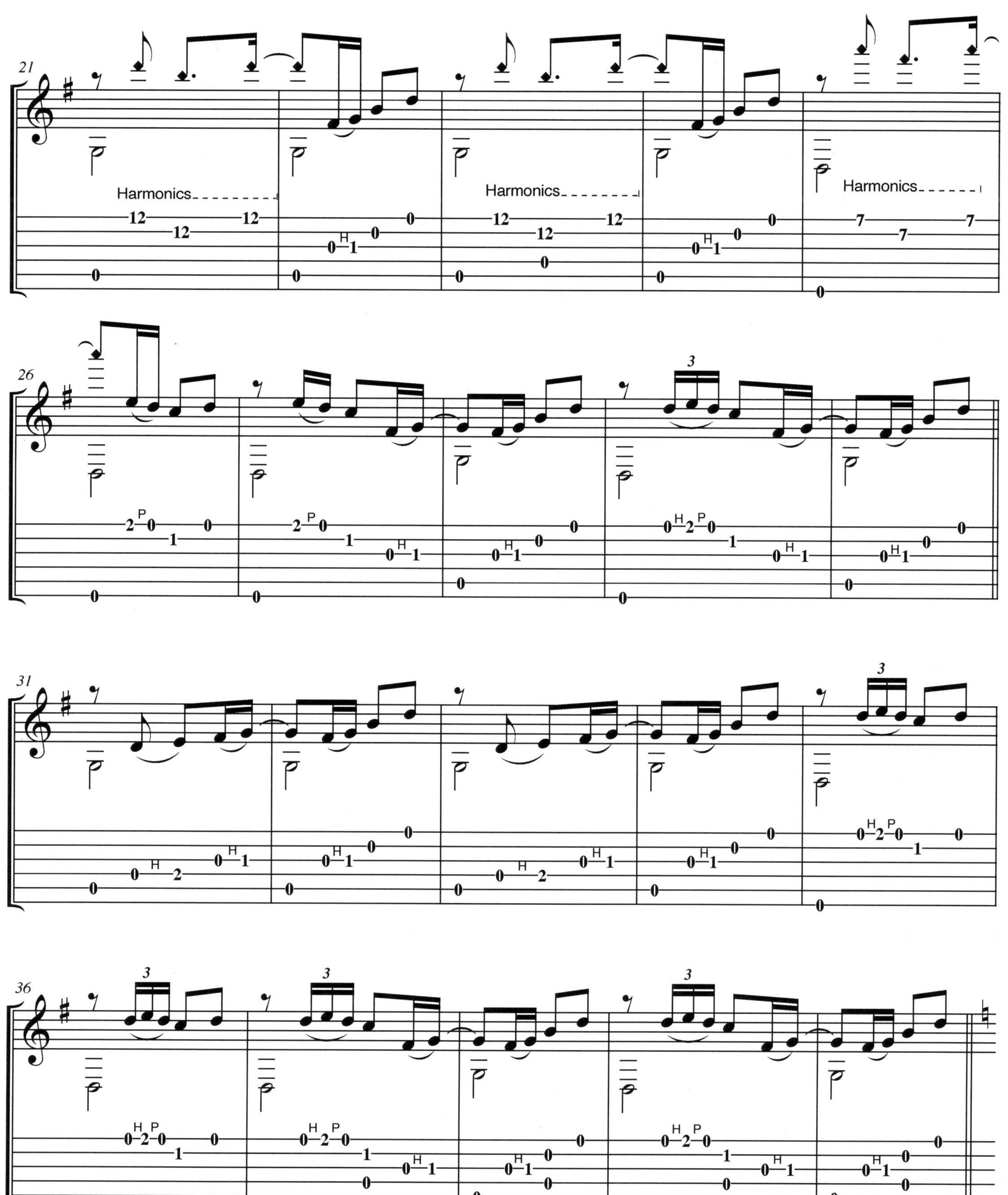
21
Harmonics
Harmonics
Harmonics
26
31
36

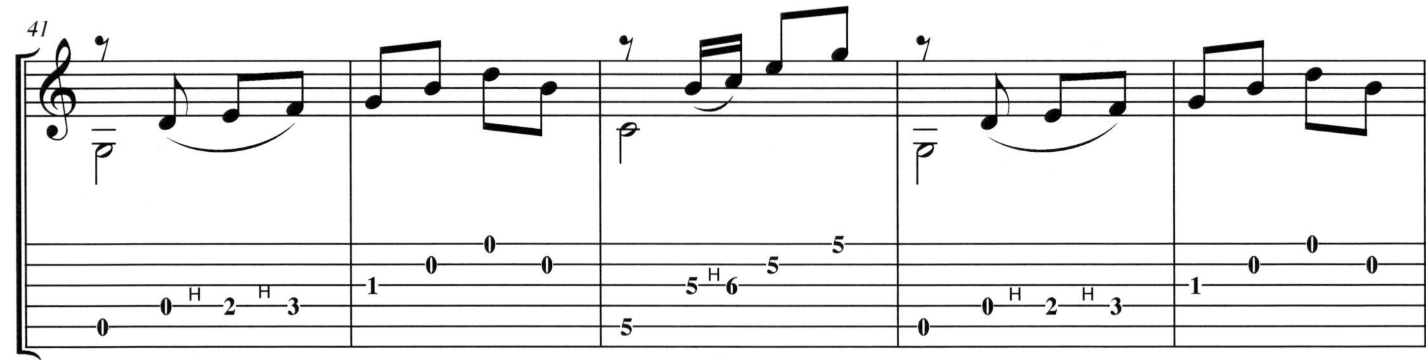
41
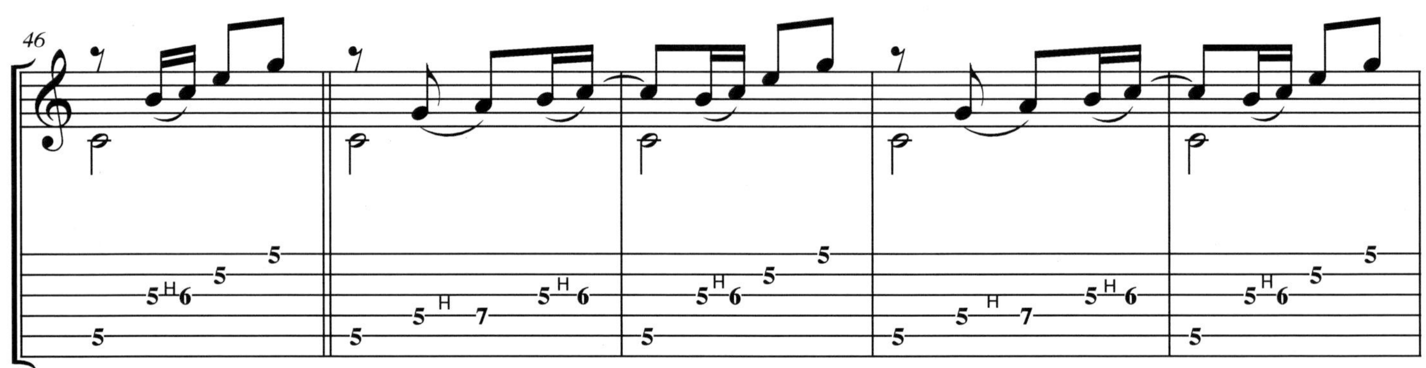
46
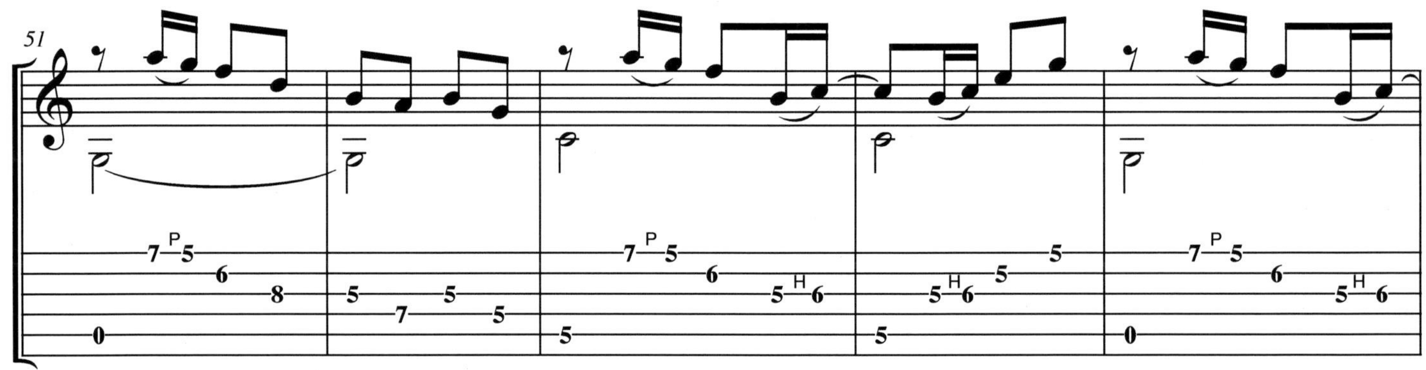
51
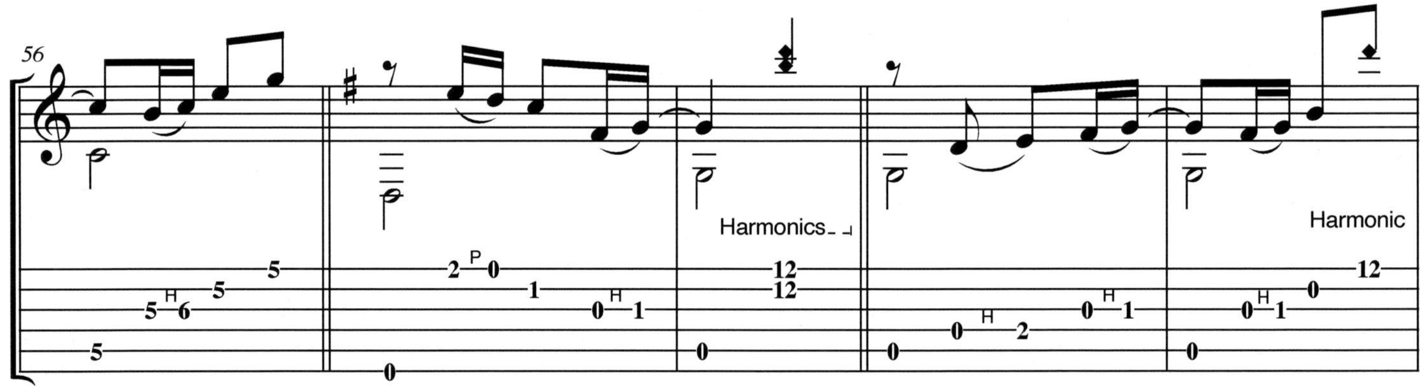
56
Harmonics
Harmonic

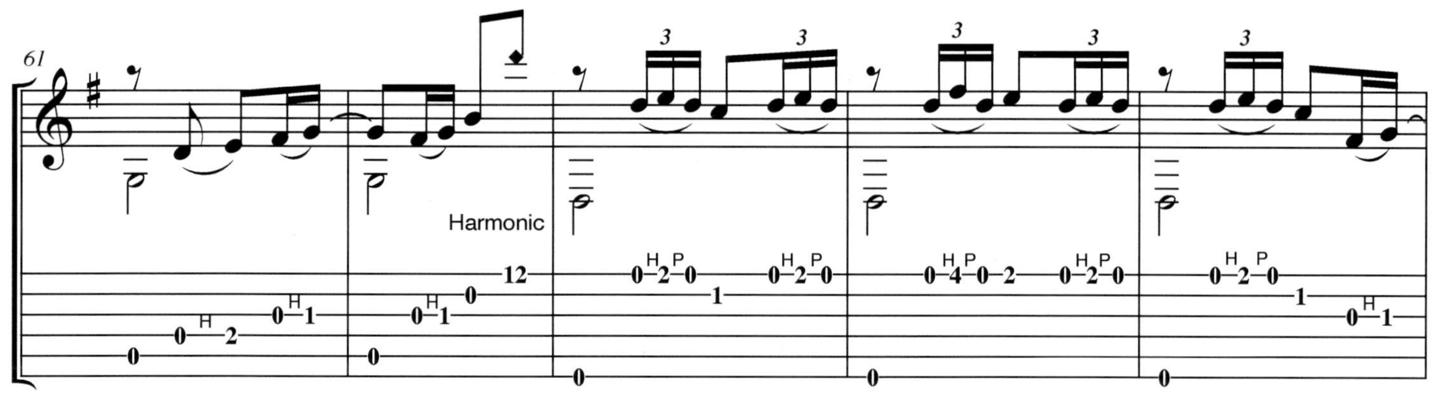
61
Harmonic

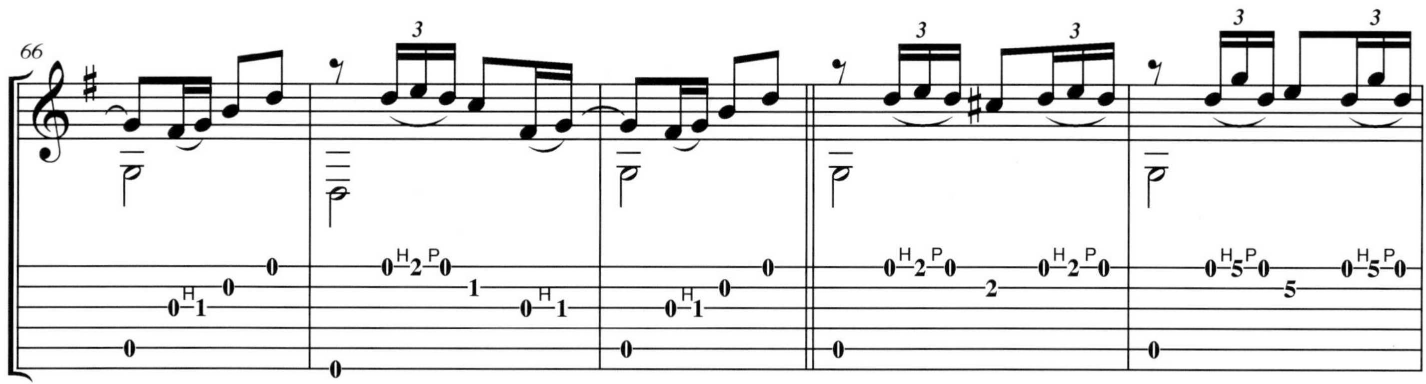
66

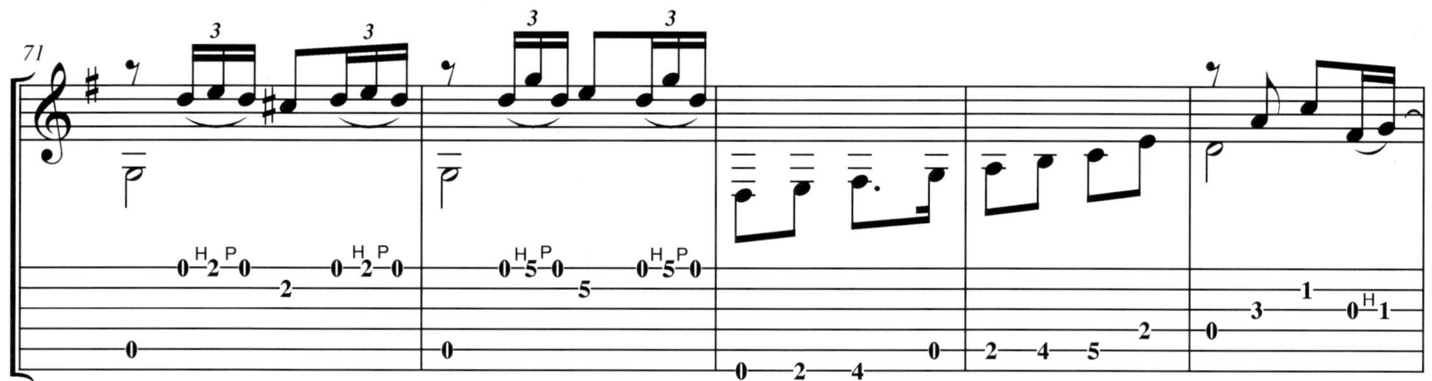
71

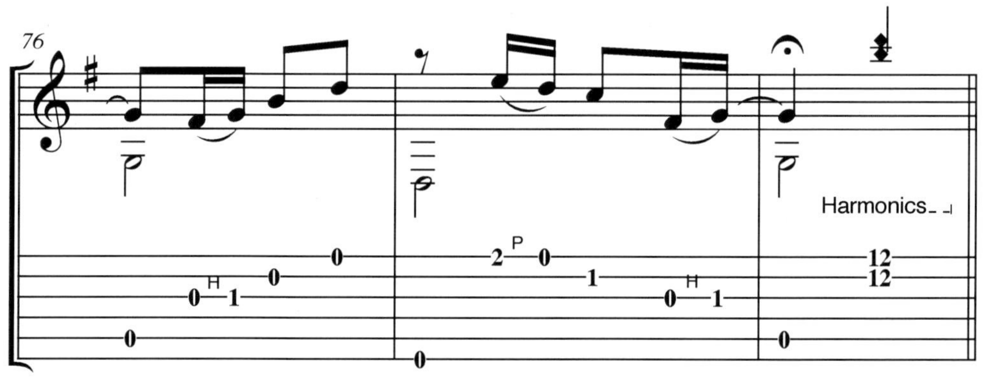
76
Harmonics

Double Slack Tuning
D-G-D-F♯-B-D

Like all Wahine tunings, Double Slack contains a major seventh interval. To tune to Double Slack from Taro Patch, simply drop your 3rd string a half step – from G to F♯. To play a G chord, hold down the 3rd string at the first fret. For the D7, move that finger to the first fret of the 2nd string. EZ, no?

Po Mahina Slack Key
Notes

"Po Mahina Slack Key" follows the same basic 10-measure "theme and variation" form as "Punahele," "Malasadas," "Whee Ha Swing," and countless other slack key instrumentals: Four measures of the tonic chord (G), two measures of the dominant chord (D7) and two quick turnarounds from the D back to the G.

Measures 1-10 are the foundation for everything that follows. These figures are based on the playing of Aunty Alice Namakelua. She would play something similar as an accompaniment to her singing. It is a very old style.

Pay attention to what notes are played out of double stops (measures 15 & 16) and which are played out of barres (measures 46-56).

Once you've played through the tab a few times, try to find your own variations.

Drop C Tuning
C-G-D-G-B-D

Drop C Tuning is essentially just Taro Patch with the lowest string dropped down to C, but it opens a whole new world!

Sanoe
Notes

Measures 1-4: The intro, which moves between C major and G minor7 chords, introduces a wistfulness to the tune. Minor chords are quite rare in Hawaiian music, so what is this about? The answer is revealed in measure 42!

Measure 8: That is not a typo; after playing the open 5th string on beat three of the previous measure, hammer-on to the 5th fret of your bass string with enough power to sound the note. The next two notes are played out of a barré at the 5th fret.

Measures 39-42: After reprising the melody, you play C, Gm7 and C chords just as in the intro. However, thanks to that bass note, the chord in measure 42 is a B♭, not a Gm7. I won't bore you with the music theory behind this, but that tiny change sets up the modulation to F in the following measure.

Measures 43-57: We are now in the key of F. Most of this is played out of closed-position chords. Measure 44 uses a barré at the 5th fret, as do measures 52, and 55-57.

Measures 57-61: This unusual modulation back to the key of C walks down in whole steps from the F/C chord at measure 57 through E♭/B♭ and D♭/A♭ chords. That sets up the final half-step bass movement to the open G and a typical Hawaiian turnaround from G7 back to C. Go back to measure 7 and play down through measure 20.

Measures 62-71: The Coda begins with a reprise of the last two measures of the melody before repeating the chord figure from the introduction.

The final chord is a C^{add2}. Contemporary slack key artists often make use of mysterious chords like this one in their arrangements.

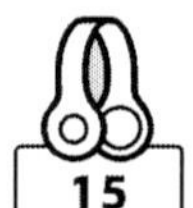

Sanoe

Queen Lili'uokalani

Drop C tuning

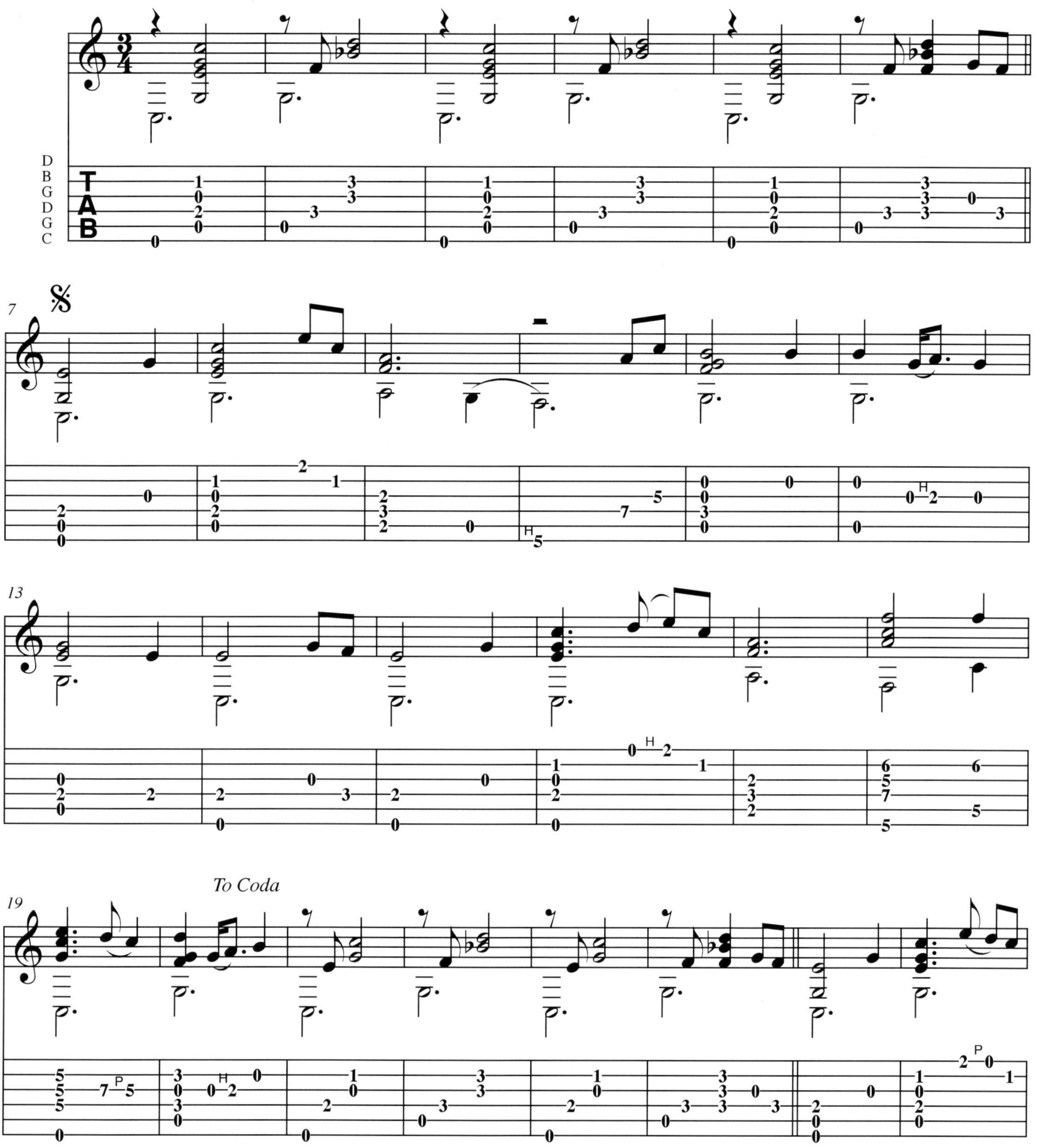

D
B
G
D
G
C

7

13

19

To Coda

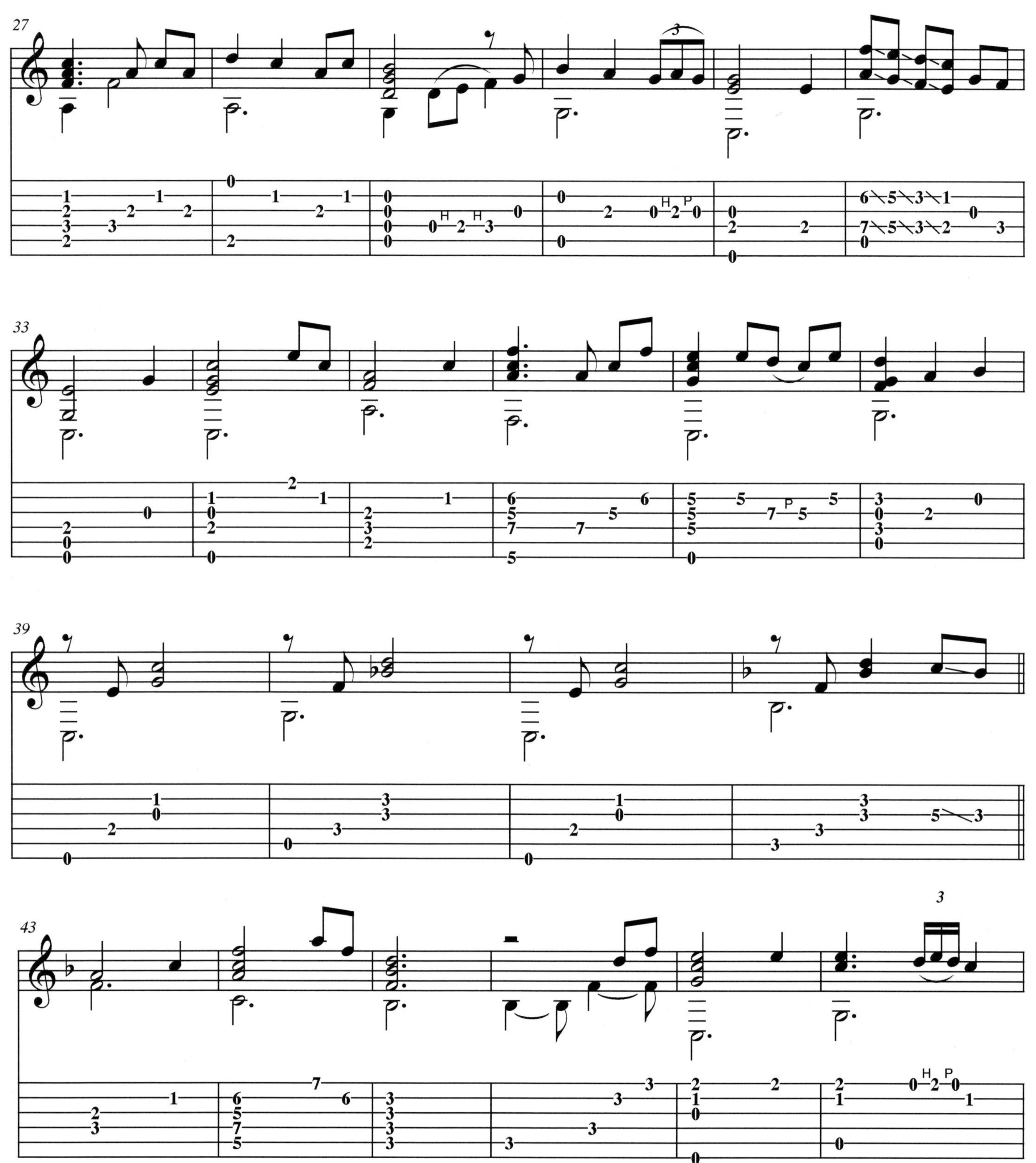
27
33
39
43

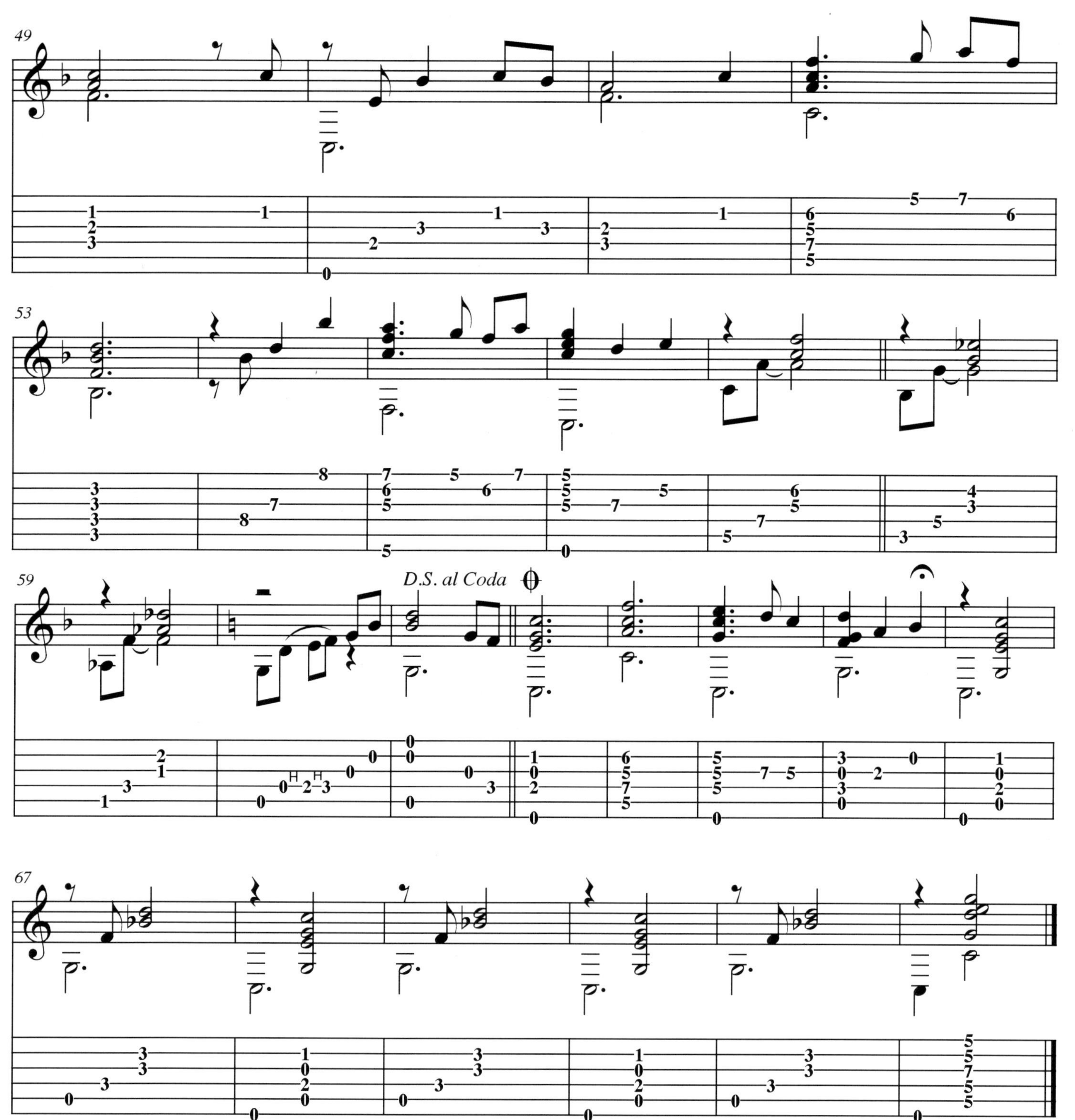
49
53
59
D.S. al Coda
67

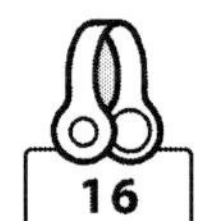

Annie's Slack Key Lullabye

Mark Nelson

Drop C tuning

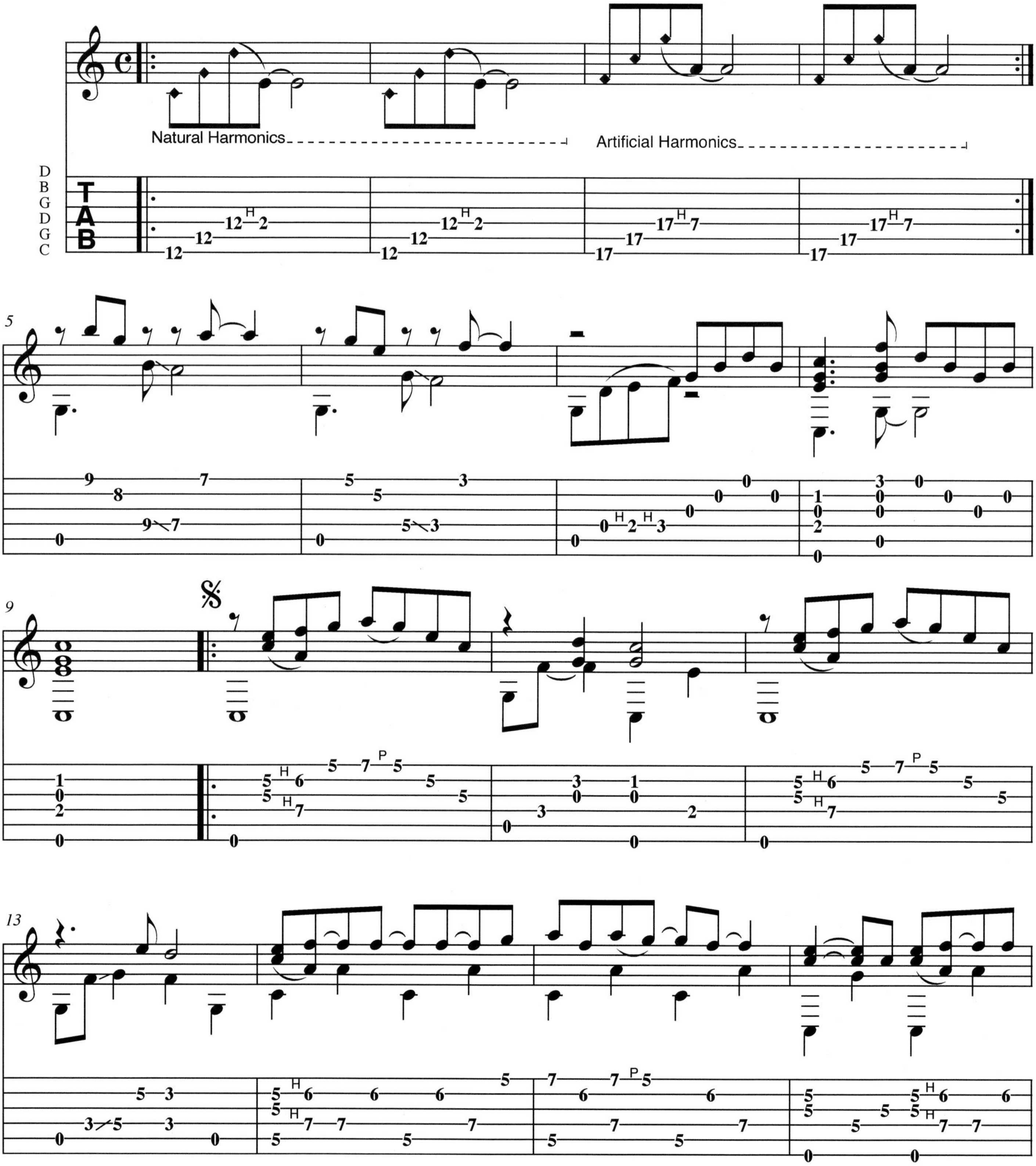

Natural Harmonics

Artificial Harmonics

D B G D G C

TAB

5

9

13

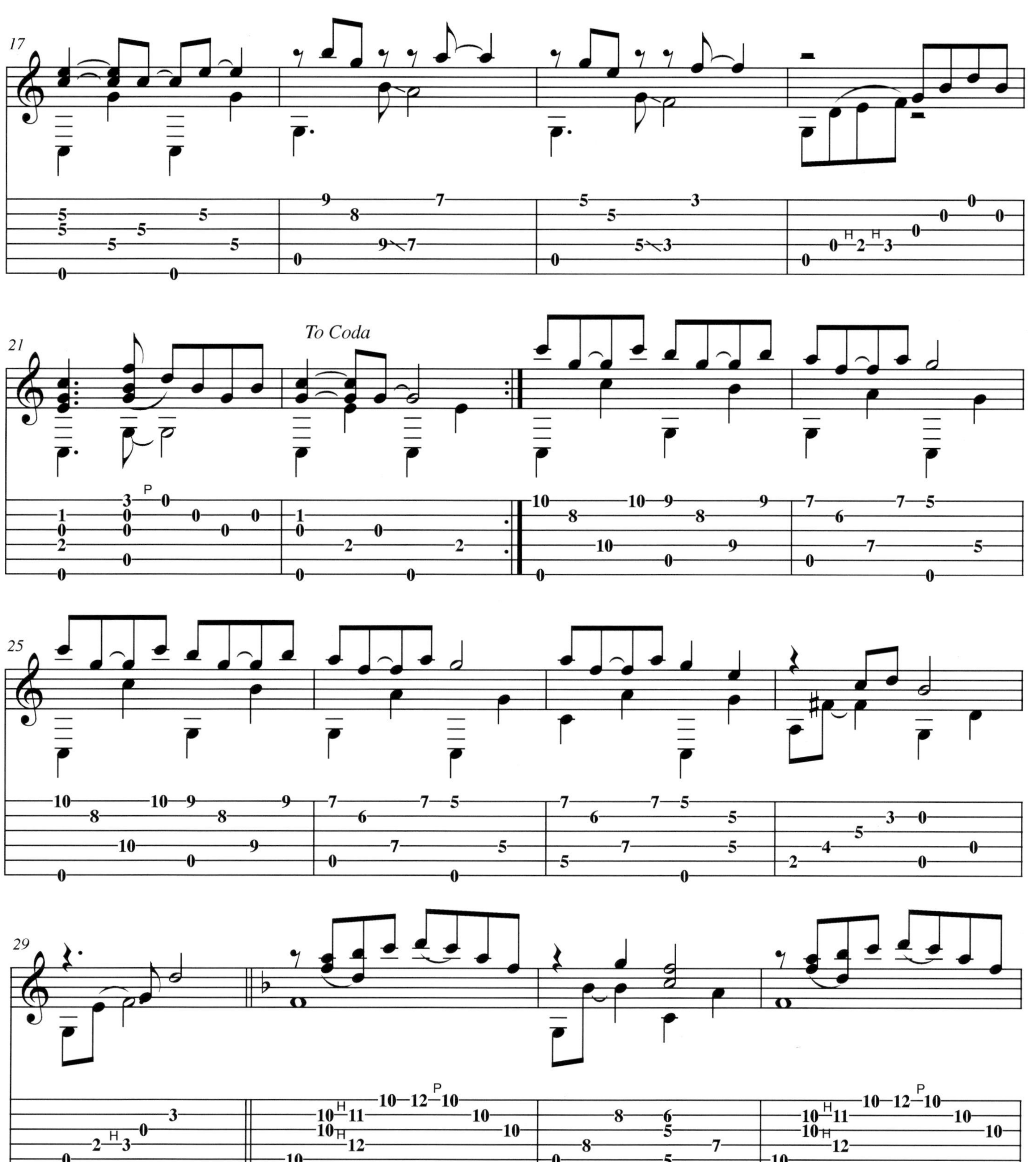
To Coda

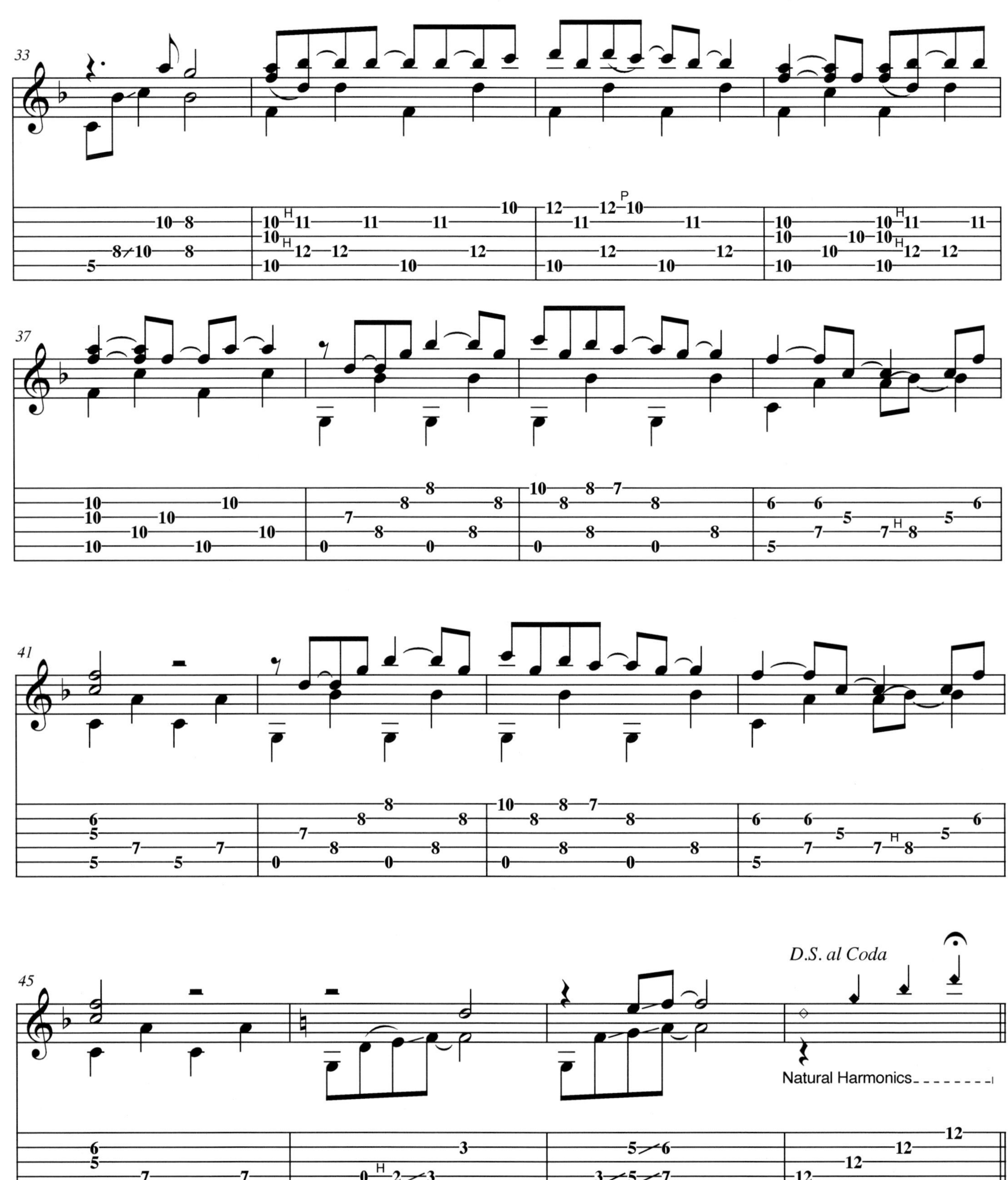
D.S. al Coda
Natural Harmonics

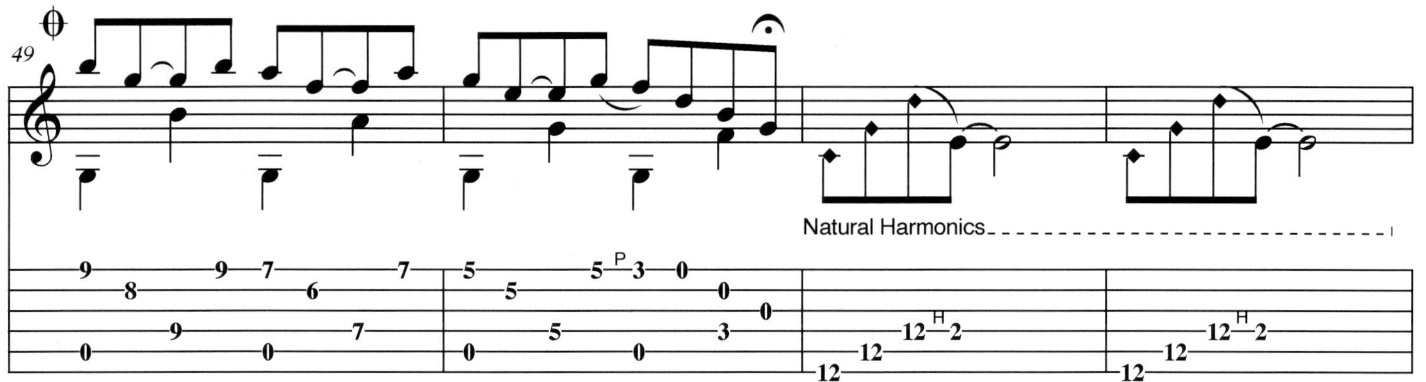

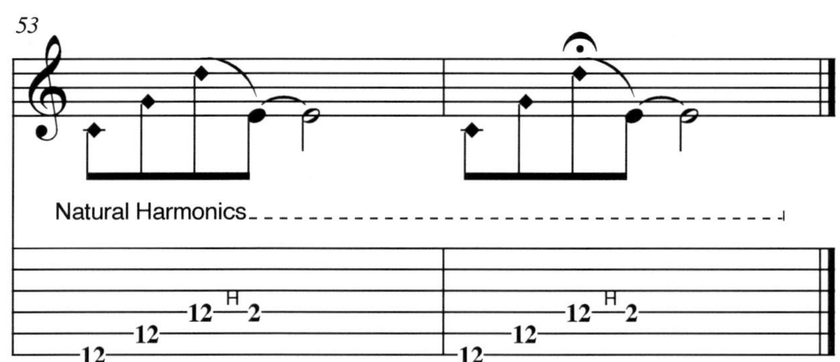

Annie's Slack Key Lullabye
Notes

I've included this original song to demonstrate some interesting techniques such as artificial harmonics, hammer-ons without a preceding plucked note, and another approach to modulation.

Measures 1-4: Play the harmonics in the first 2 measures as you normally would, then hammer-on with enough force to sound the next note. At measure 3, place a barré at the fifth fret and play artificial harmonics one octave higher, at the 17th fret. I use my right-hand index finger to touch the string at the harmonic node, plucking behind the finger with my thumb. Alternately, use your index and pluck with your middle finger. Hammer-on as before.

Measures 5-9: This descending lick is a great feature of this tuning, as is the turnaround back to the tonic.

Measure 10: Here is the first example of a hammer-on from empty space. Place a barré at the 5th fret, play the bass note and brush upwards to the double stop. Then hammer down on the 2nd and 4th strings with enough force that you can hear the A note clearly. This technique is the basis of the song, so take some time to get it right.

Measures 23-29: The bridge walks down the scale a couple times, then plays a II-V vamp (D7-G7) in the key of C. So how does that set up the modulation to F in the next measure? It doesn't, really – but it works because the long pause in measure 29 alerts you that something is about to happen.

Measures 30-48: This section is essentially the main theme transposed to the key of F. Notice that the harmony changes slightly in measures 38 & 39 and 42 & 43. The modulation back to the key of C is pretty straightforward: three measures of G, the dominant chord of the key of C.

After playing through the song one more time, jump to the coda and bring the song to a restful conclusion.

Aunty's Christmas Goose

Mark Nelson

Drop C tuning

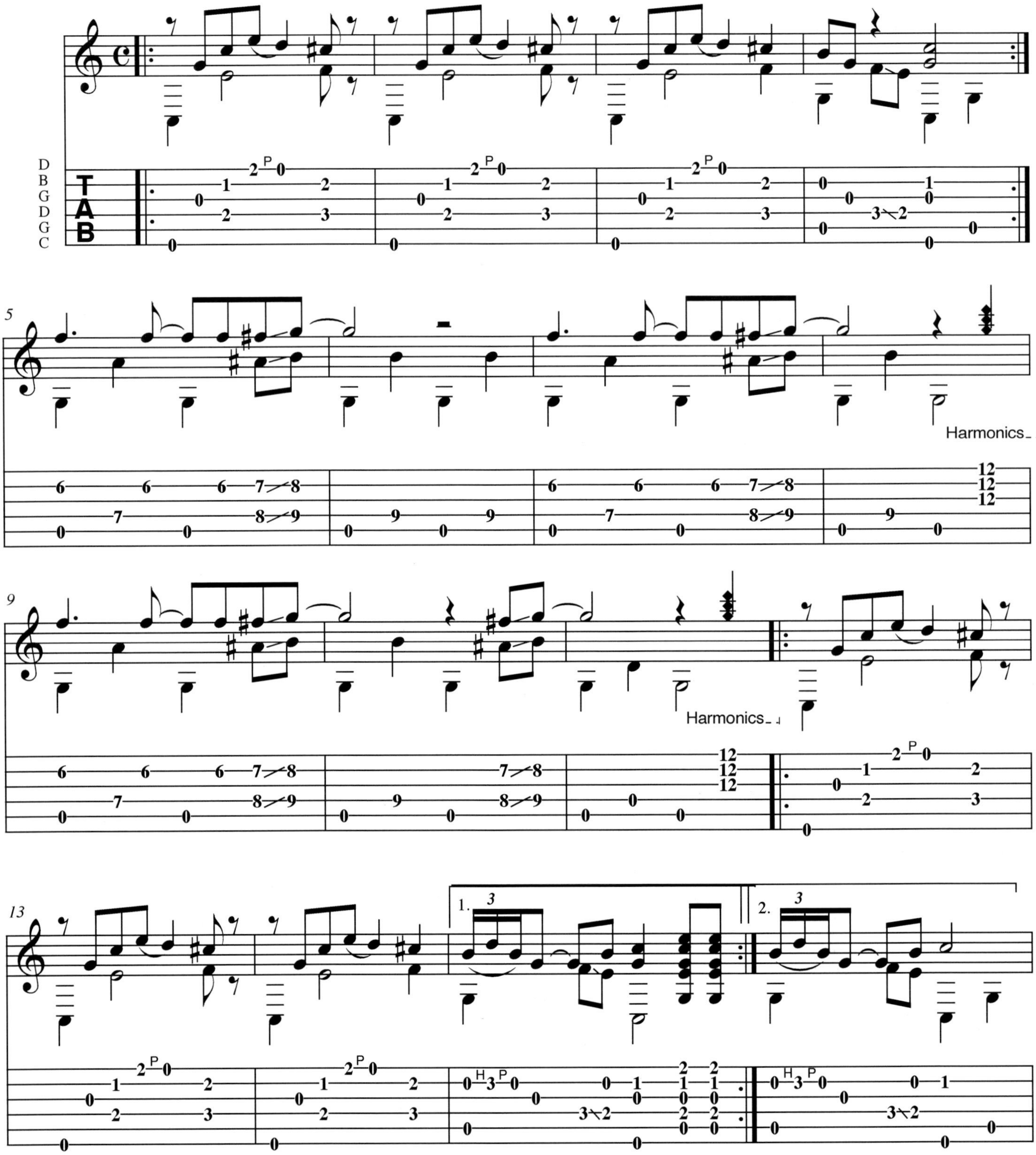

D B G D G C
TAB

5

Harmonics

9

Harmonics

13

1. 2.

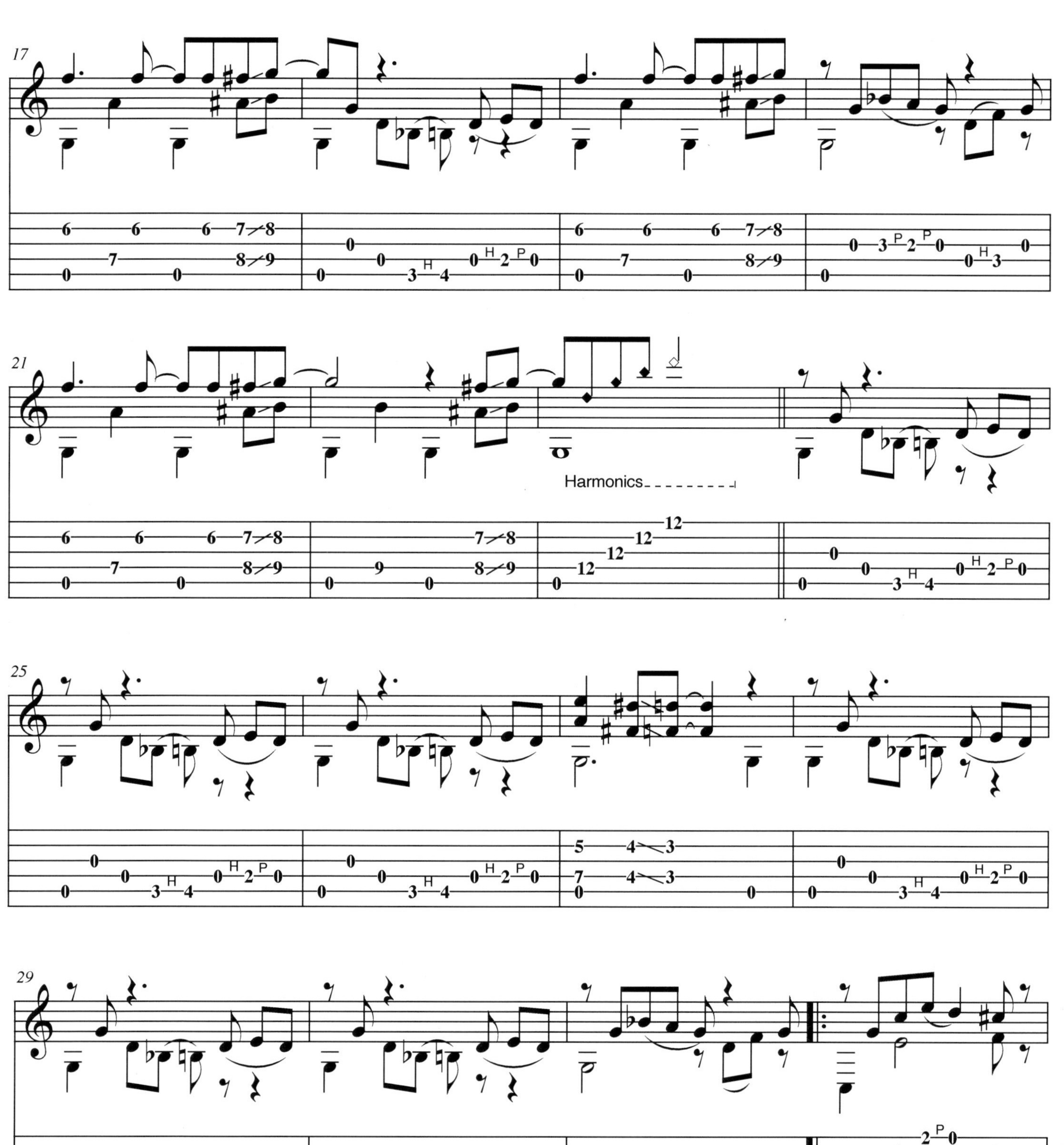
Harmonics

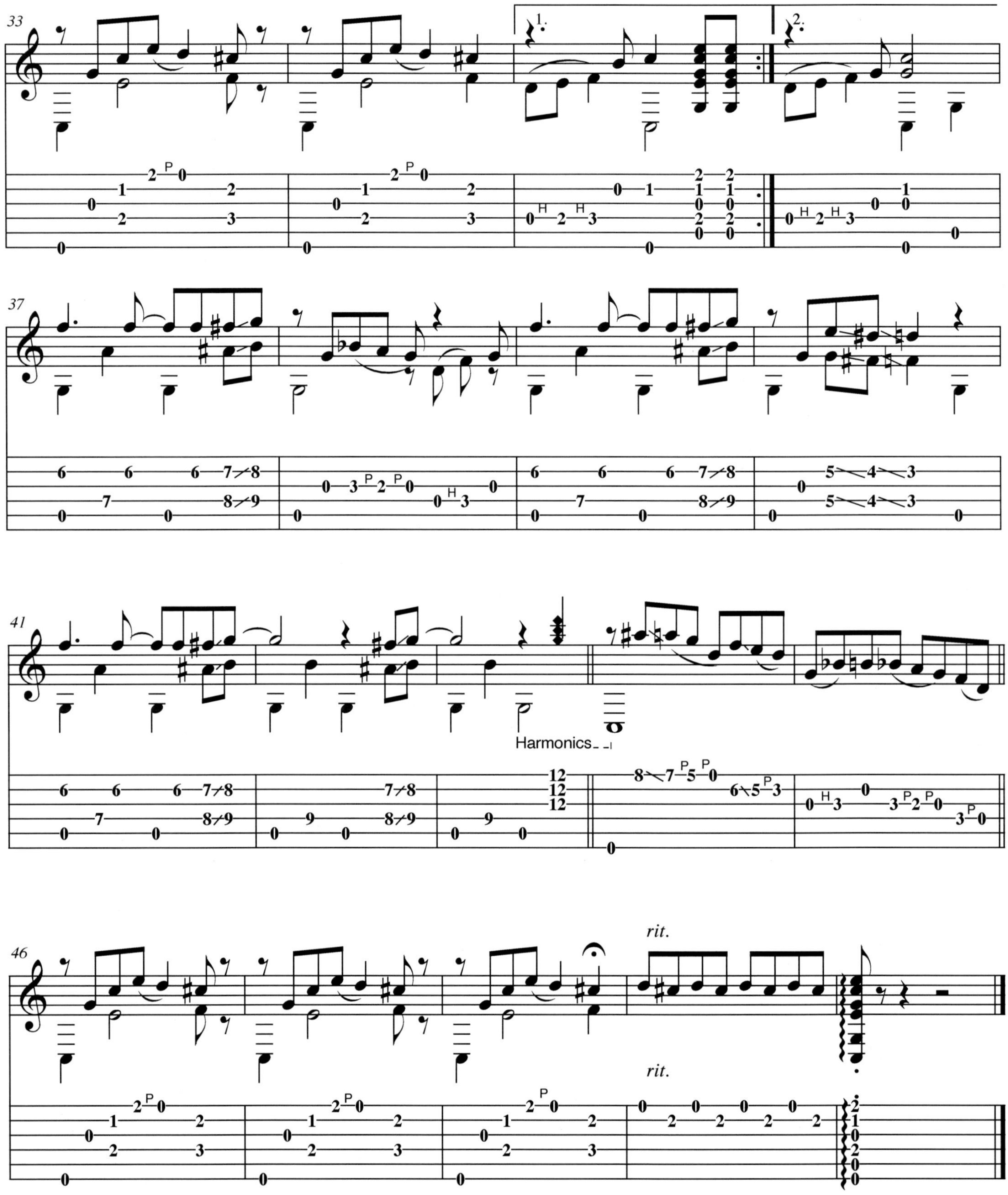

33

37

41

Harmonics

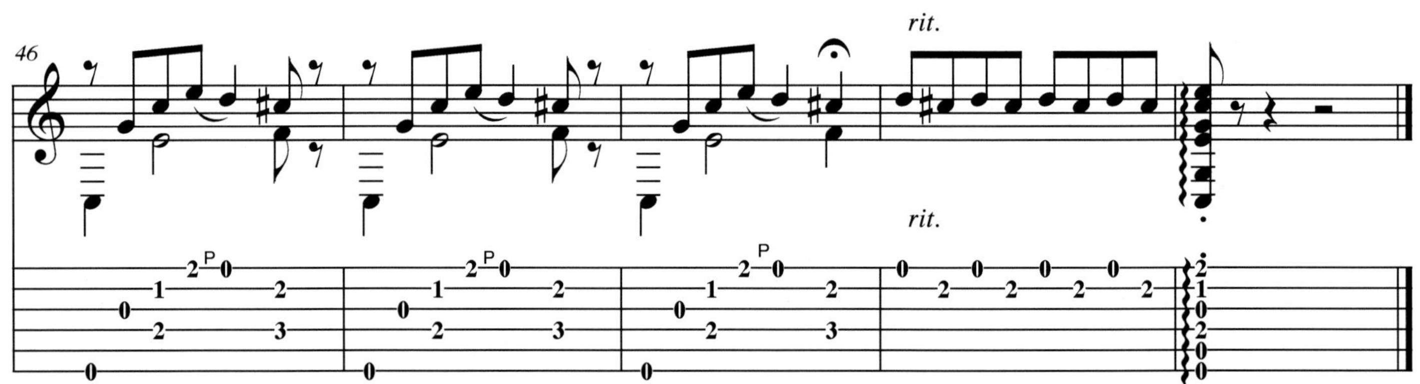

Aunty's Christmas Goose
Notes

Although it may not be apparent at first, "Aunty's Christmas Goose" is related to such instrumental slack key standards as "Whee Ha Swing" and "Opihi Moemoe." Like those songs, it is a series of short themes with many variations. And just like in Leonard Kwan's gem, the bass strings get a real workout.

The obvious dissonance is another feature common to slack key, though I'll admit I take it to the extreme. Years ago I played this onstage at a slack key festival in Kaunakakai, and every time I hit those goosey notes all the Aunties in the audience erupted in laughter!

Measures 1-4: You'll be revisiting this theme often. The discordant notes on beat four are played staccato.

Measures 5-11: This is the second theme. It will get twisted around a bit before you are done. Pay attention to the way the variations build on each other as the song progresses.

Measures 24-29: The bridge – derived from a little bit of R&B bass playing – is a workout for your thumb and index finger.

Measures 44 & 45: This somewhat chromatic run serves as a turnaround back to the main theme. Try to play that long string of eighth notes in one fluid sweep.

When you reach the end, gradually slow down to heighten the tension. Then strum the final chord and quickly mute the strings. Poor goose!

Lesson Five – Jus' Press: Improvisation in Slack Key

Improvisation – the spontaneous expression of the player's personality – is as essential to slack key as the ocean is to life. With only one or two exceptions, no true slack key player will ever play a song the same way twice. In fact, I have heard it said of Led Ka'apana that he never plays a song the same way *once*. But what exactly do we mean by *improvisation*, and how does it apply to the music you are learning?

A common misperception is that the improviser creates something entirely new out of thin air. But even jazz musicians rely on the harmonic and rhythmic structure of the song to build their flights of fancy.

Most folk musics incorporate some degree of improvisation, and slack key is first and foremost a folk tradition. What that means is that the improviser will stay true to the music. He or she will know the melody and chord structure – and the lyrics, if any – of the song and make sure not to stray too far. The improviser will know the ins and outs of the style – what makes slack key *sound* like slack key.

As with many folk styles, much of what constitutes improvisation in slack key is really plugging in pre-existing licks or patterns where they fit. The more experience you have playing and listening to slack key, the more tricks you will have up your sleeve that you can employ at a moment's notice.

Although slack key has become largely a solo art, it really comes alive when playing in a group. Each musician will listen and react to the others as the music swirls around. I touched on that with the two duets; but truly the only way to learn is to get out there and play with your friends. And listen; always listen.

So what do you do when someone turns to you and says, "Take one?"

Relax, smile, and play what you know. You might play a simple picking pattern while following the chords. Or play the melody the way you learned it, with maybe a different turnaround thrown in. As you become more confident, try throwing in some licks you have learned from other songs – such as a long descending pattern to fill in a couple of measures of the dominant chord – or use different inversions of the chords from the original melody.

If you have always played from tab, try to wean yourself. After you've played through something, turn the paper over and play it again, in time and without stopping. Chances are, you will make a few mistakes. Congratulations, you are now improvising.

Kawohikukapulani

Helen Desha Beamer

C Wahine tuning

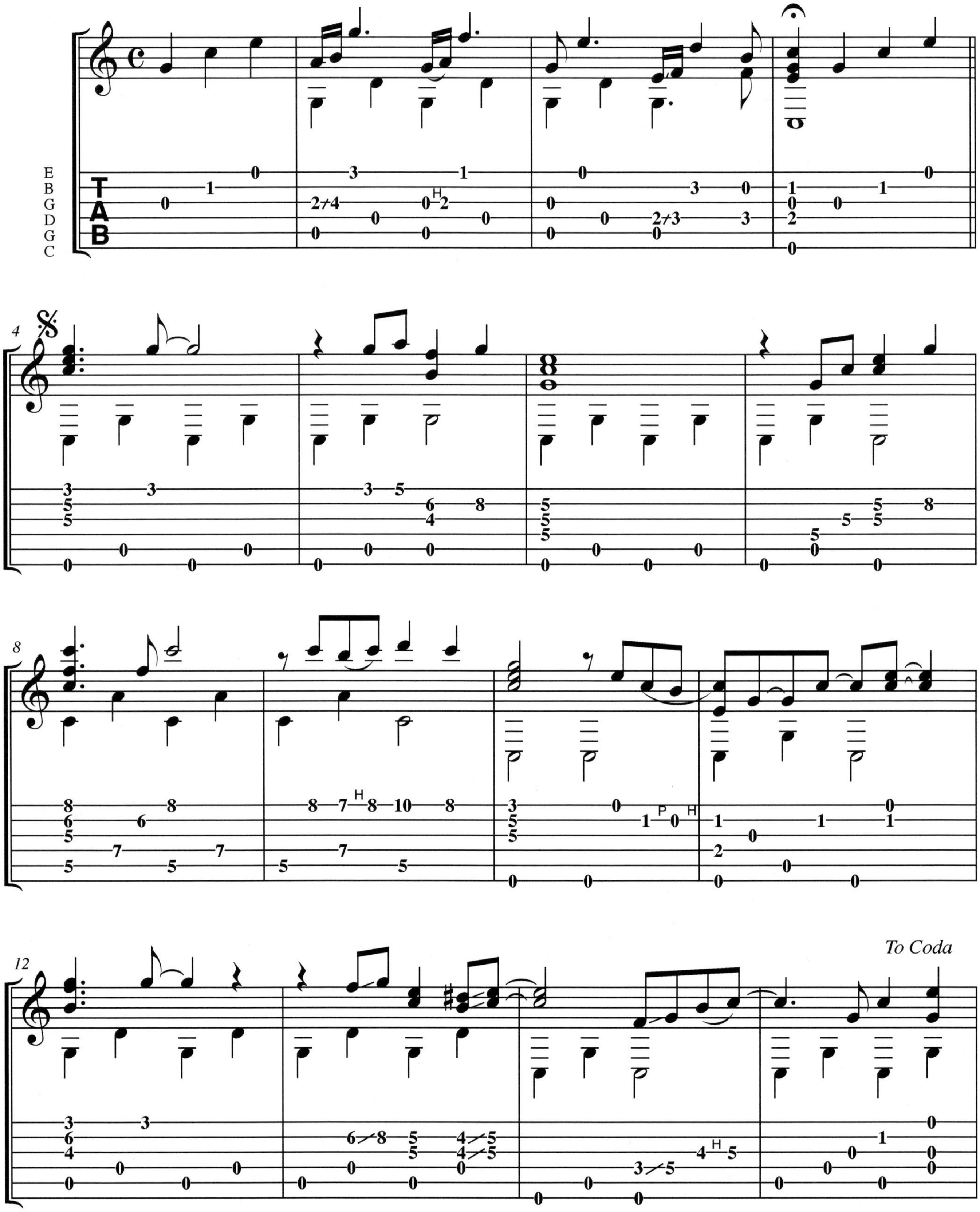

To Coda

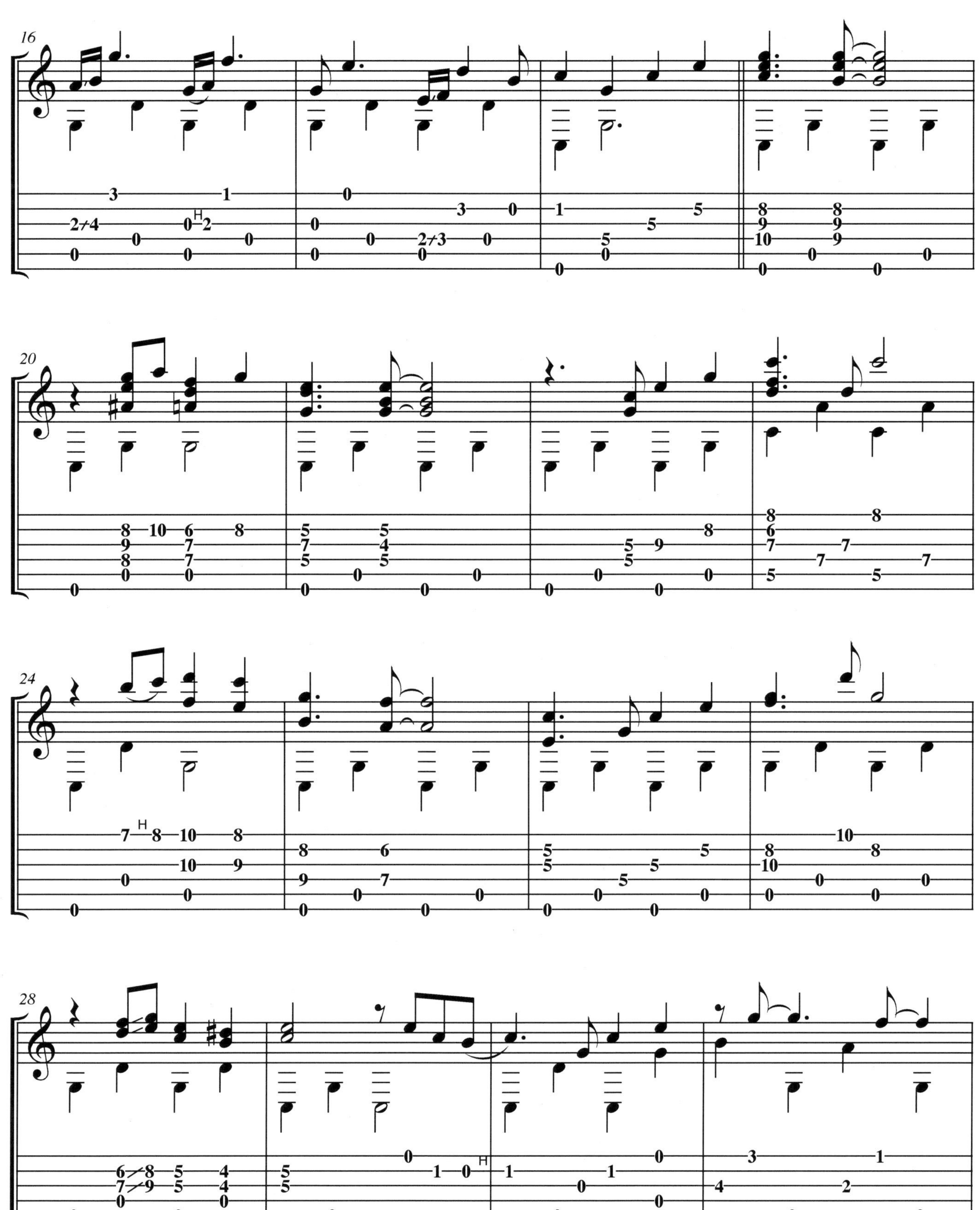
16
20
24
28

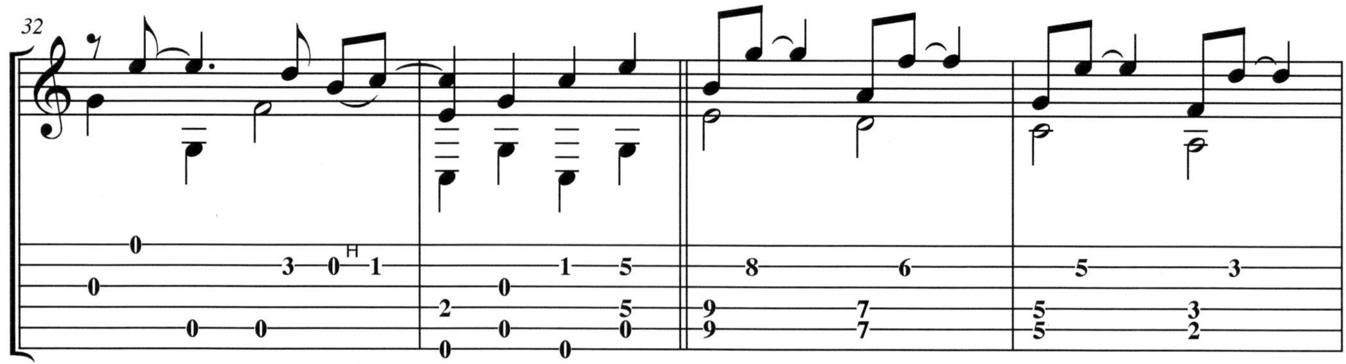
32

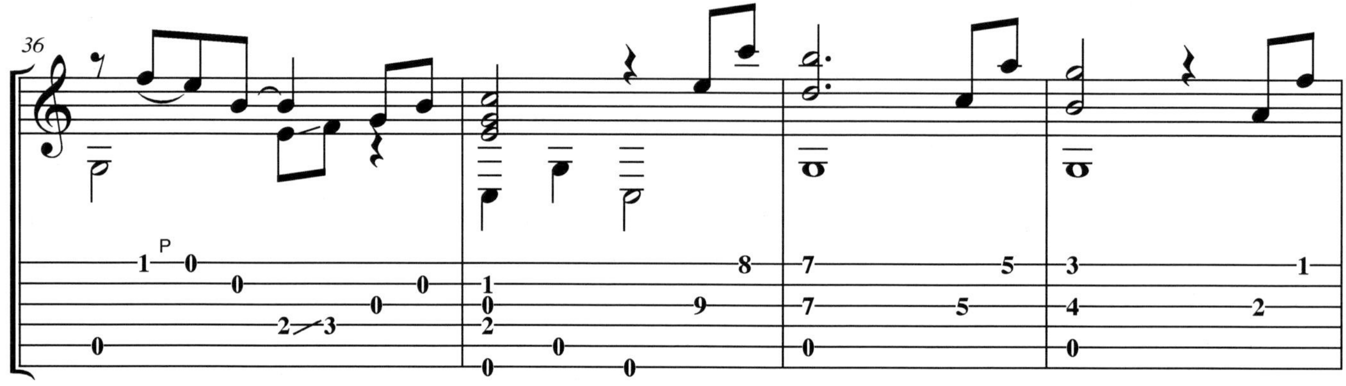
36

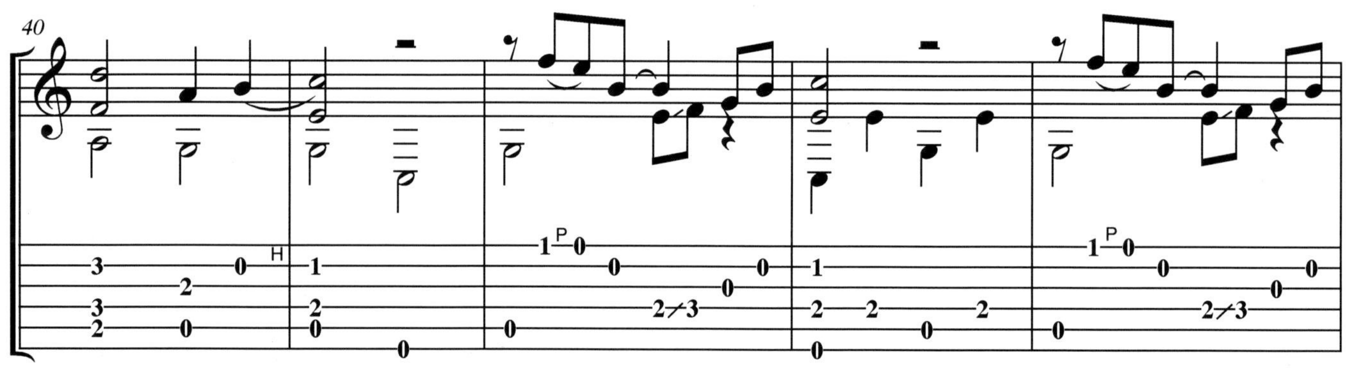
40

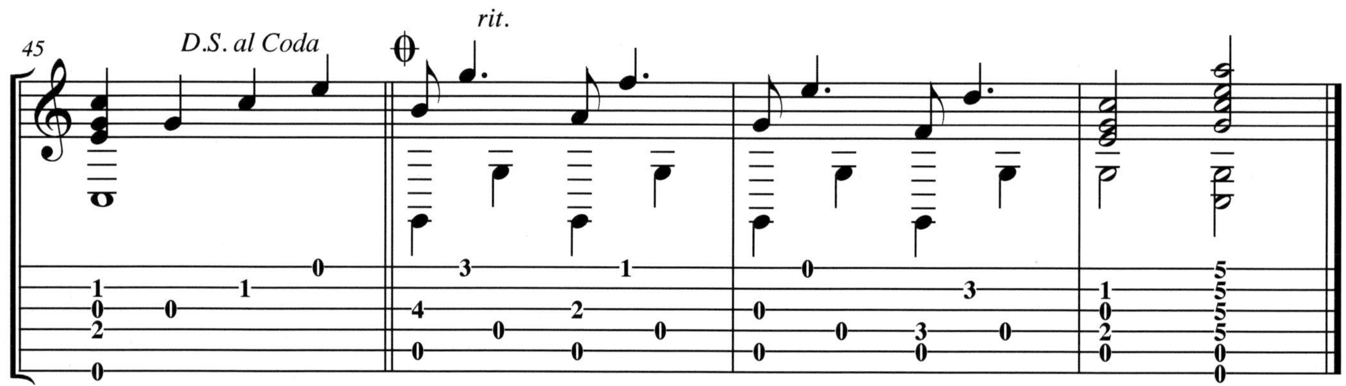
45
D.S. al Coda
rit.

C Wahine Tuning
C-G-D-G-B-E

To get to C Wahine tuning from standard tuning, lower the 5th string a whole step to G and drop the bass string all the way down to C. From Drop C, simply raise the top string a whole step.

Kawohikukapulani
("Sacred Virgin Standing in Heaven")
Notes

Because C Wahine maintains the top four strings from standard tuning, you can use many of the chord shapes and licks you already know. I've arranged this lovely old song to showcase some of the common licks used in this tuning.

Measures 4-18: The first time though the arrangement sticks pretty close to the melody as written. Note the G7 chord on beat 3 of measure 5. The half-step movement in Measure 13 is an echo of an earlier time in Hawaiian music. Many composers in pre-War Hawai'i used this motif; it was particularly prominent in Hawaiian steel guitar playing.

Measures 19-21: I've filled out the harmony for the repeat using some tricks from the jazz guitar styles contemporary with the song. The chords move in half-steps from C major through Cma7, C7 to C6 before jumping to a quick G7. The resolve back to the tonic in measure 21 is delayed by the initial Csus2 chord.

From there things are pretty straightforward.

Measures 34 & 35: This lick, a reharmonization of the main motif of the song, is a good one to have in your bag of tricks.

Measures 36 & 37: This lovely turnaround figure takes full advantage of the tuning.

Las Blancas Flores
Notes

The song "Las Blancas Flores" was popular in 1830's California. We know that the guitar was common in the pueblos and ranchos at this time, but we have no way of knowing exactly how it was played. Since the origin story of slack key involves Spanish-speaking cowboys sailing from Monterey, it is certainly possible that the original *paniolo* would have played this song. Accordingly, I have arranged it to include some elements of the slack key style.

"Las Blancas Flores" has three parts. The first two parts stay firmly in a major key, while the third moves to the relative minor, in this case Am. Songs in a minor key are very rare in Hawaiian music.

Measures 5-20: This is the first strain of the melody. You keep up a steady pulse with your thumb for most of the song, so practice playing the bass part in isolation if you need to.

Measures 21-36: The reprise of the first strain simply adds a little more complexity.

Measures 37-52: For more contrast, the second strain drops the steady pulse in the bass.

Measures 53-68: The song moves to the relative minor of C. After playing through this section, go back and play the first part again before jumping to the coda.

Las Blancas Flores

Traditional Californio

C Wahine tuning

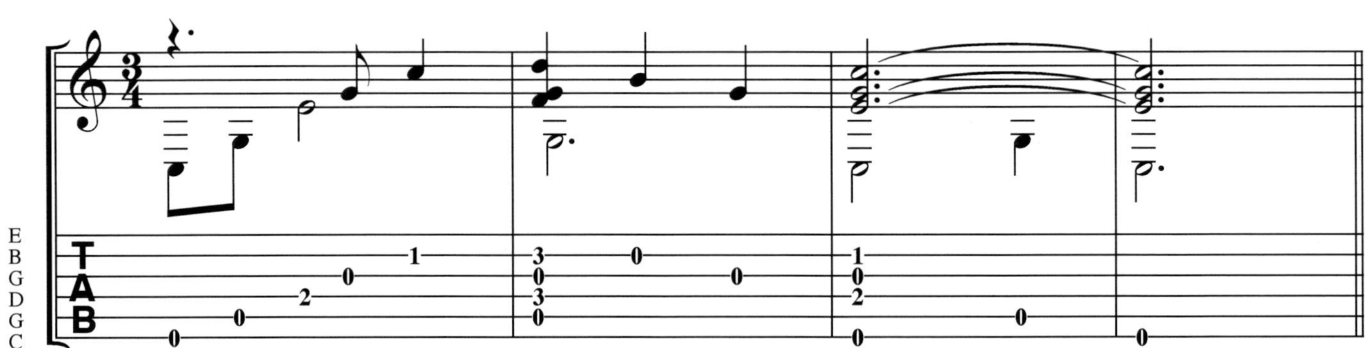

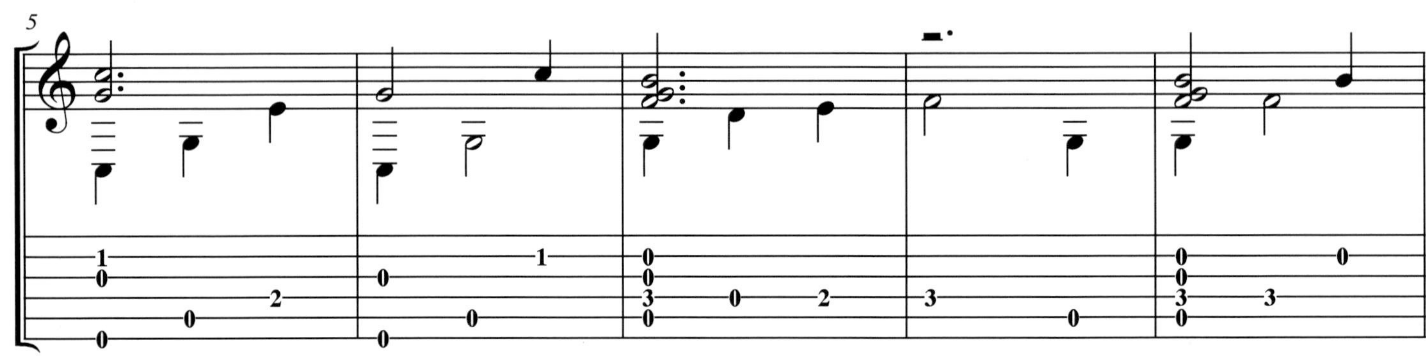

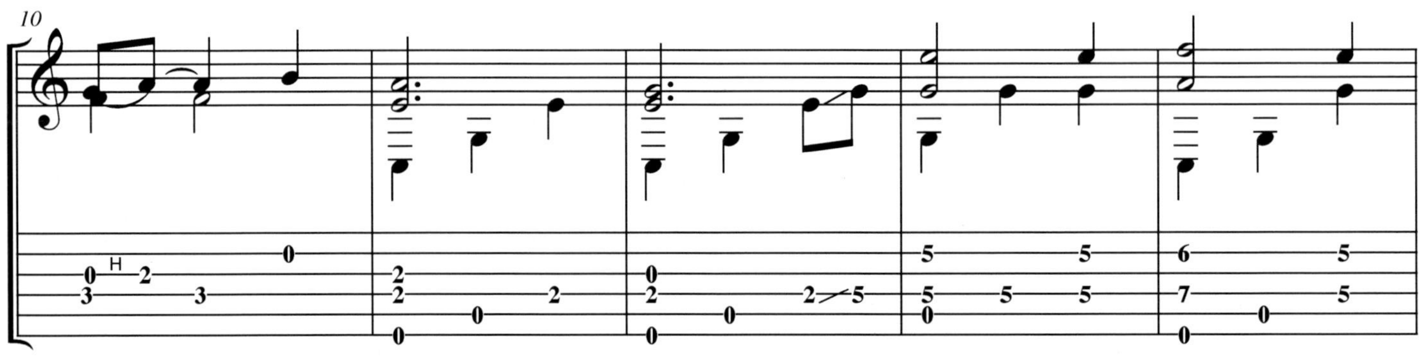

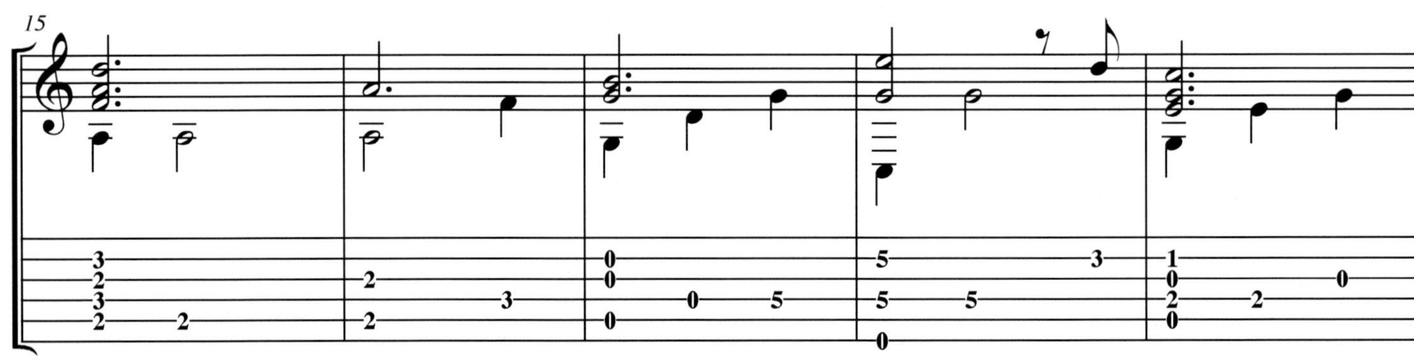

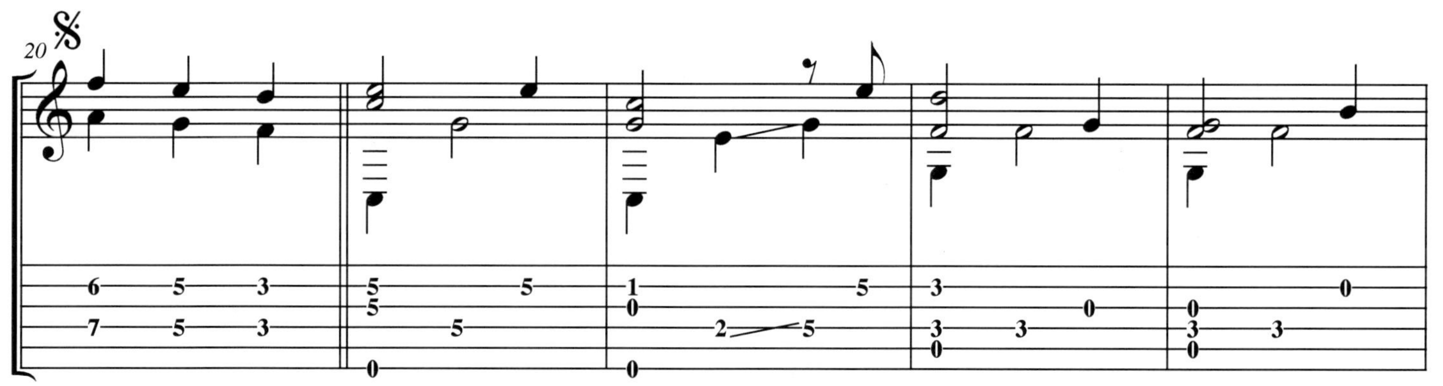
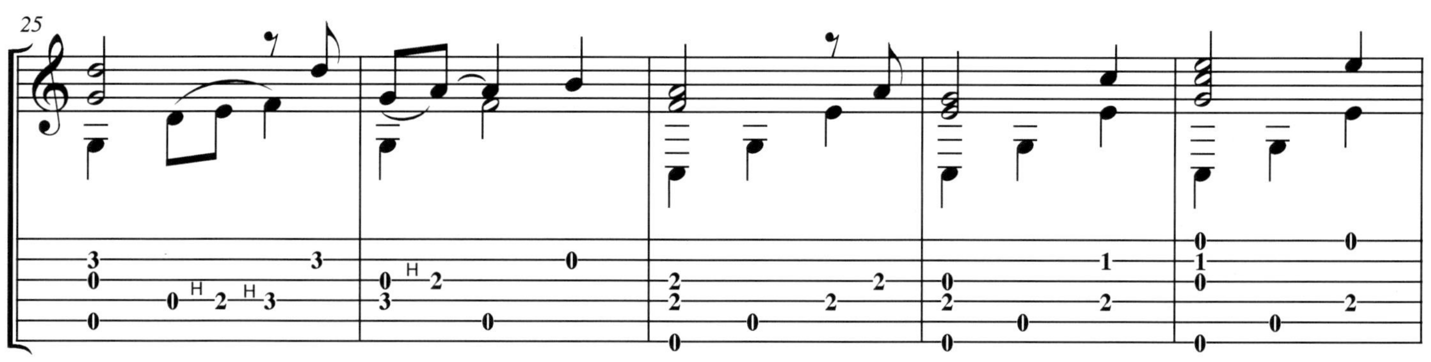
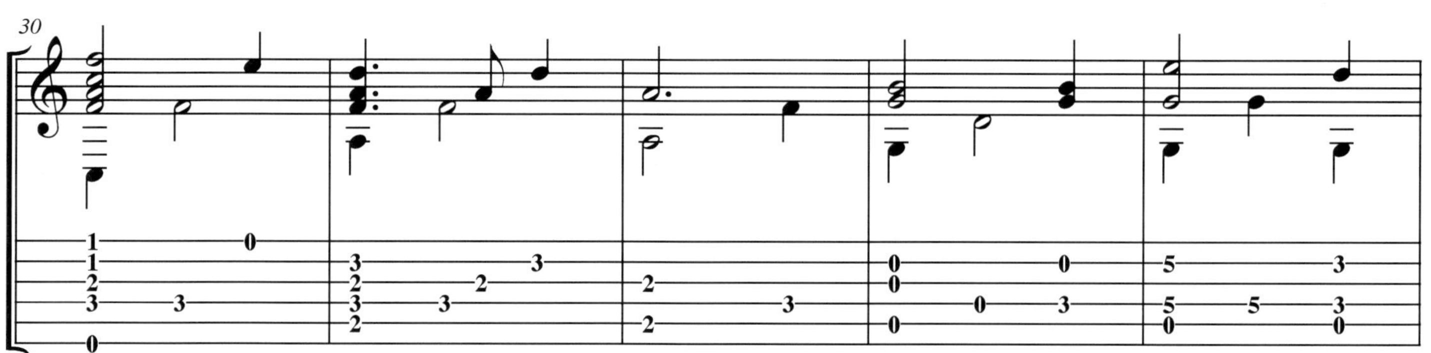
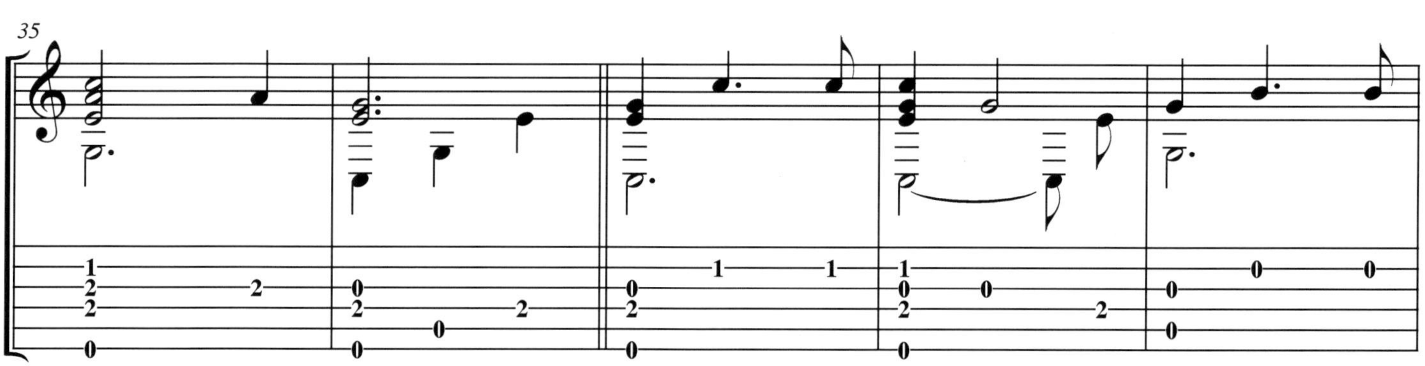

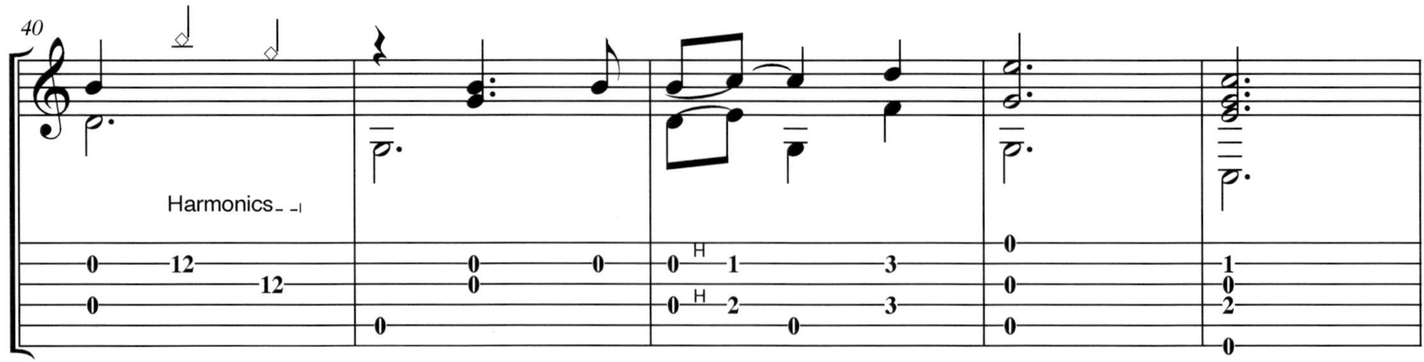
40
Harmonics
H
H
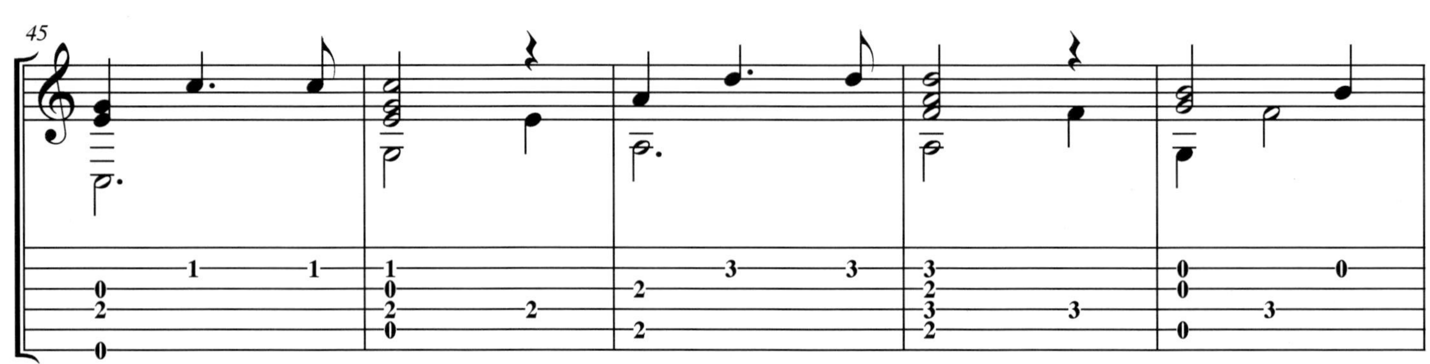
45
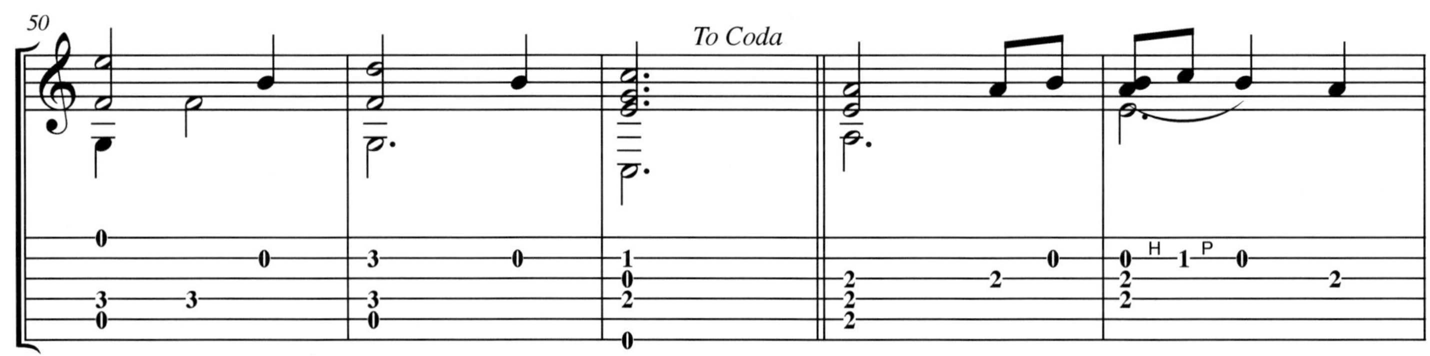
50
To Coda
H
P
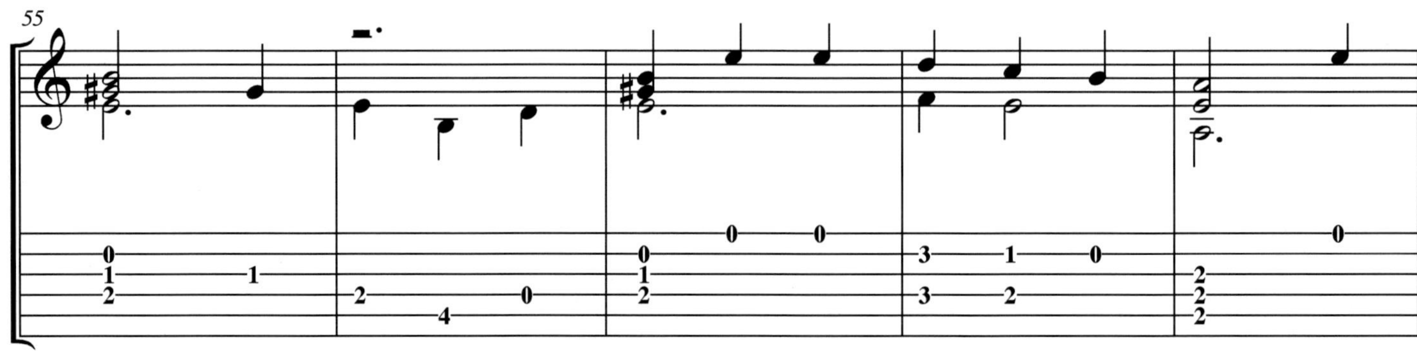
55

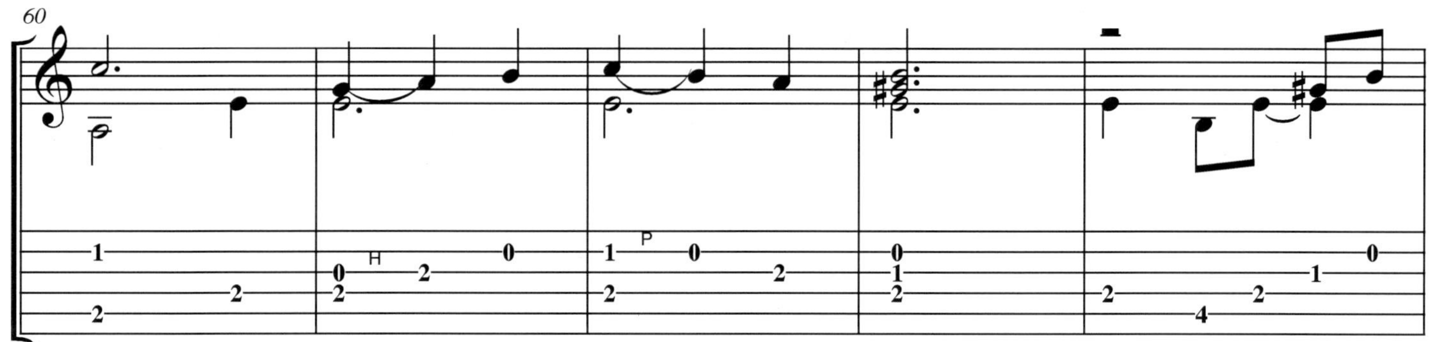
60
H
P

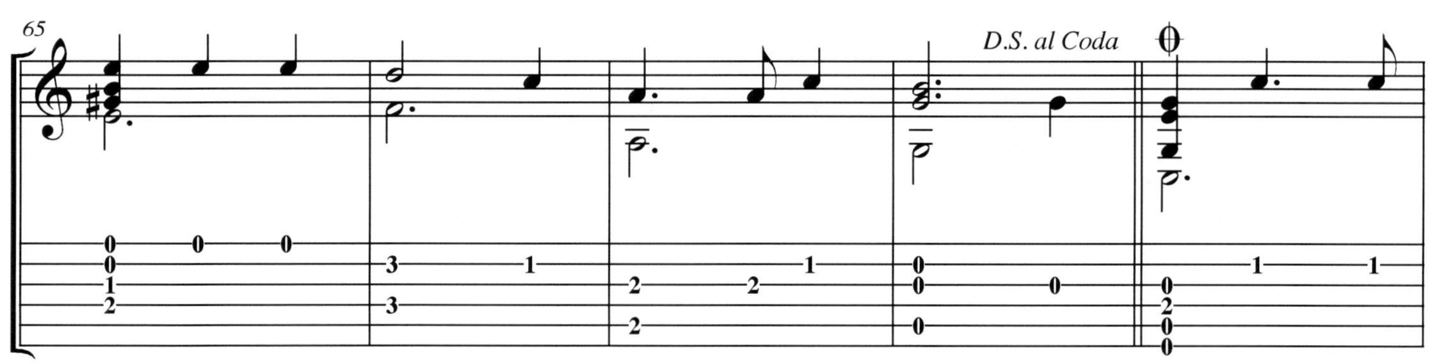
65
D.S. al Coda

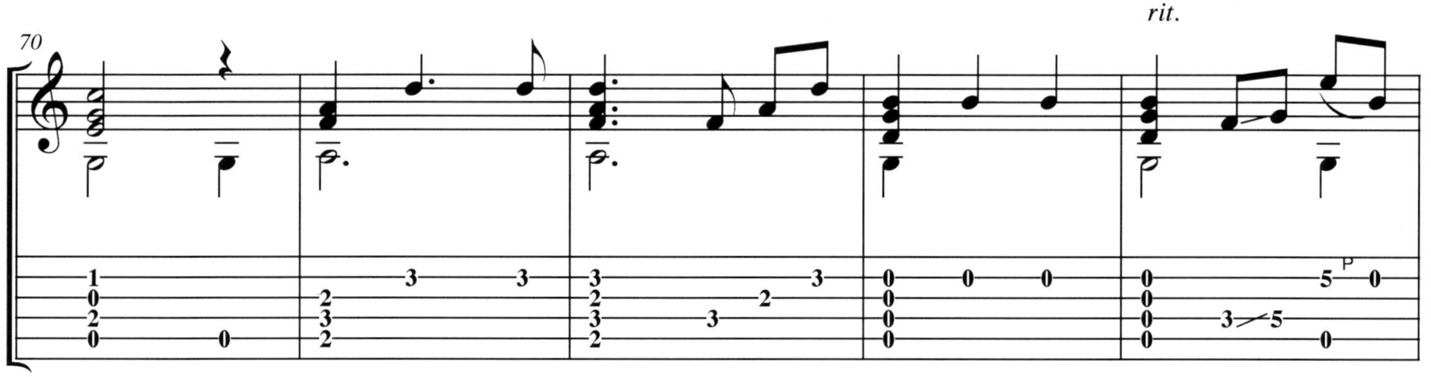
70
rit.
P

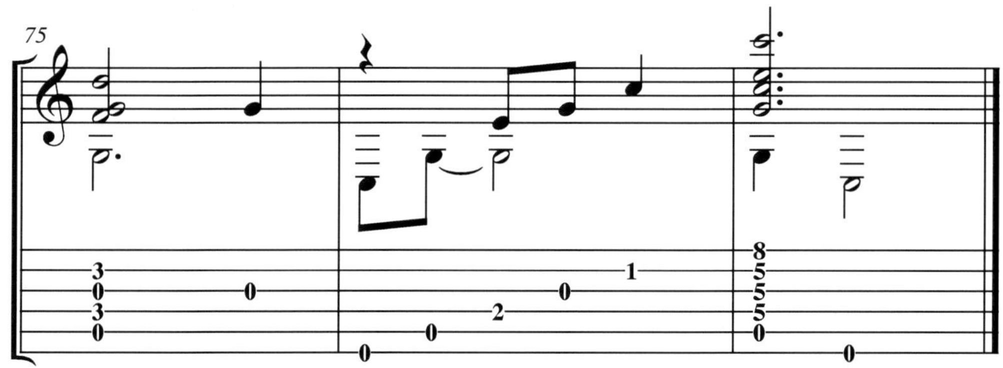
75

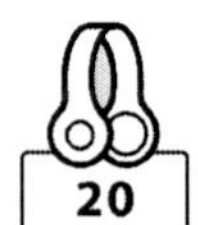

He Aloha Noʻo Honolulu

F Wahine tuning

Lot Kauwe

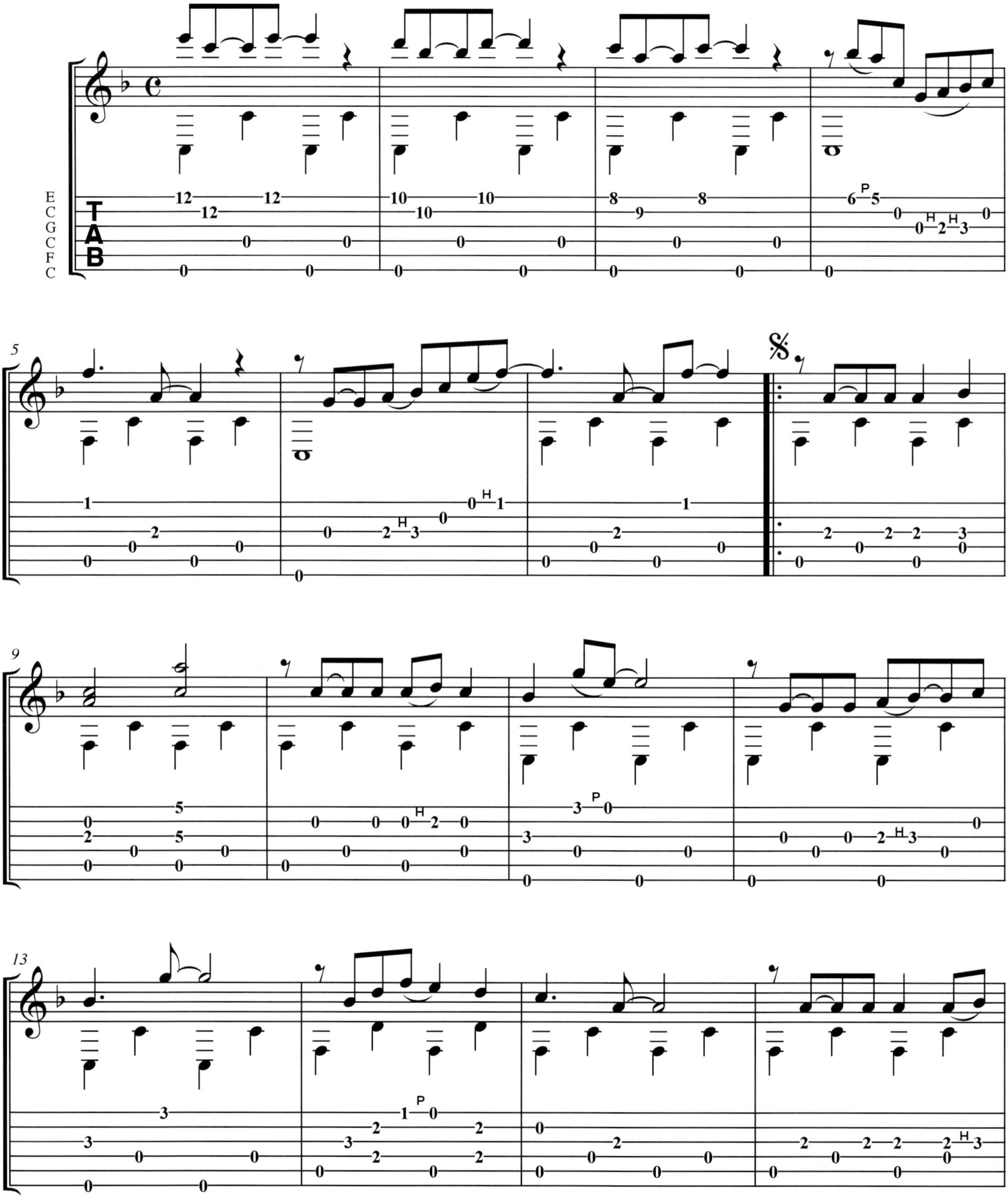

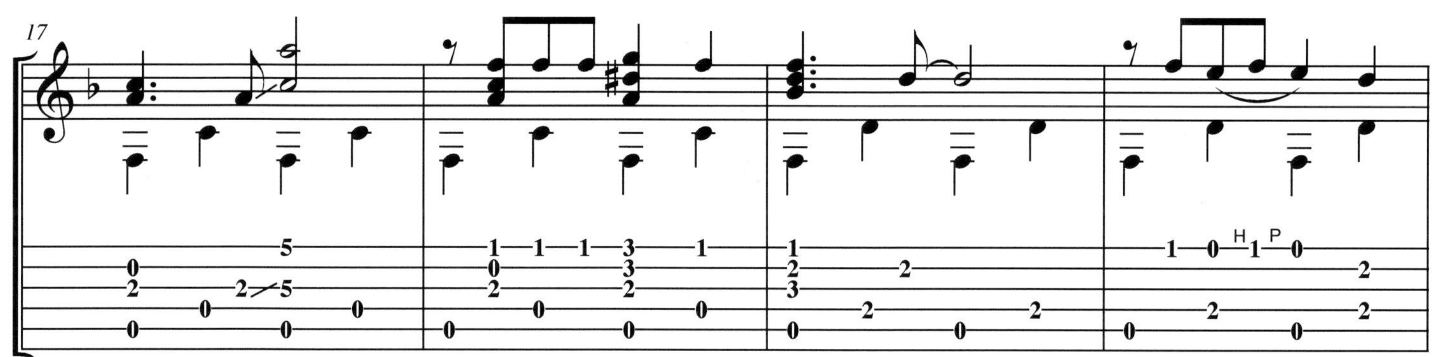
17
H
P
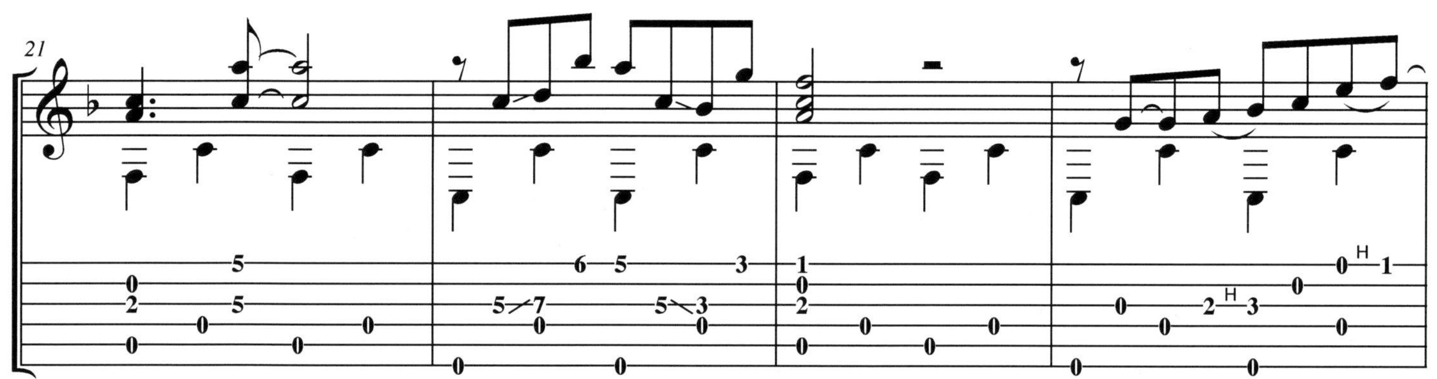
21
H
H
H
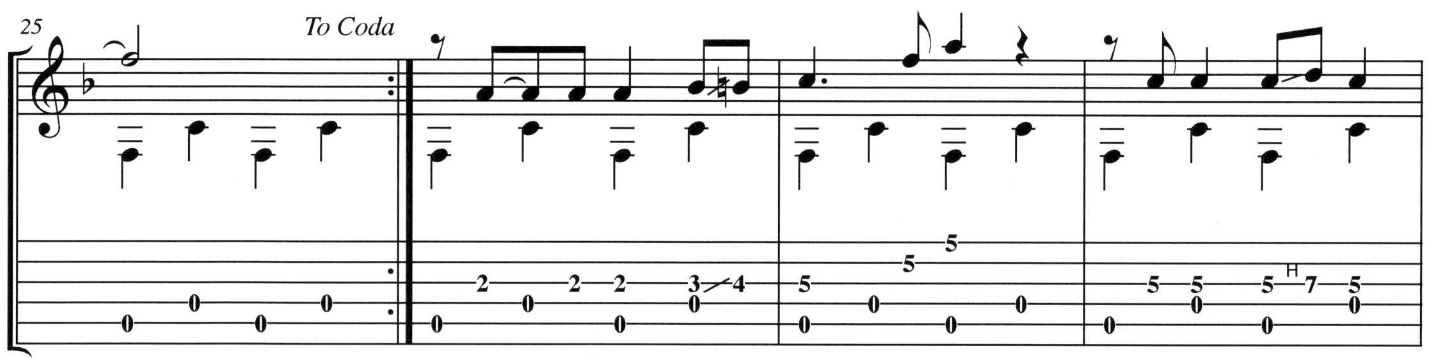
25
To Coda
H
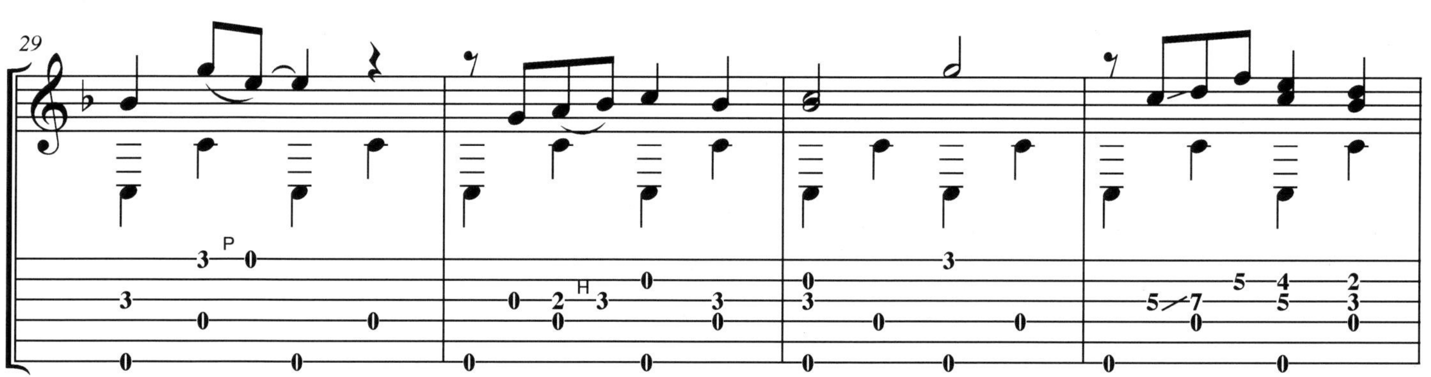
29
P
H

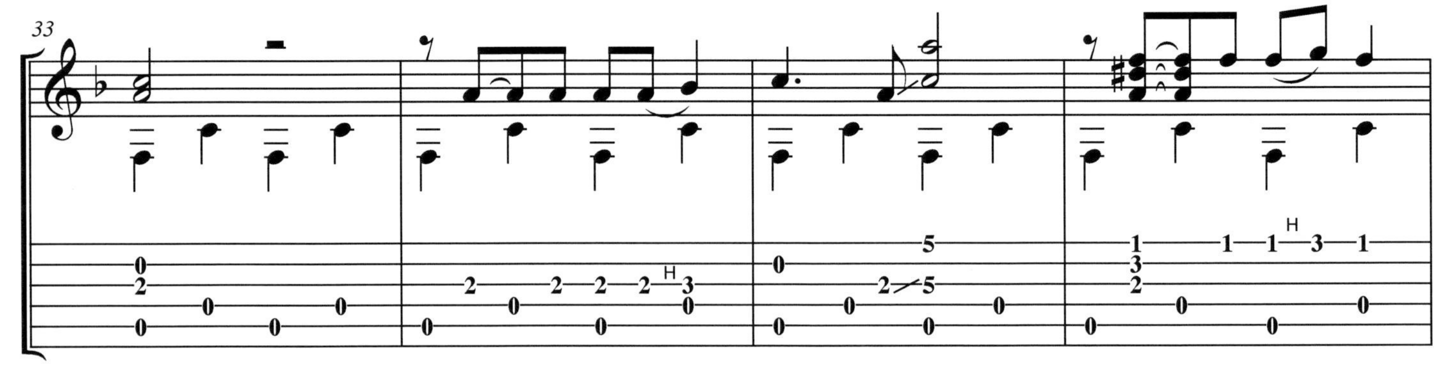
33

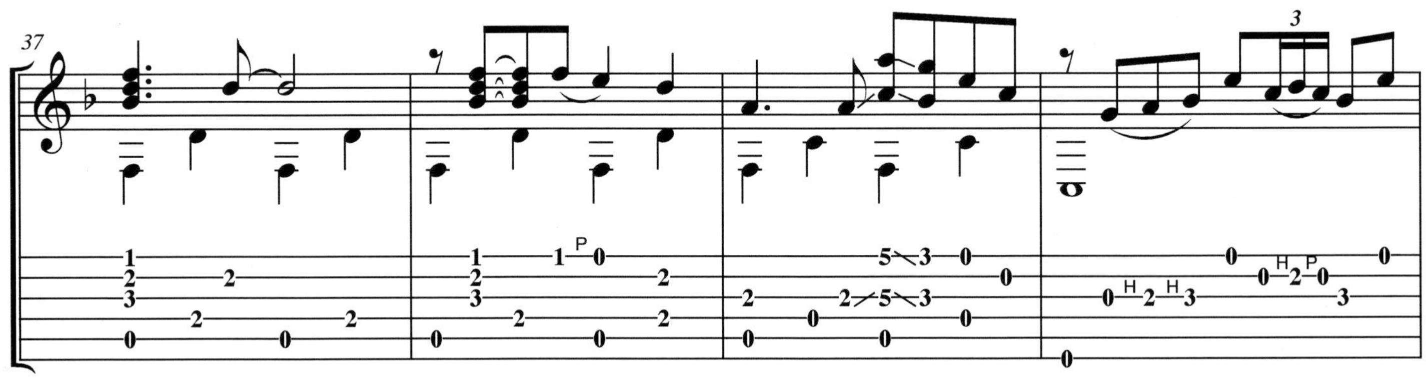
37

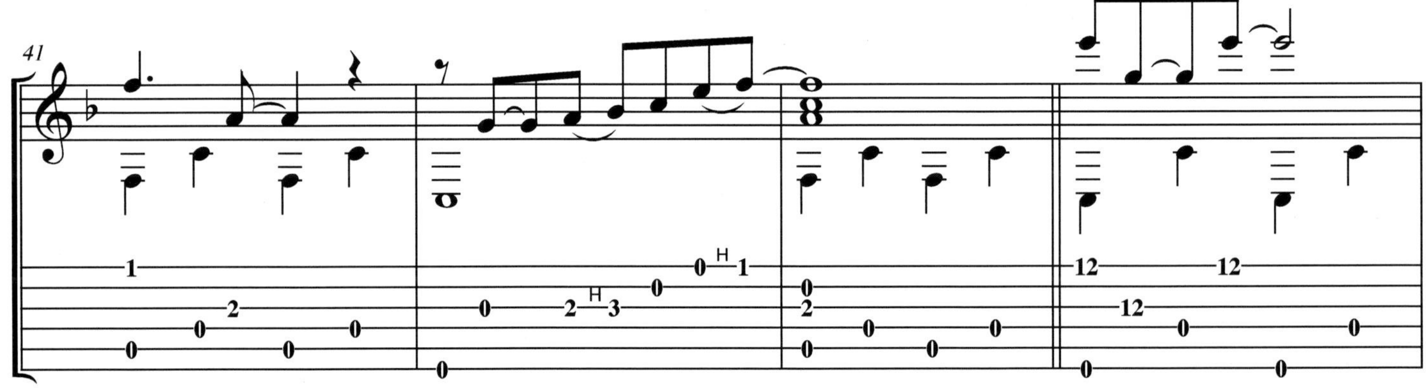
41

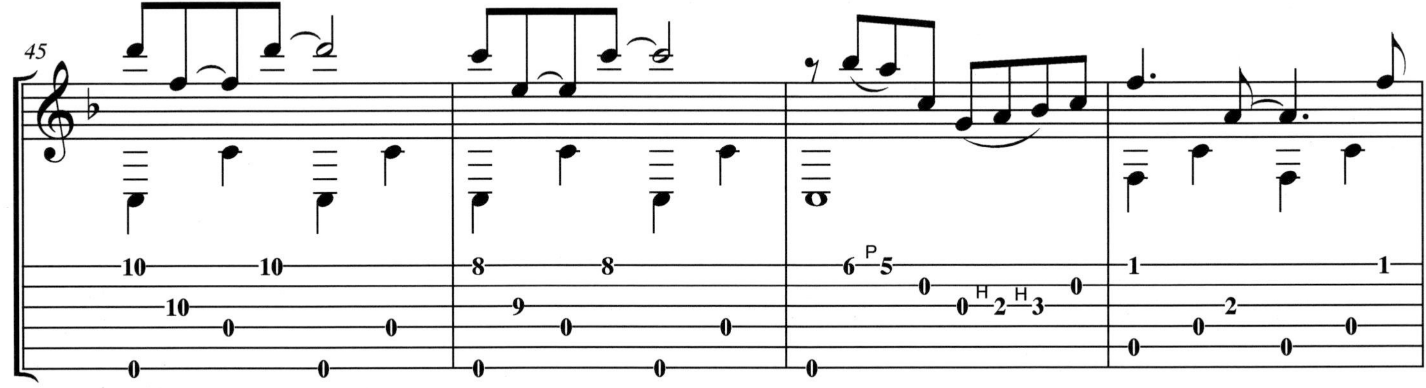
45

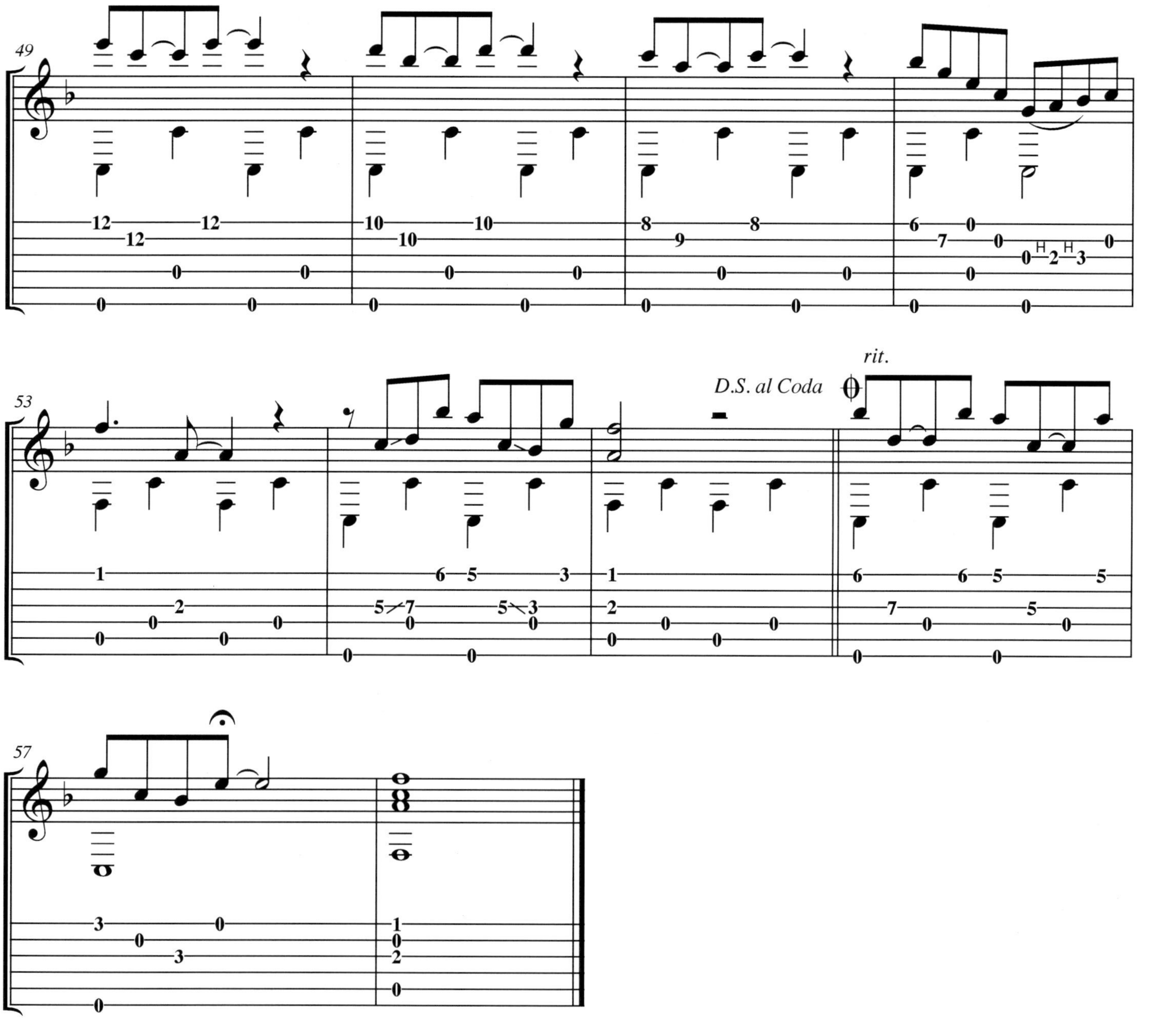

He Aloha Noʻo Honolulu
Notes

F Wahine tuning truly makes your guitar sing. From standard, raise your 2nd string one half step to C. Then drop the 4th string down to C; the 5th two whole steps to F and the bass all the way down to C. You might wish to string your guitar with heavier strings on the bass end to handle this tuning.

Note that this tuning lets you play alternating bass in the tonic and dominant keys, just like in Taro Patch. Notice, too, the similarities between this tuning and C Wahine. Many licks – double stops, vamps, chord shapes, etc. – are easily transferred from one to the other.

"He Aloha Noʻo Honolulu" is arranged to show off some of the typical licks and finger positions used in this tuning.

Makee Ailana

James K I'i

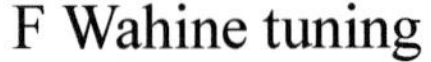

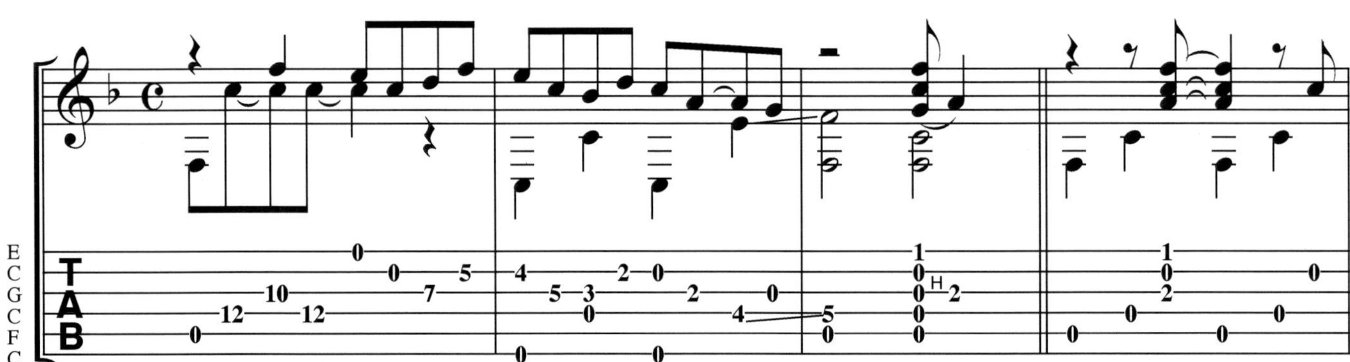

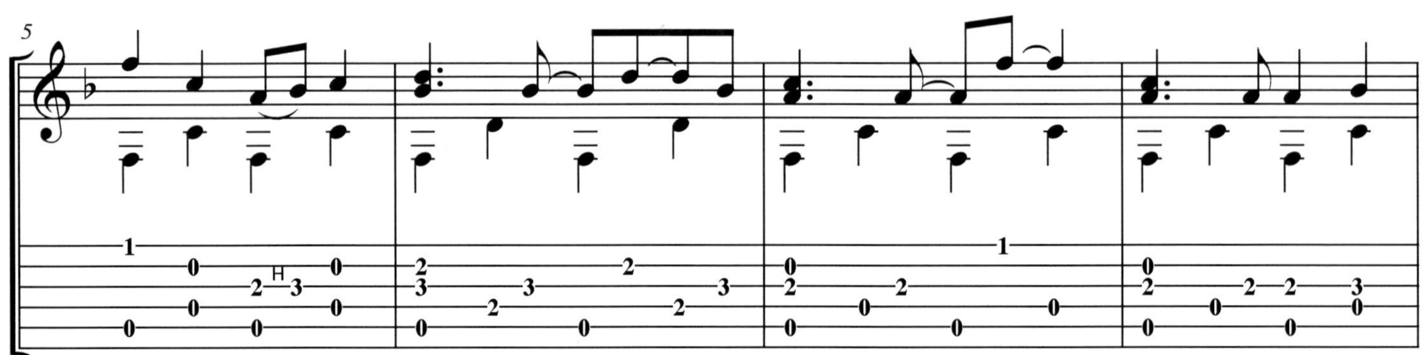

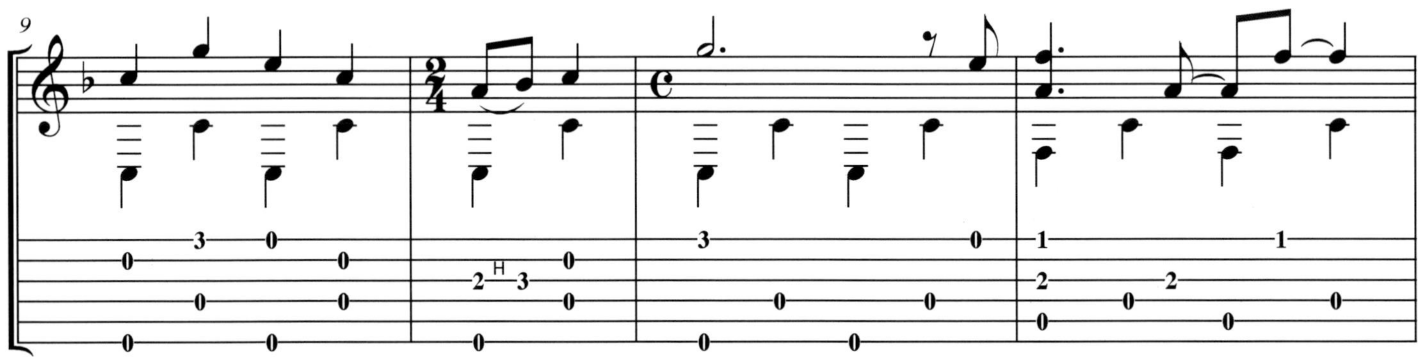

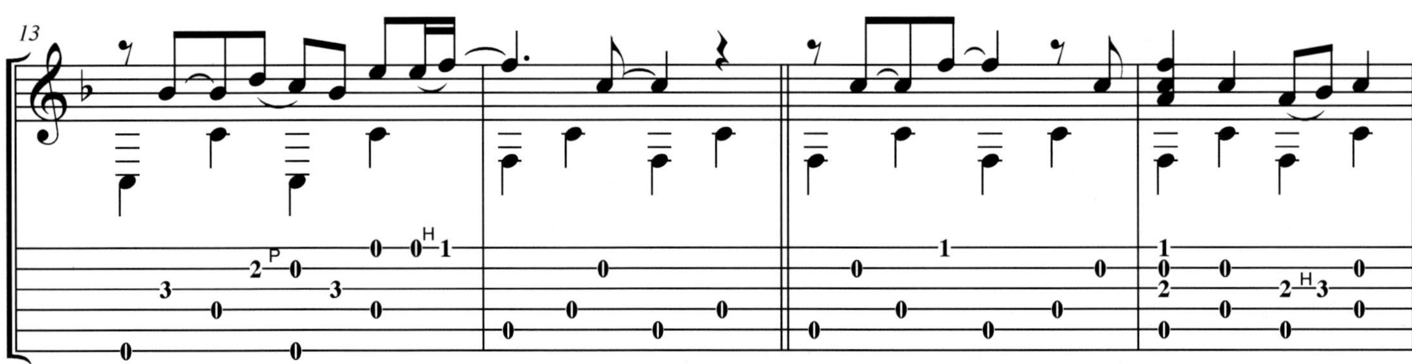

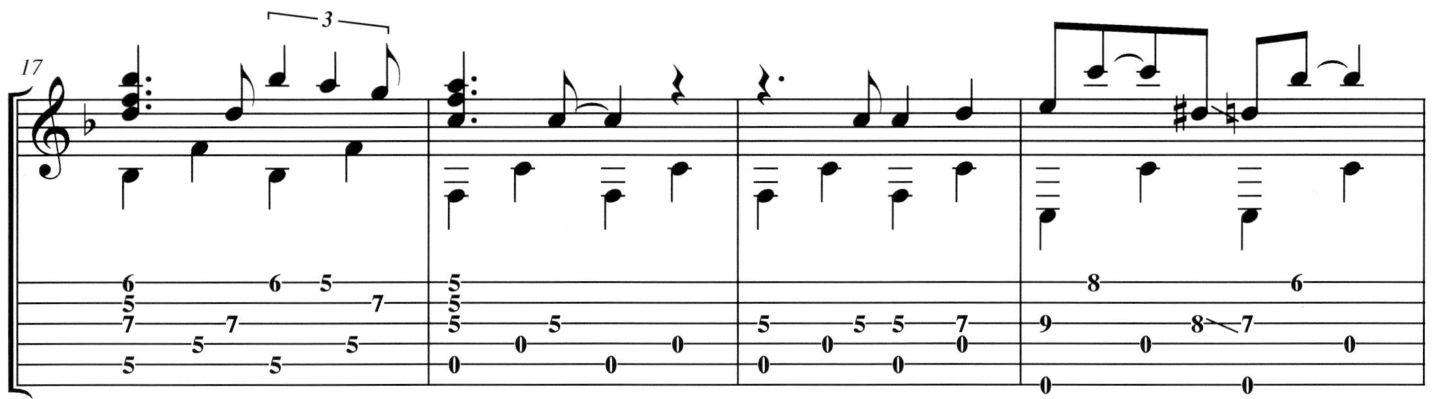
17

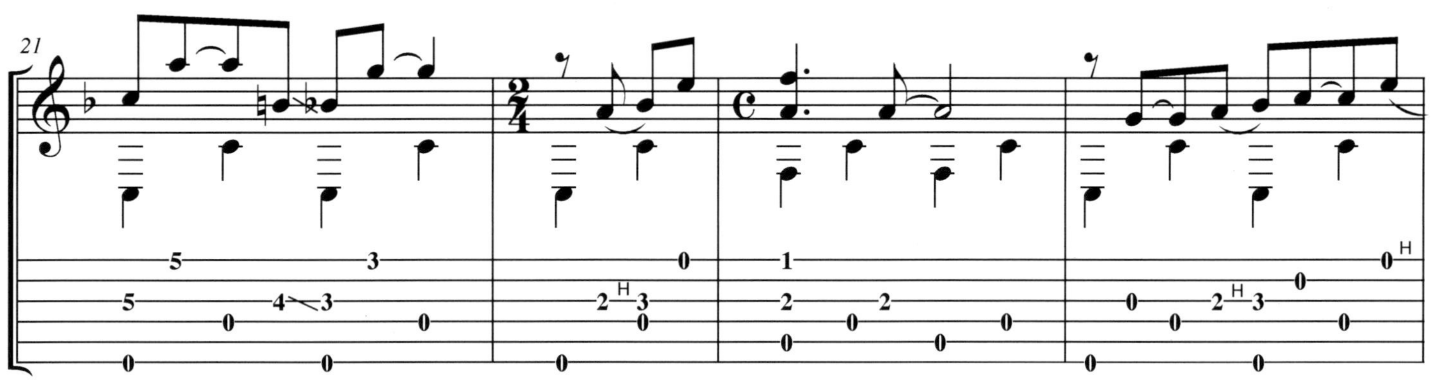
21

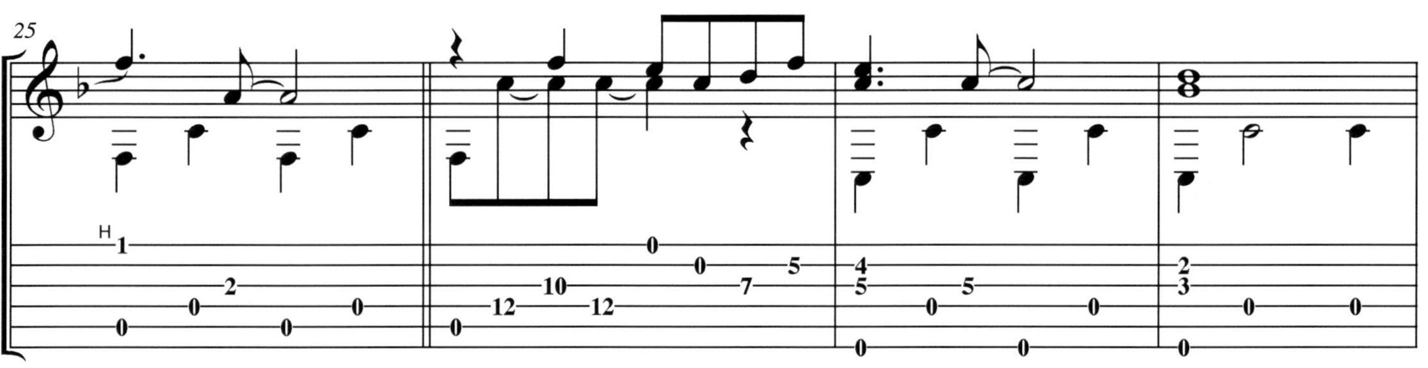
25

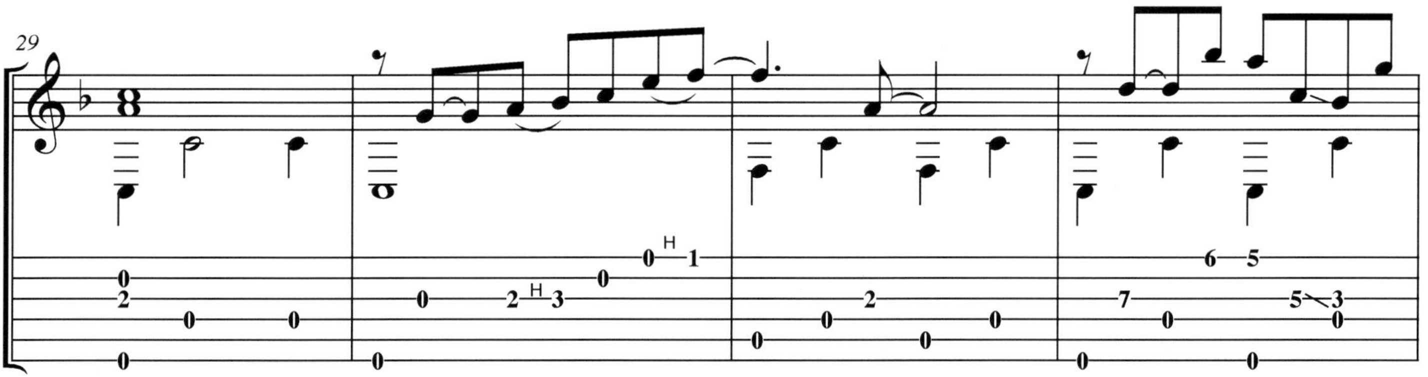
29

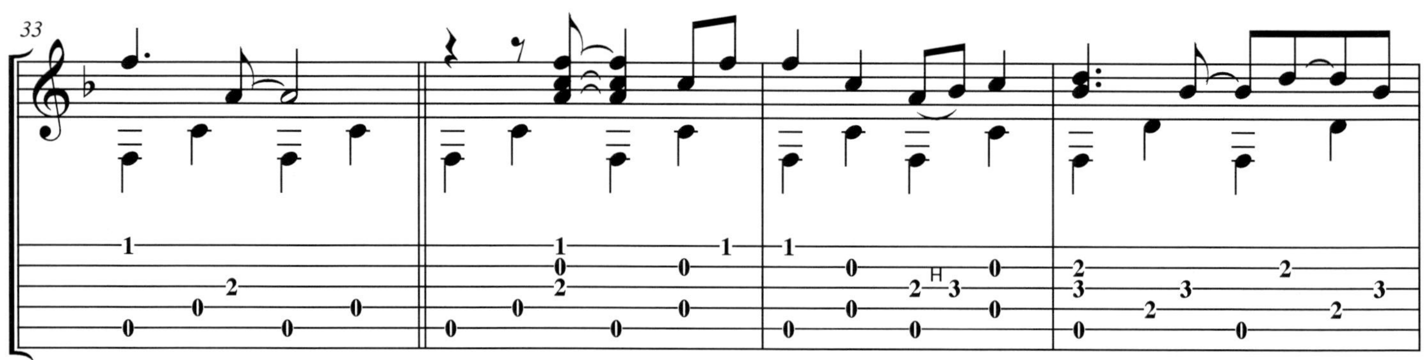
33

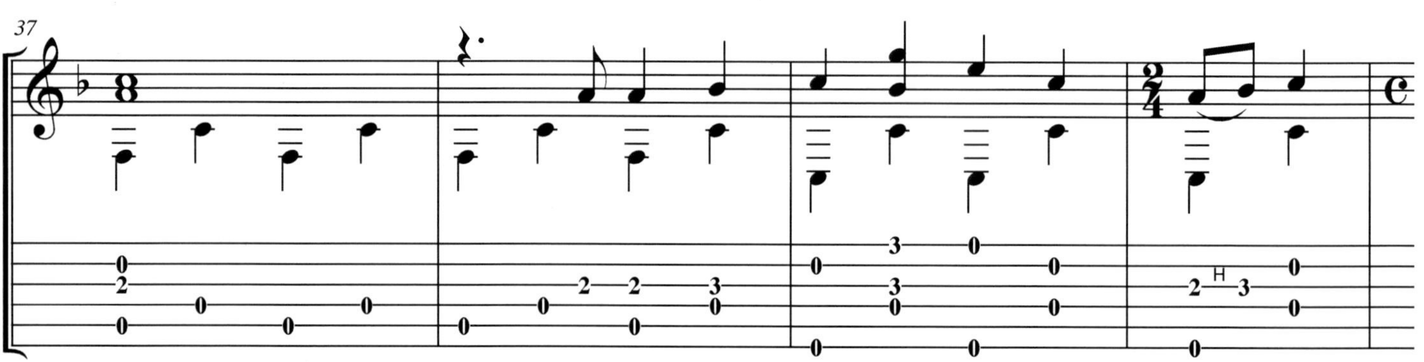
37

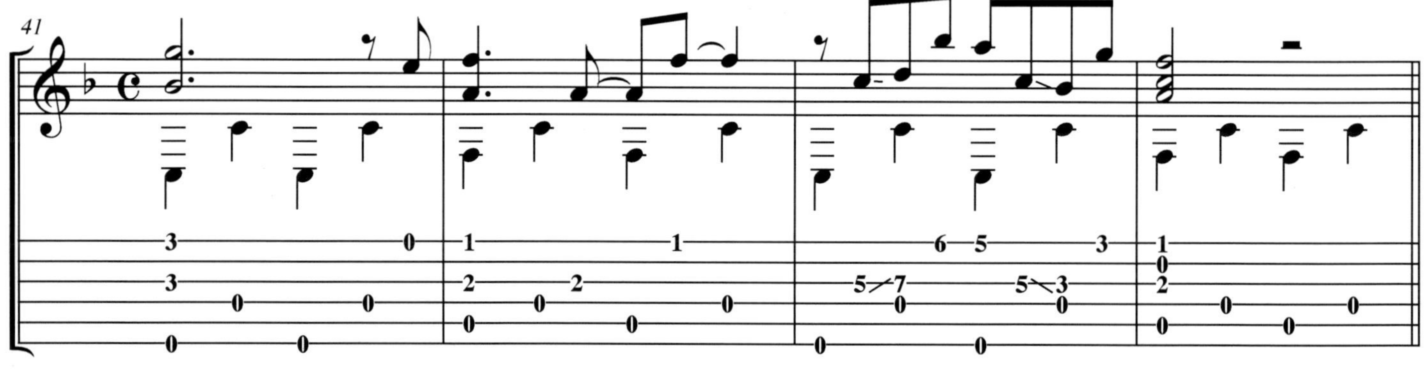
41

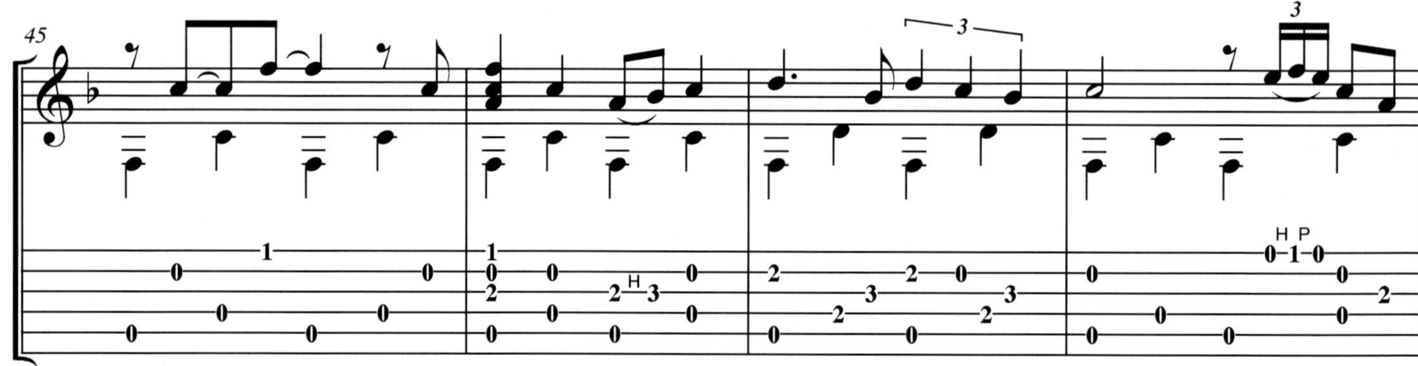
45

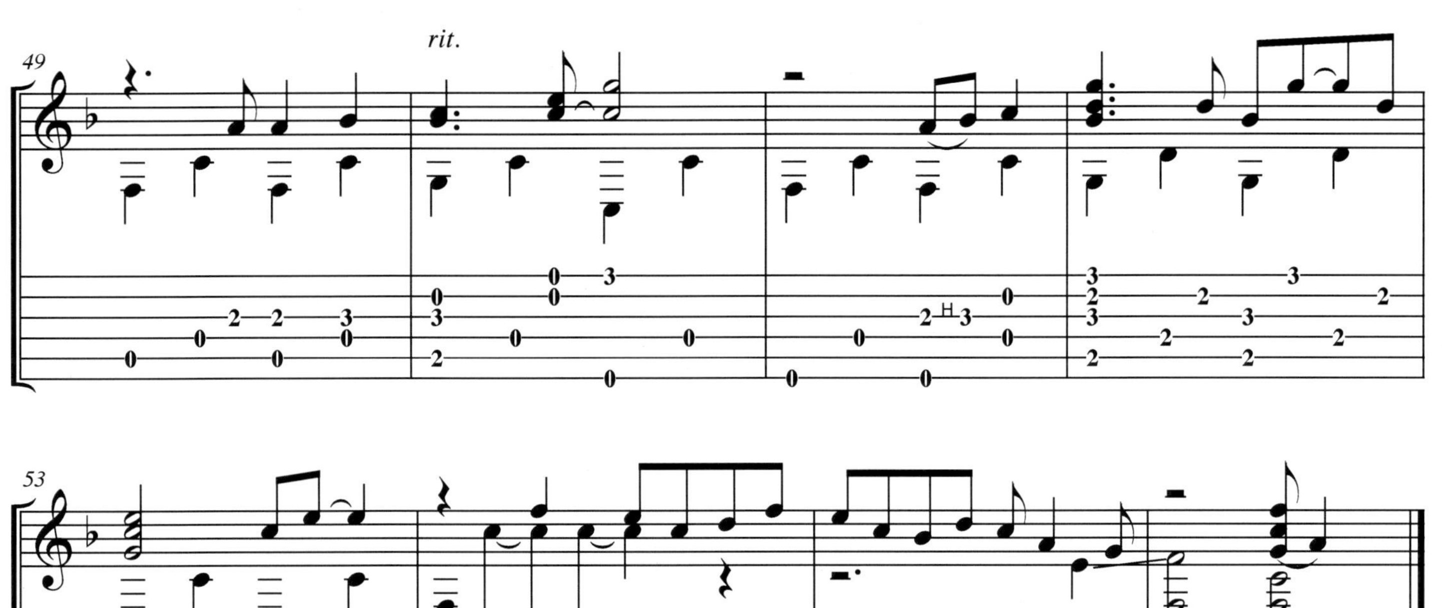
rit.

Makee Ailana
Notes

"Makee Ailana" starts off with an unusual descending melodic motif. The same riff – with slight modifications – shows up again as a bridge and a coda. This piece represents a more modern approach to slack key than arrangements such as "Gabby's Hula Medley" and "Green Rose Hula." Some players go out of their way to create elaborate introductions, bridges, interludes, and codas to offset and frame the main melody.

Other than that, the arrangement is made up of several variations on the melody using licks typical of slack key stylings in this tuning. Pay attention to the double stops and chord shapes in both this and "He Aloha Noʻo Honolulu."

Measures 1-3: This initial descending lick sets up a cascading flurry of notes moving between the bass and treble strings. To begin, hold down notes on the 12th and 10th frets. Play the initial open 6th string, then roll the next three notes between your thumb and index finger. Let these ring while you play the two open strings, then move up to the next double-stop position at beat 4.

That puts you in position for measure 2. Play the first four notes on the treble strings out of double-stop positions – take a look at measures 26 & 27 if you need help finding these.

Resolve the sequence by sliding into the downbeat of measure 3, then strum the final chord and quickly resolve it with the hammer-on.

Strive for a smooth flow between all the notes. You will encounter a few more variations of this lick, so take some time to get it right.

Measures 4-14: Here is the essential melody of "Makee Ailana." I play the chords in measure 4 either as an upwards brush or with a quick rolling motion using three fingers.

Take note of the time change in measure 10. Just keep a steady quarter-note pulse in the bass and you will be fine.

The turnaround in measure 13 is just one of the many F Wahine vamps you will encounter.

The melody repeats beginning at measure 15.

Measures 17 & 18: Play these out of a partial barré at the 5th fret. The triplets in measure 17 are easier to hear than to read, so be sure to listen to the audio file.

From there, the arrangement substitutes a two-measure descending run for the melody. Play these out of double stop – or two-note "chord" – positions.

Measures 26-33 are a bridge based on the opening figure, with a couple of F Wahine vamps thrown in.

From there, you play through the melody a couple of more times before reprising the introduction.

B♭ Major Tuning
F-B♭-D-F-B♭-D

Unlike most of the other tunings in this book, B♭ Major requires tuning three strings higher – the 2nd, 5th and 6th – from standard tuning. Depending on your guitar, you may want to put on a lighter-gauge string set.

B♭ Major tuning is made up of a pair of major chords on strings 1, 2 & 3 and strings 4, 5 & 6. Although you do not have bass strings sounding roots and fifths on the tonic and dominant chords, the symmetrical nature of the tuning more than makes up for this deficiency. Anything you play on the top 3 strings can be played on the bottom three strings. Double-stop positions on any adjacent string pairs – 1 & 2 and 2 & 3-repeat on strings 4 & 5 and 5 & 6. Similarly, double-stop pairs on strings 1 & 3 repeat on strings 4 & 6.

As you play through the next two arrangements, take note of all the various double stops and where they fall. The best way to get to know a new tuning is to try to find those all-important positions.

"Green Rose Hula" and "Pua Lilia" demonstrate two different approaches to this tuning.

Green Rose Hula
Notes

Although composed around 1935, "Green Rose Hula" sounds far older. The basic melodic form is related to any number of songs built around an ancient two-line chant structure.

Measures 1 & 2. Nothing says "slack key" quite like this classic vamp. Pay attention to the bass notes.

Measures 3-8: The first four bars constitute the melody to which the words to "Green Rose Hula" would be sung. The two vamps are for the dancers to make their turns to set up for the next verse. As such, they are essential.

Measures 9-14: This variation is intended to introduce some of the double-stop positions found in this tuning.

Measure 15 & 16: If you are playing instrumentally, you can get away from the requirement to always play two vamps at the end of each verse. These extra turnarounds give your ear a rest before launching into the next two variations on the melody.

From here on, you play a few more variations, one in the upper octave and another that makes use of chimes for some of the melody notes. Once again, pay attention to the various chords and two-note "chords" you encounter so you can use them in your own explorations.

Pua Lilia
Notes

In contrast to "Green Rose Hula," "Pua Lilia" has a fairly complex melody and harmony. It was composed in 1916, at the height of the Golden Age of Hawaiian composition.

The arrangement is fairly straightforward, with a strong waltz time feel in the bass. Play it with a stately grace befitting this tender love song.

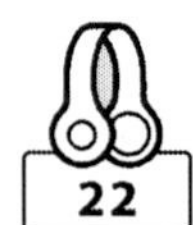

Green Rose Hula

Laida Paia & John K. Almeida

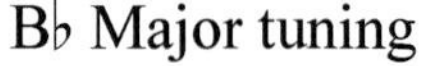

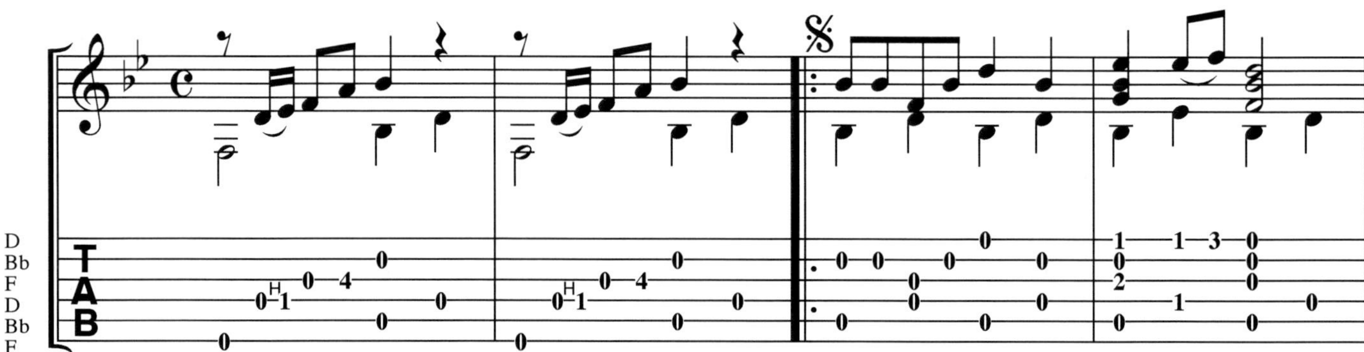

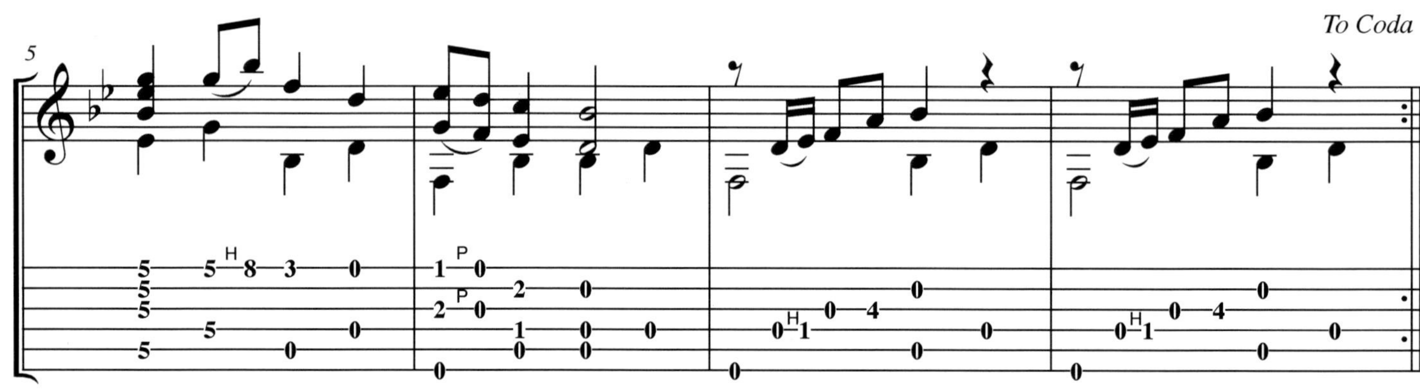

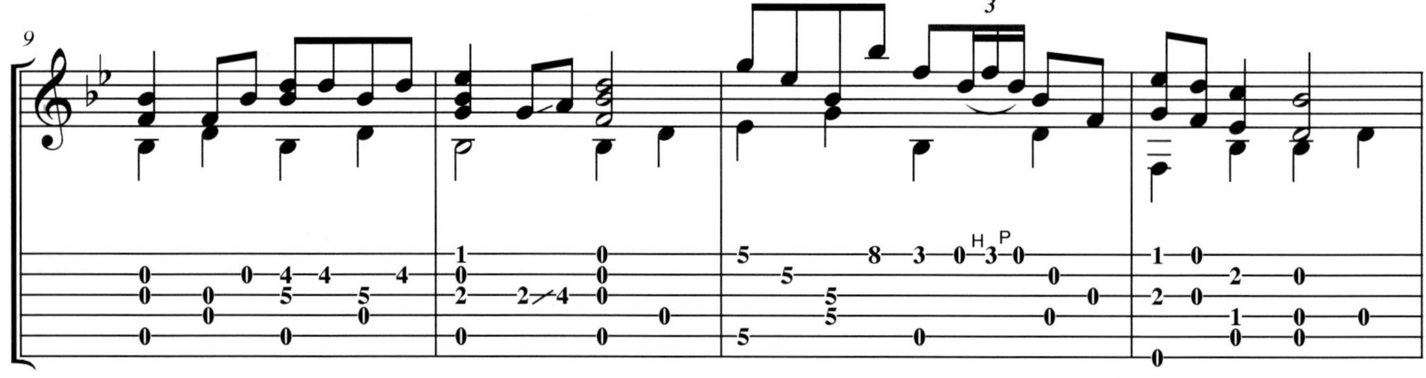

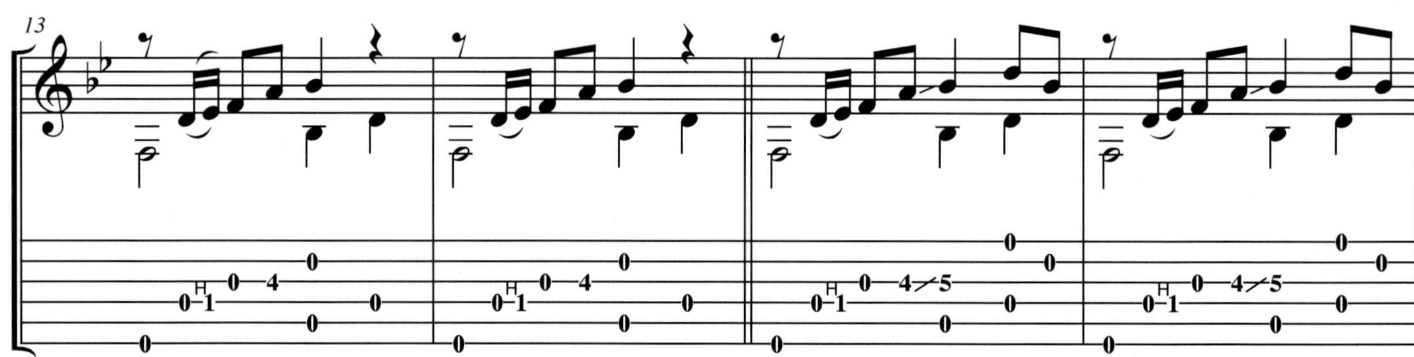

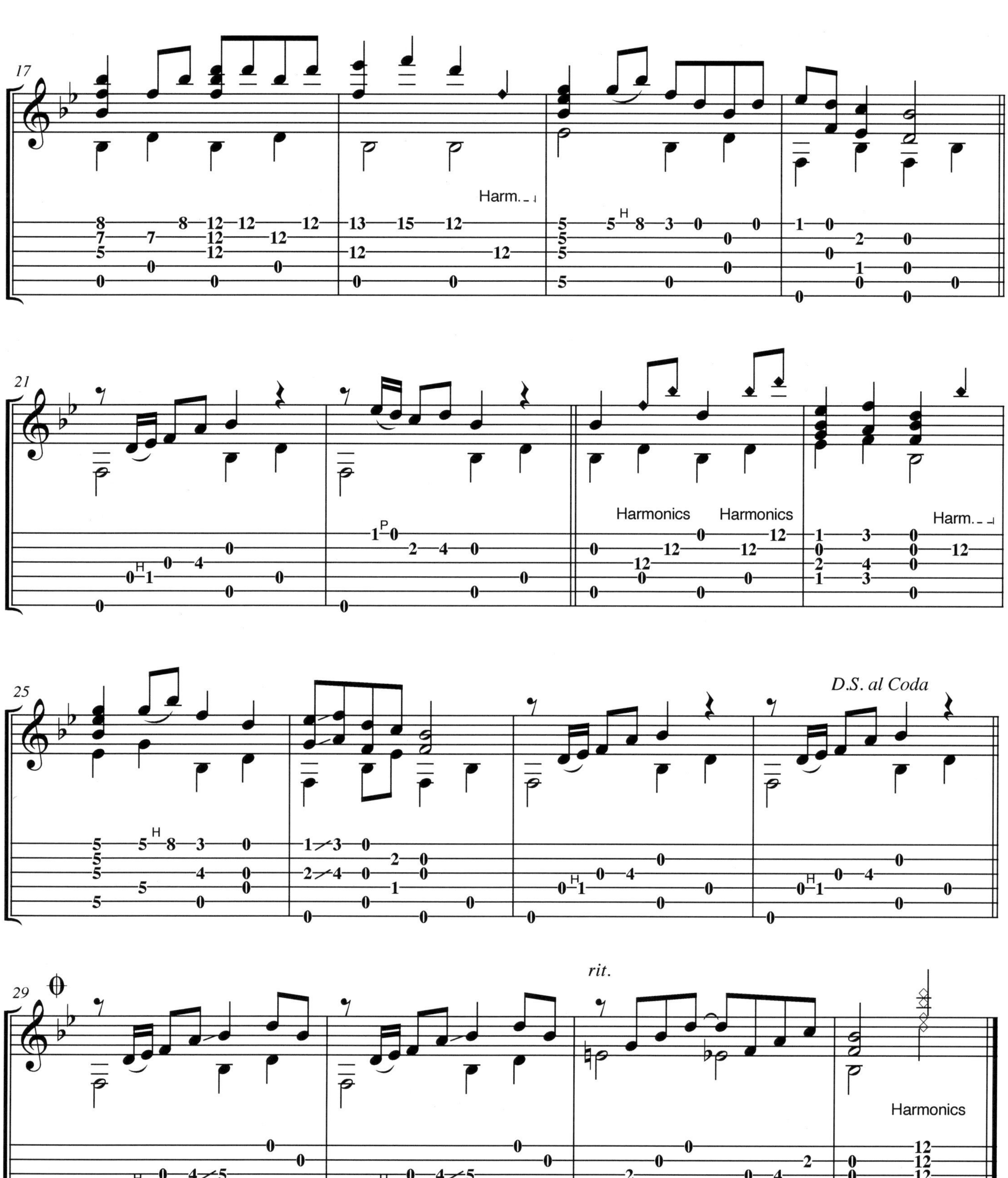
17
Harm.
21
Harmonics
Harmonics
Harm.
25
D.S. al Coda
29
rit.
Harmonics

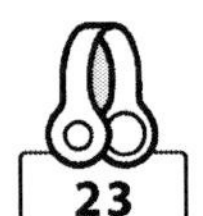

Pua Lilia

Alfred Unauana Alohikea

B♭ Major tuning

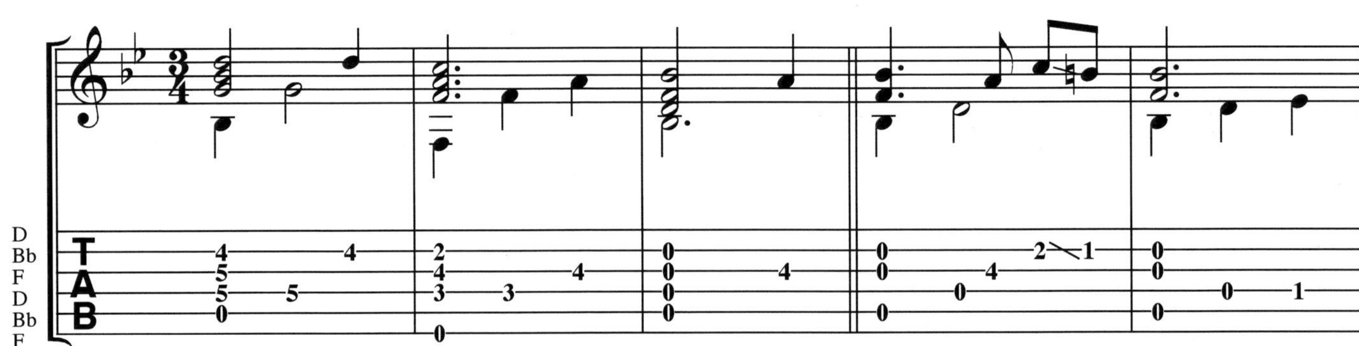

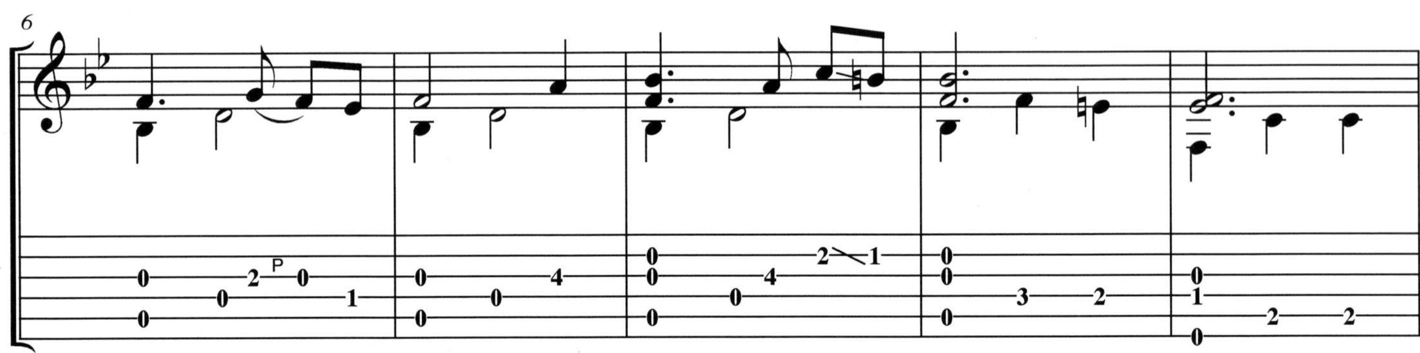

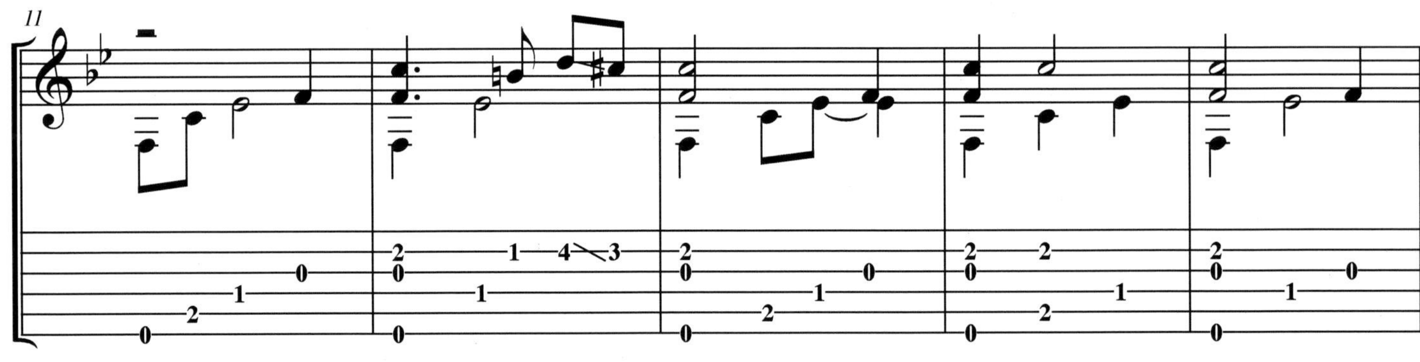

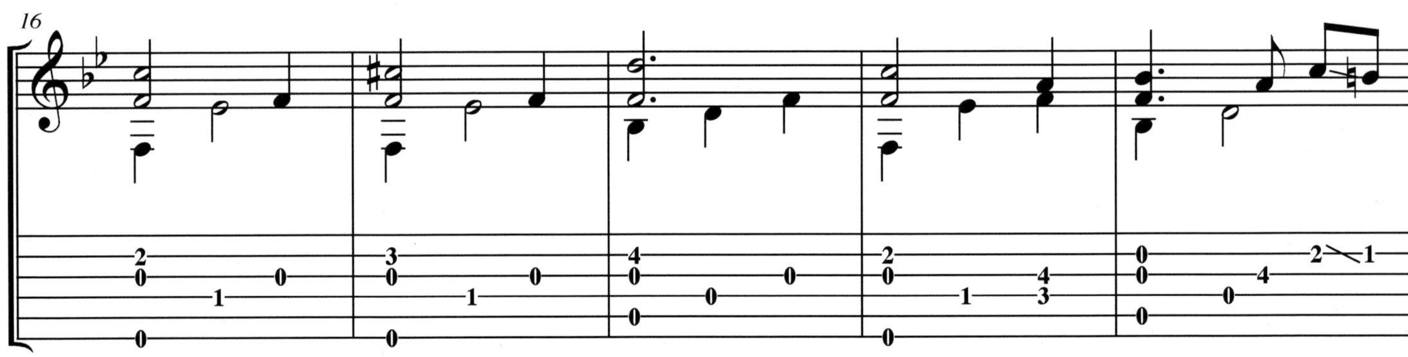

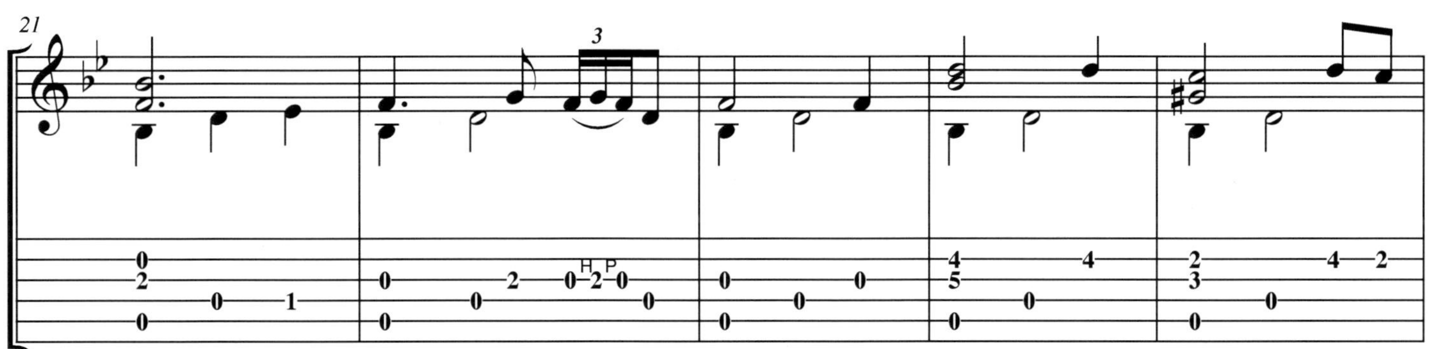
21

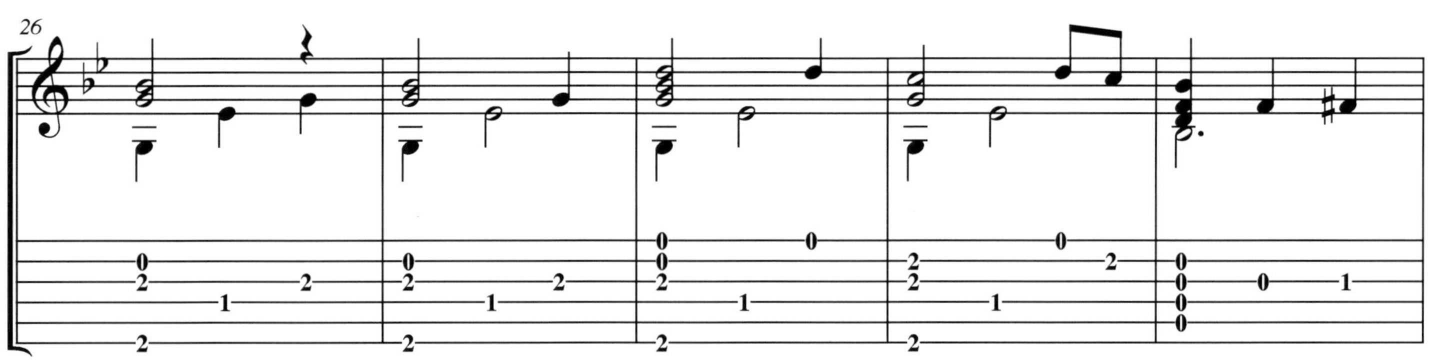
26

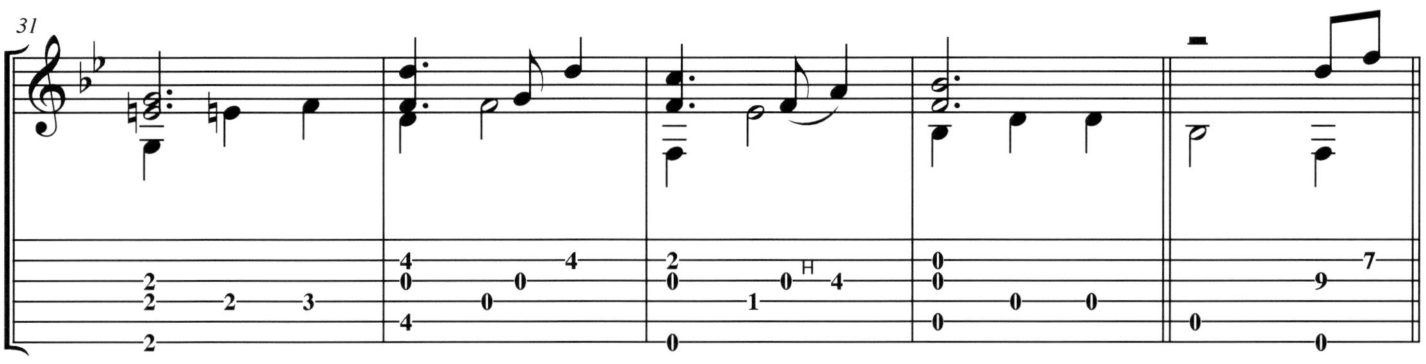
31

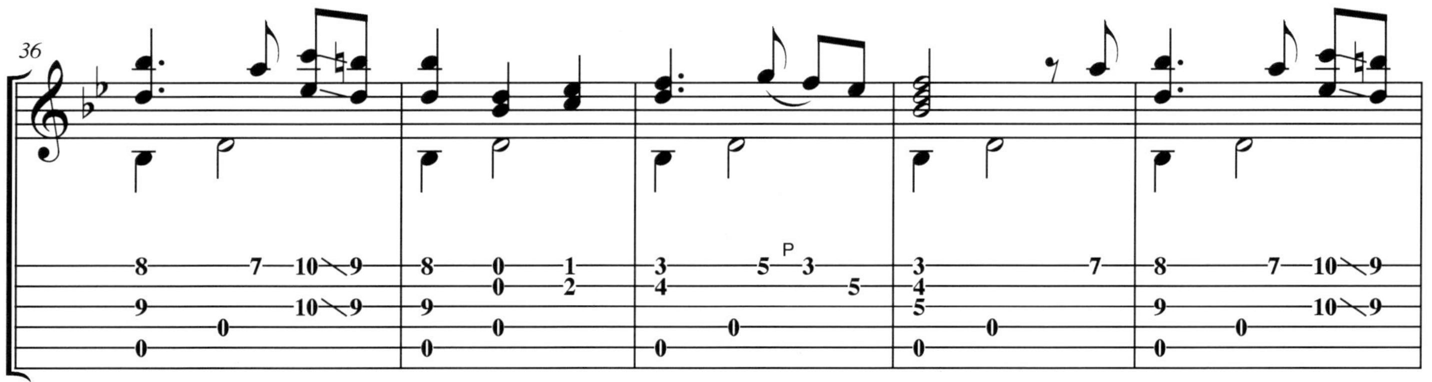
36

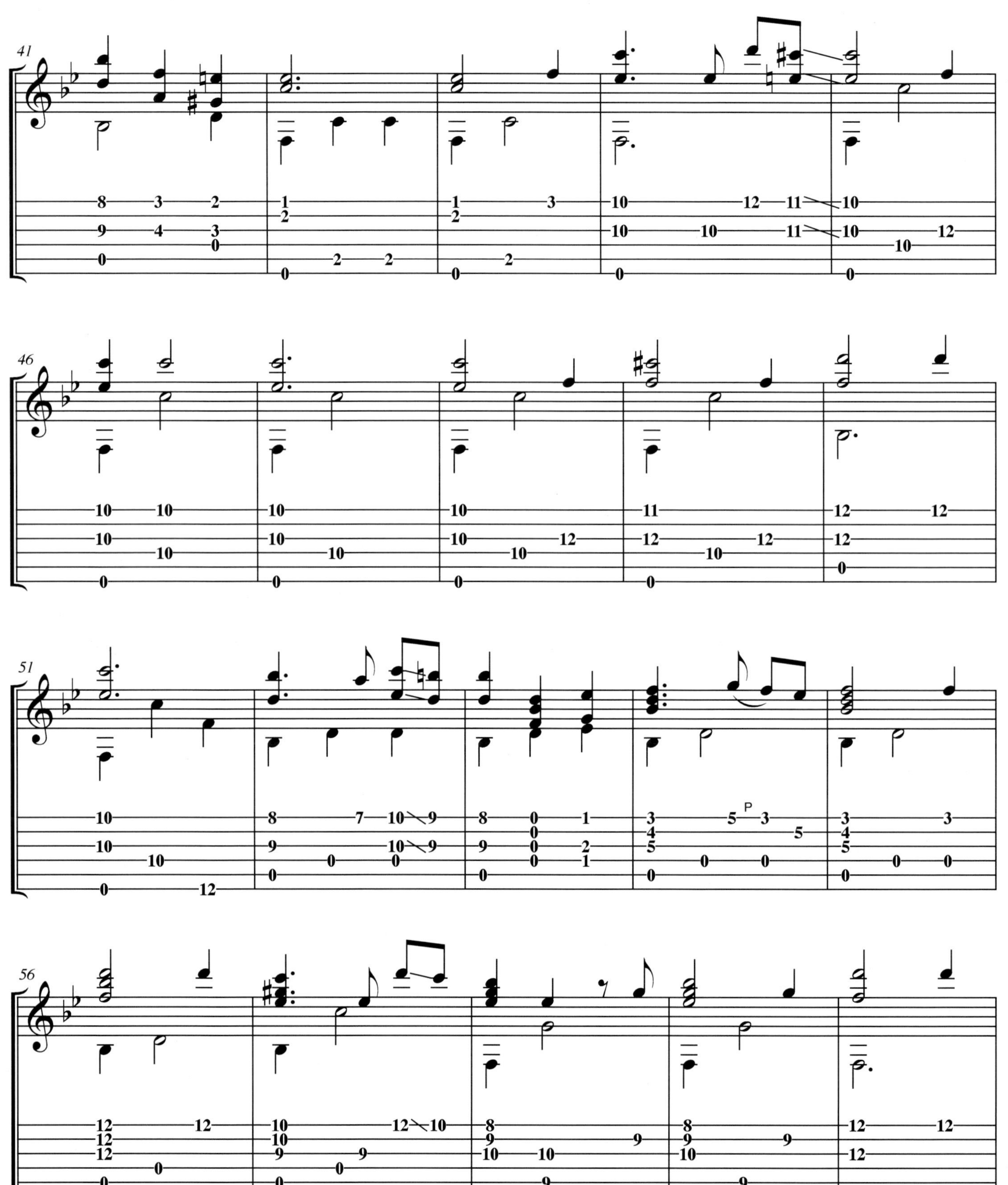
P

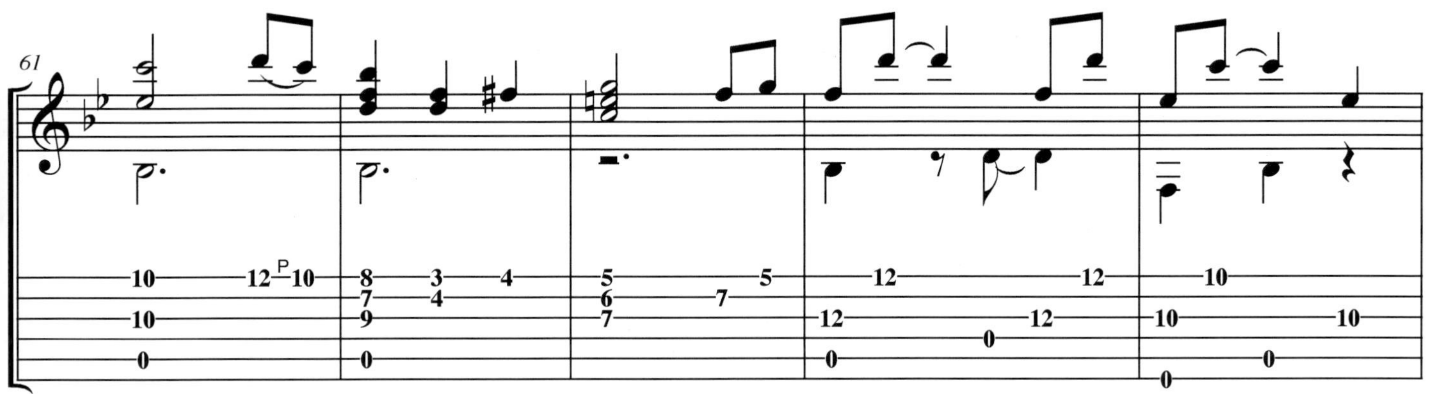
61
10
12
P
10
8
7
9
3
4
4
5
6
7
7
5
12
12
0
12
10
10
0
0
0
0
0

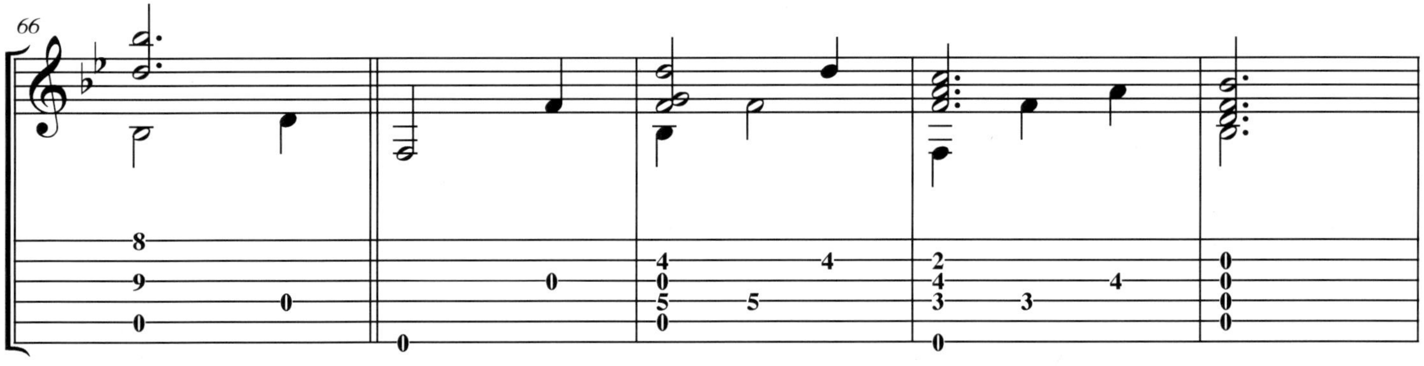
66
8
9
0
0
0
4
0
5
0
4
5
2
4
3
0
3
4
0
0
0
0

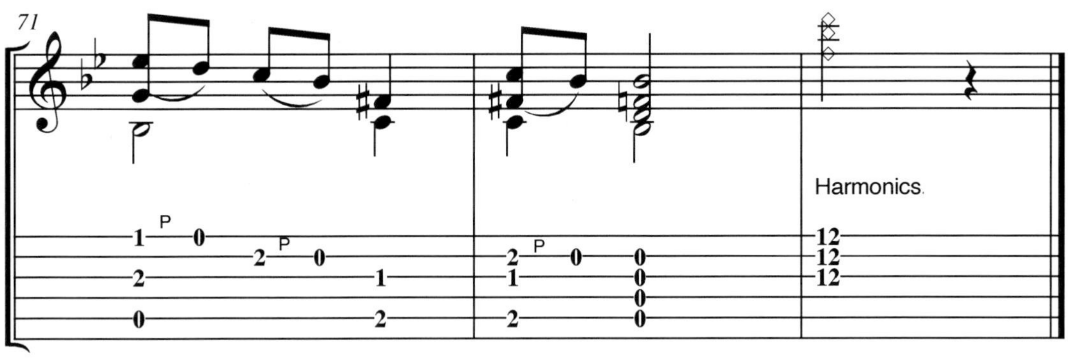
71
Harmonics.
1
P
0
2
P
0
2
1
0
2
2
P
0
1
2
0
0
0
0
12
12
12

D Major Add9 Tuning
D-A-E-F♯-A-D

This unusual tuning is a modification of the more common D Major tuning (D-A-D-F♯-A-D). Raising the 4th string a full step to E gives you tonic and fifth bass notes for both the D and the A chords on open strings.

Slack key players will often create a special tuning that they use for only one or two songs.

To tune from standard tuning, drop both your outside strings a whole step to D. Drop the 2nd a whole step to A and the 3rd a half-step to F♯. Finally, raise the 4th string to E.

Ku'u Lei Awapuhi Melemele
Notes

"Ku'u Lei Awapuhi Melemele," which translates as "My Yellow Ginger Lei," is one of the most beloved slack key songs of all time. The timeless melody just lends itself to *kī hōʻalu.* So let's get started.

The introduction is composed of a repeated two-measure harmonics pattern – notice the indeterminate chord suggested by measures 1 & 3 – followed by a descending pattern played using broken double stops. If you have played through most of the arrangements in this book, this should feel pretty familiar by now. You will find variations on this theme everywhere you look in slack key. Having a number of similar options at your finger tips allows you to spontaneously create your own arrangements.

Measures 12-21: This is the melody of "Ku'u Lei Awapuhi Melemele" as it is sung. Later on, you will encounter a couple of typical slack key style variations on this melody.

Measures 29-38: After another short interlude, here is a reprise of the melody. Notice that the harmony changes, dropping the quick move to the G chord. Pay attention to how the sliding turnaround licks in measures 31 & 35 substitute for a fair amount of the melody.

These ten measures represent the usual way this tune is played, regardless of the tuning. I can point to any number of examples that sound similar, including recordings by Leonard Kwan, Keola Beamer, and Ledward Ka'apana. For my arrangement in F Wahine, see *Old Time Hawaiian Slack Key Guitar.*

Measures 39-48: Here is another way to play the melody that is slightly different than the previous ten measures. I've added little pieces of the original melody here and there, while retaining some of the old time slack key stylings.

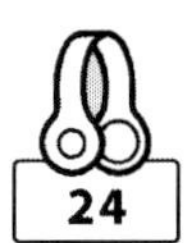

Ku'u Lei Awapuhi Melemele

John Keawehawai'i

D Major add9 tuning

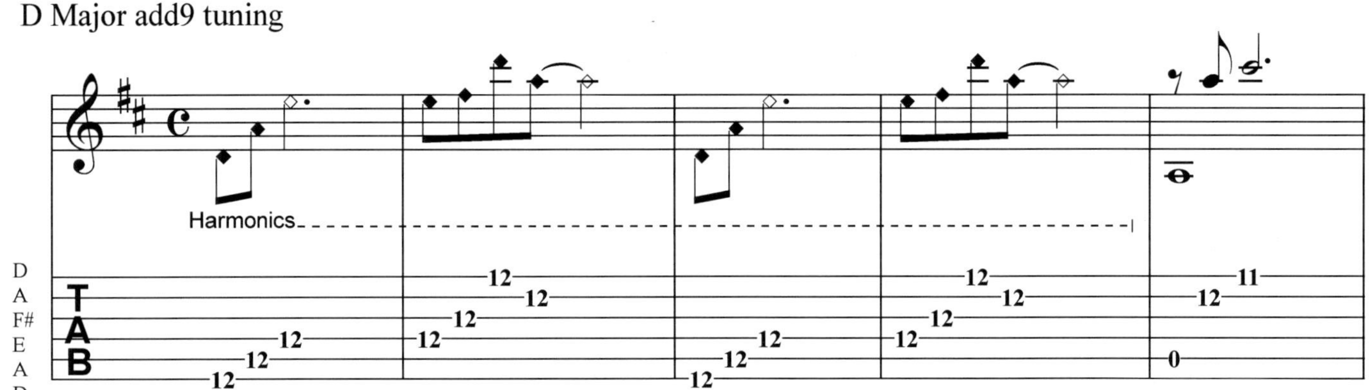

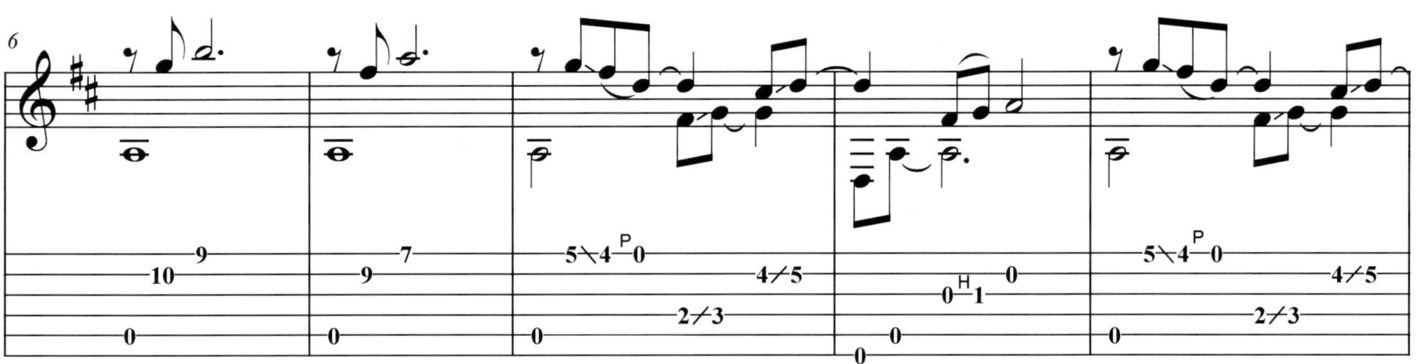

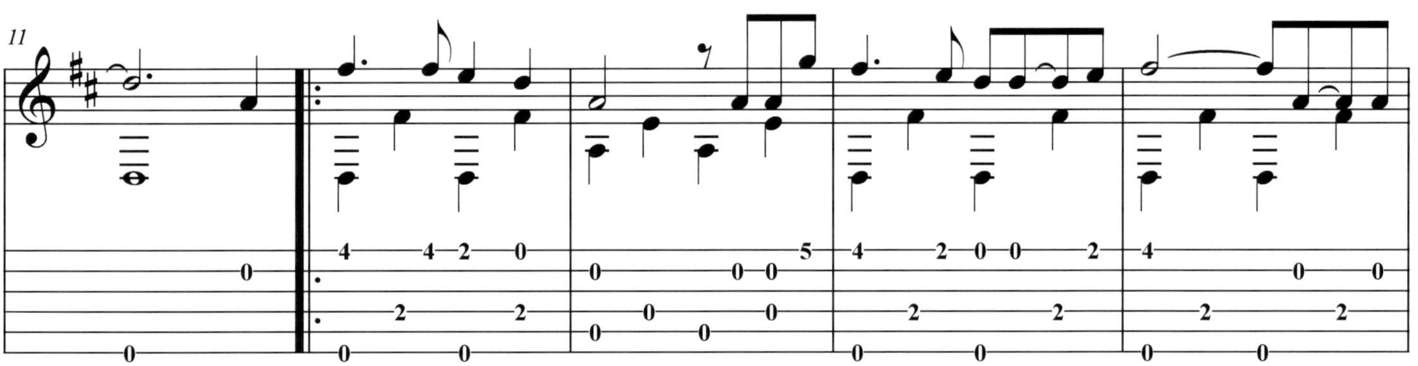

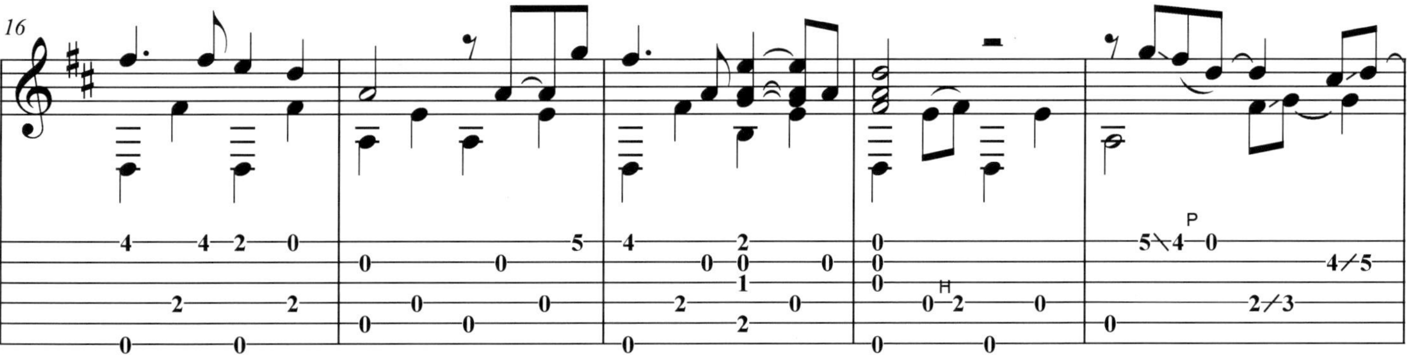

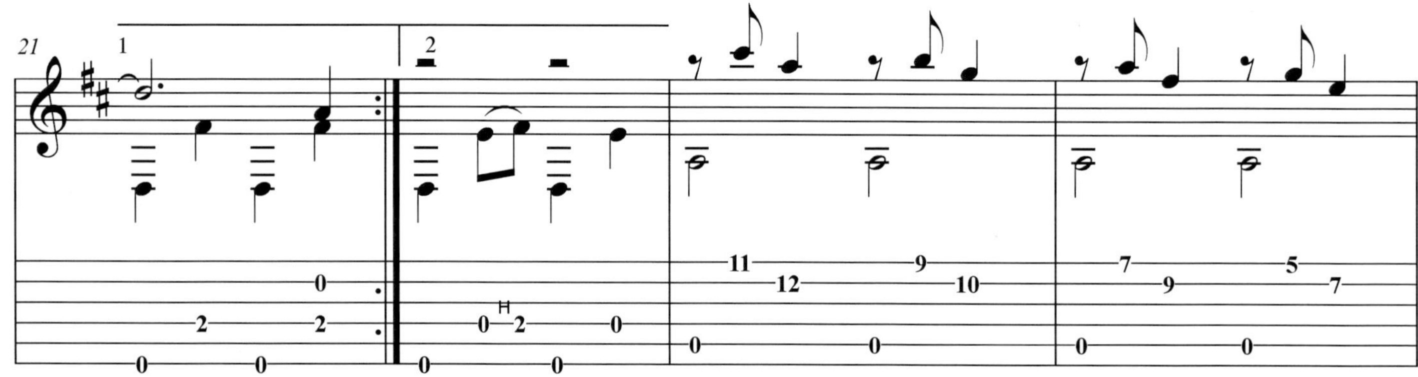
21
1
2
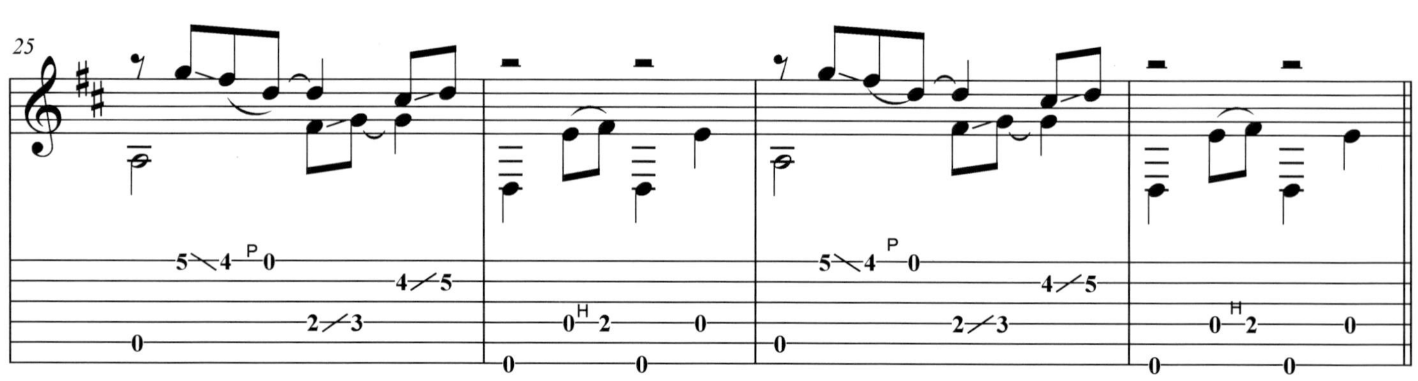
25
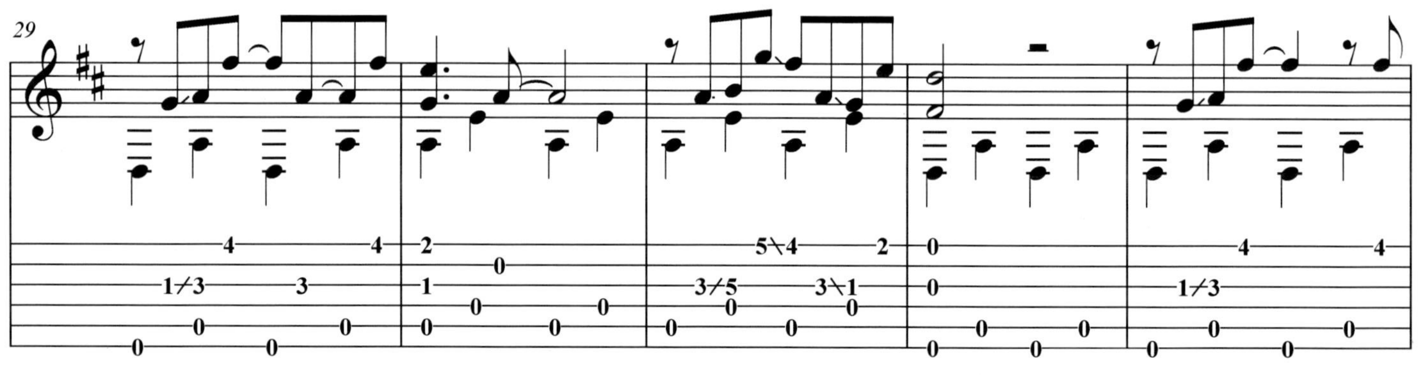
29
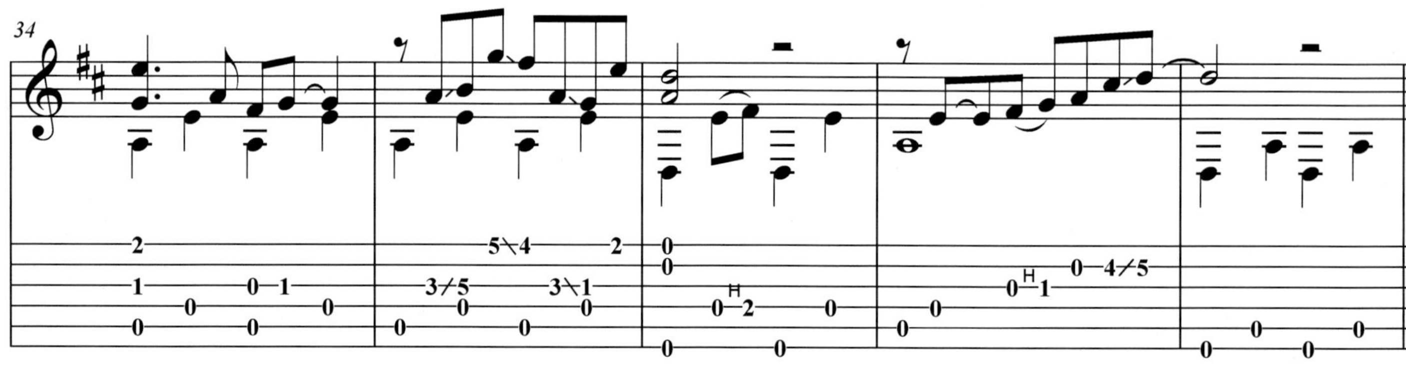
34

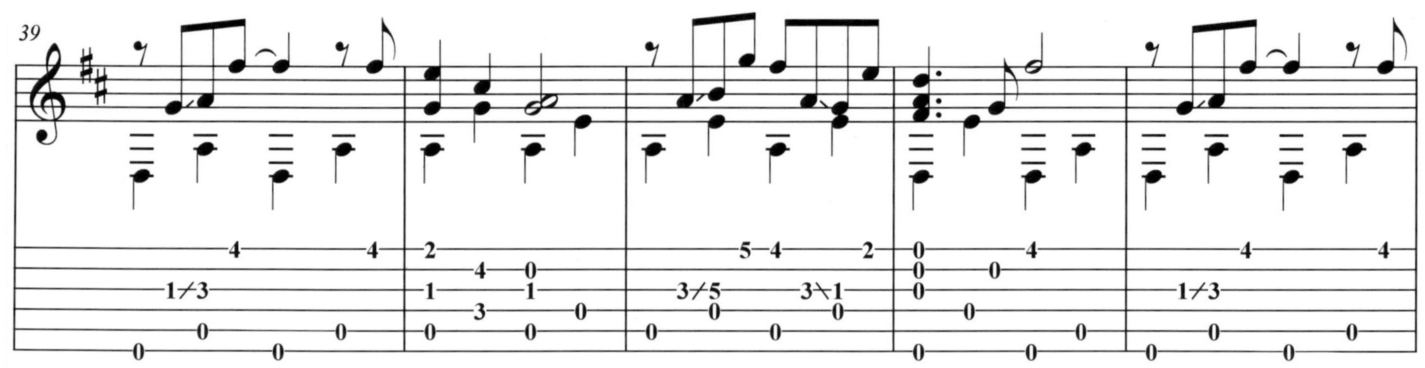
39

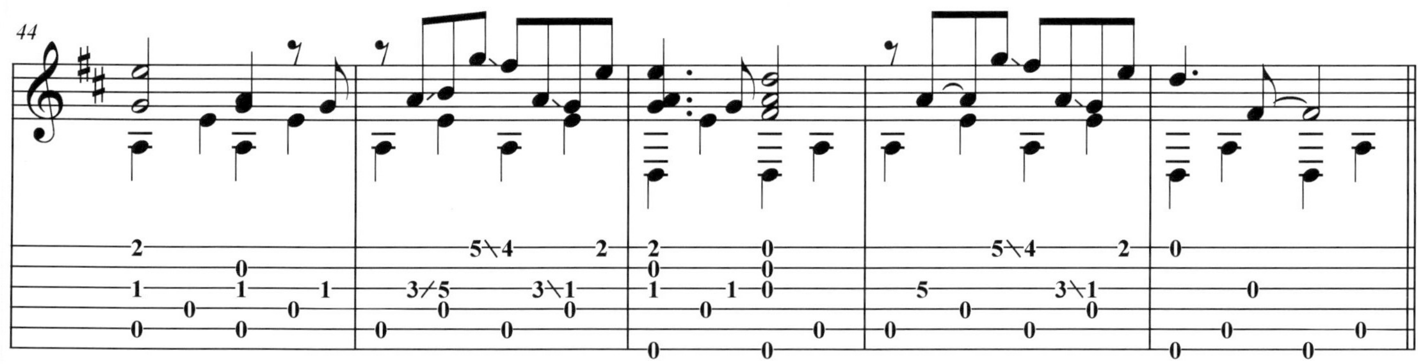
44

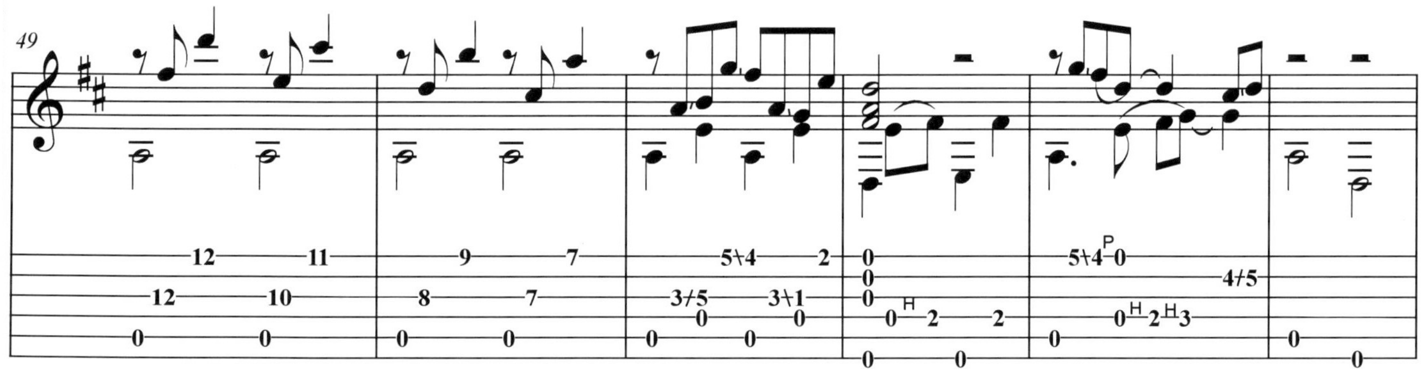
49

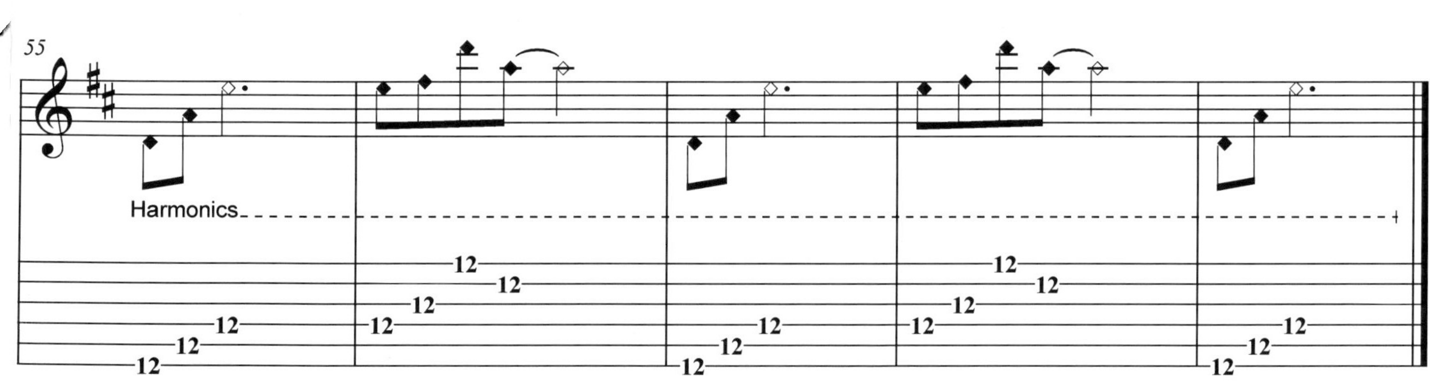
55
Harmonics

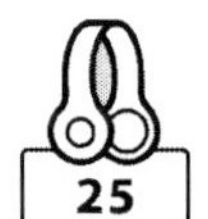

Aloha Medley
Isa Lei/Aloha 'Oe

Traditional Fiji
Queen Lili'uokalani

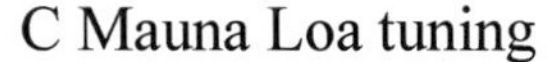

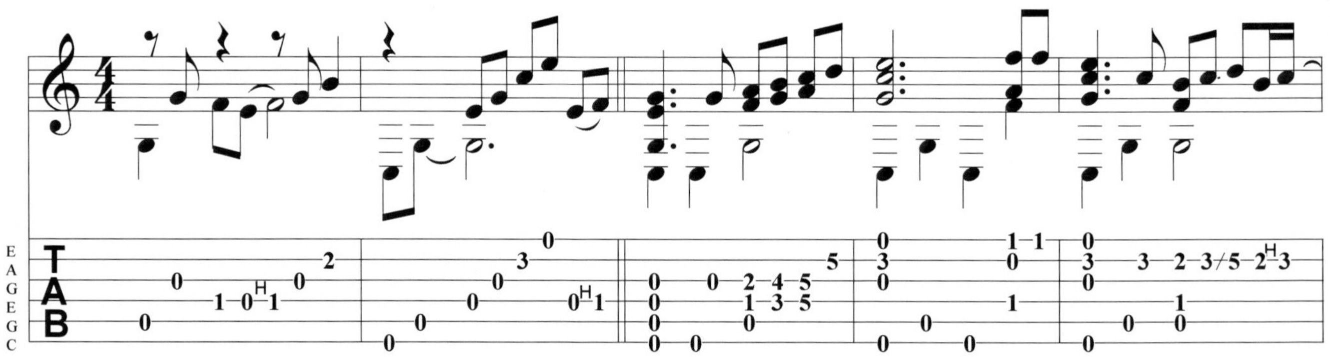

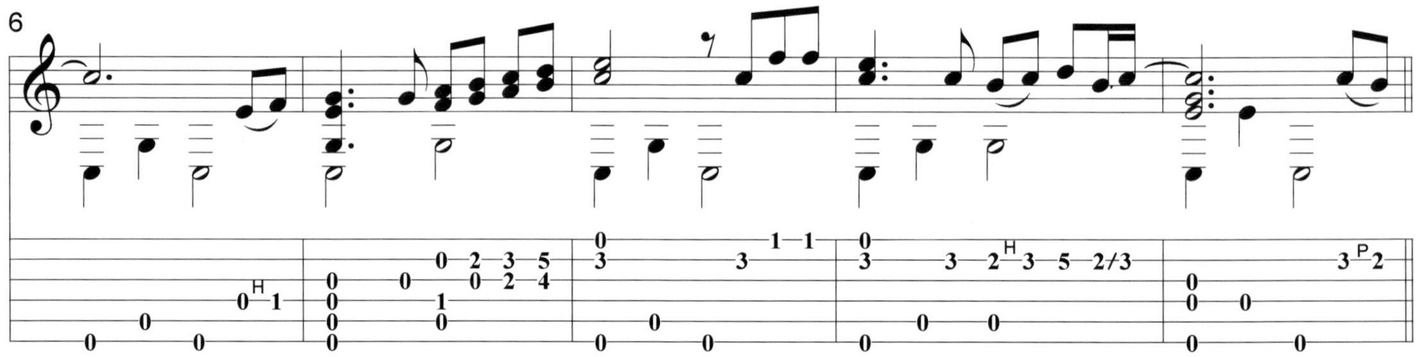

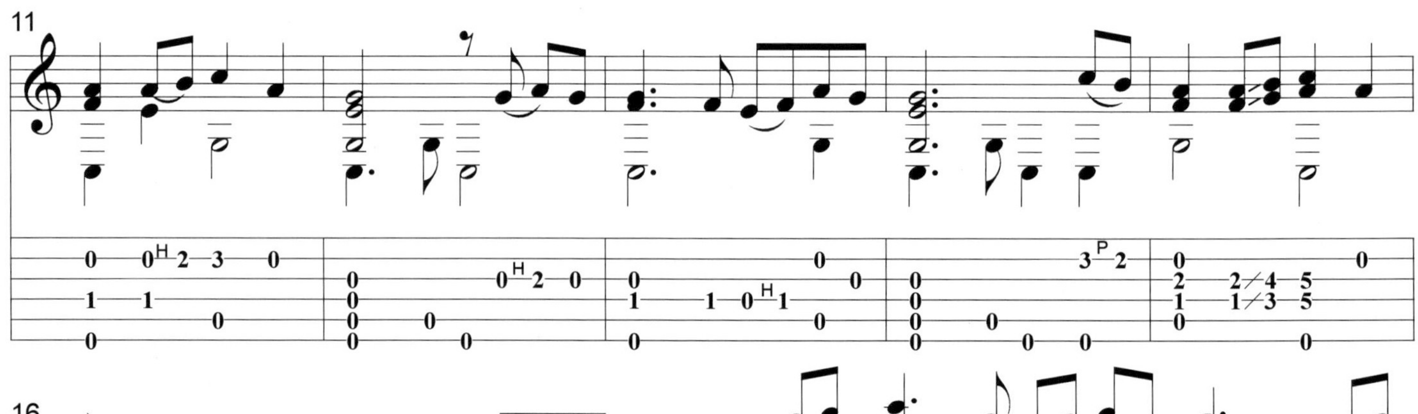

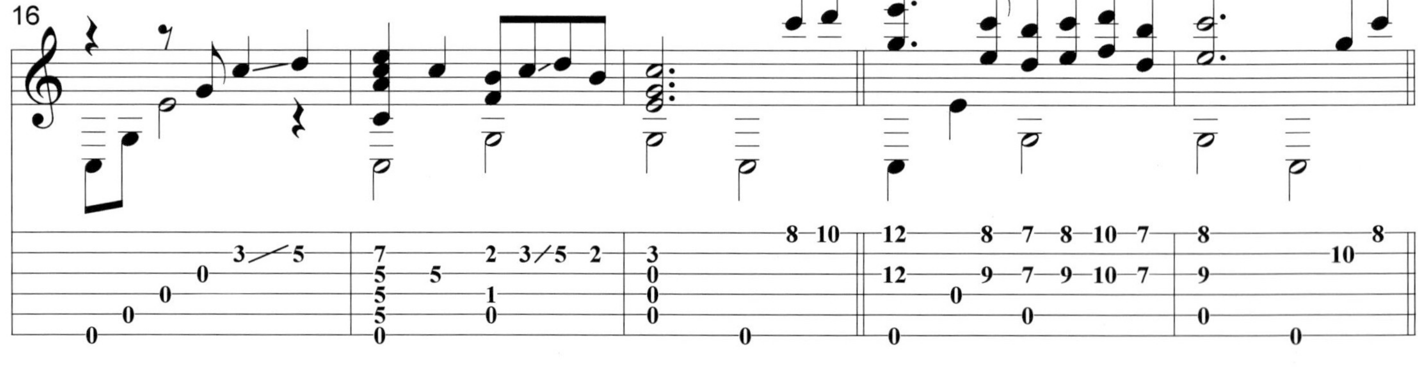

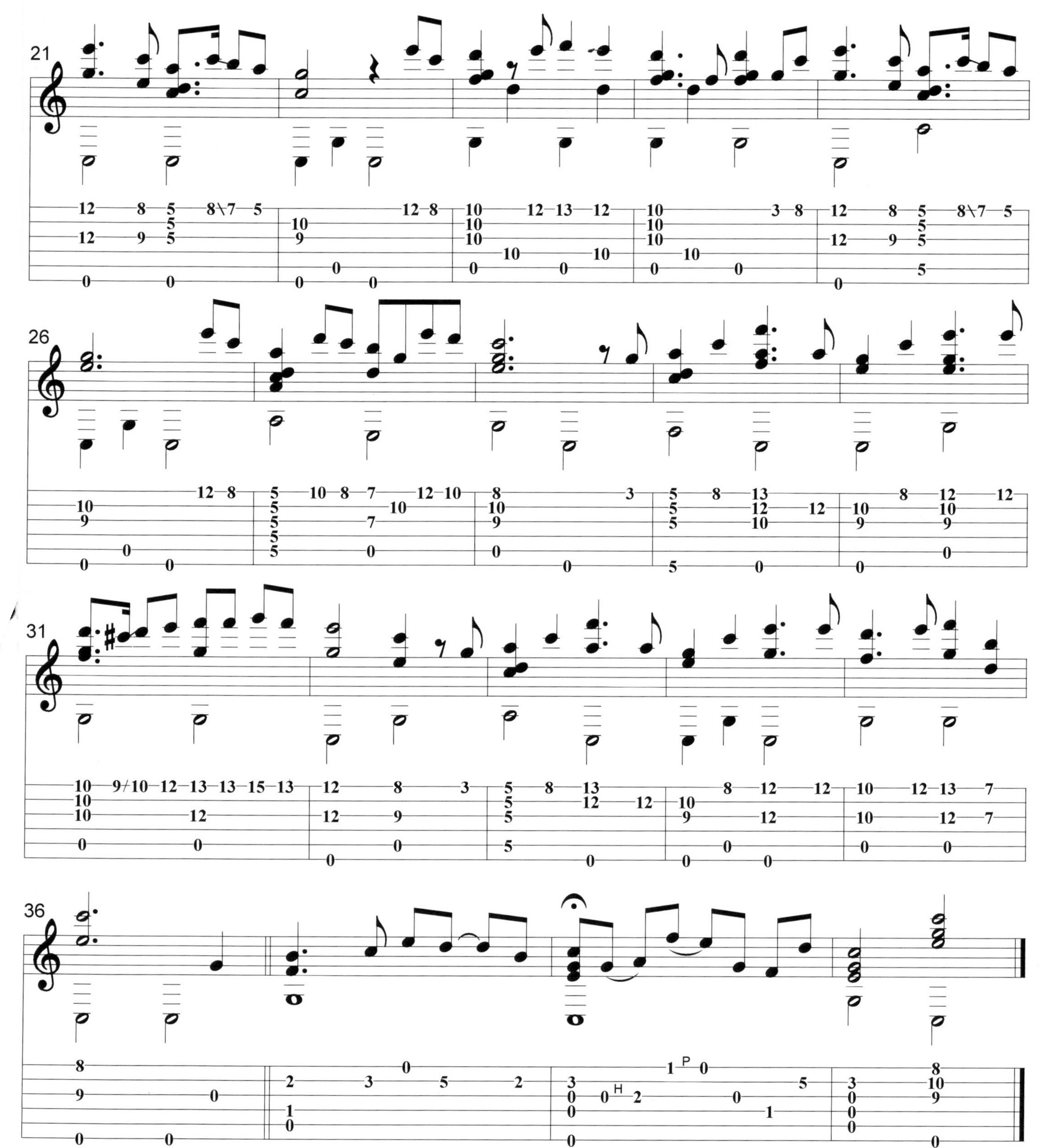

C Mauna Loa Tuning
C-G-E-G-A-E

Like all Mauna Loa tunings, the two top strings are a fifth apart. From standard, begin by dropping your 2nd string a full step to A. Next, slack the 5th string to G and the bass all the way down to C. Finally, raise your 4th string up to E.

Aloha Medley
Notes

This medley is associated with Gabby Pahinui, although this particular setting is my own. I've known these two songs since I was young. A friend told me that when she was a child, her mother sang "Isa Lei" as a lullaby. And "Aloha 'Oe" is simply one of the best-loved melodies in the world.

These two lovely songs of parting make a fitting end to this stage of your slack key journey. The arrangement is designed to show off some of the double stops and chord positions in C Mauna Loa Tuning. Play the songs slowly and with a great deal of feeling.

Afterword

Thank you for taking the time to work through this book. I hope I have been able to point out a few tips and techniques that will help you on your way. May you find great joy from this music.

So where do you go from here?

There is a saying in Hawai'i that translates as "Not all knowledge comes from a single school."

Each of the authors whose instructional books I've listed on the next page offers a different point of view. I encourage you to sample a few of the valuable resources to learn how each teacher approaches the music.

The same goes for online or video instruction. Try as many different styles as you can – and then go back and apply what you have learned to some of the older songs in your repertoire.

If you have not been to Hawai'i to attend a slack key concert or festival, start saving today. Although it's possible to hear live Hawaiian slack key artists in concert almost anywhere in the world, there is nothing like hearing the music in the land of its birth. Even better, plan to attend one of the Hawaiian music camps that have sprung up in the past twenty years.

Above all, please treat this music with respect. It isn't just about the notes – slack key is the essence of Hawai'i.

And so, until the next time we meet: stay tuned and "Jus' Press!"

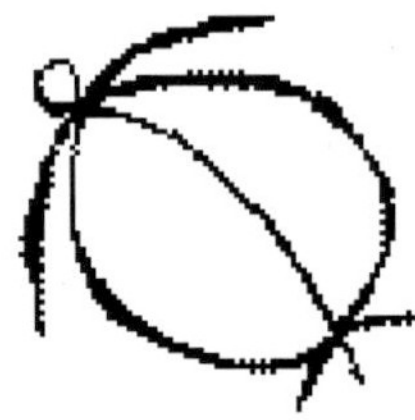

Resources

Mark-o.com

Be sure to check out Mark's free slack key and finger-style ʻukulele video lessons.

JamPlay.com

A huge guitar instruction site. Mark has 65 slack key lessons on this extensive guitar site.

Taropatch.net

Online community for lovers of slack key, ukulele and Hawaiian music.

DancingCat.com

Outstanding recordings of Hawaiian slack key players. Look for the *Dancing Cat Slack Key Info Book,* with lists of recordings, tunings, essays and more.

Huapala.org

Online lyrics resource for Hawaiian music.

Mele.com

"The World's Online Source for Hawaiian Music Since 1995"

A quick search on YouTube will yield hundreds of videos featuring slack key guitar, many with instruction.

Selected Slack Key Artists

Aunty Alice Namakelua, Gabby Pahinui, Raymond Kane, Leonard Kwan, Sonny Chillingworth, Dennis Kamakahi, Atta Isaacs, Cindy Combs, Cyril Pahinui, Jeff Peterson, Ledward Kaʻapana, Owana Salazar, Keola Beamer, Kapono Beamer, Ozzie Kotani, Makana, George Kahumoku, Jr., Keoki Kahumoku, Brittany Paiva, Sonny Lim, Gary Haleamau, Kevin Brown, Amy Hanaialiʻi, John Keawe, George Kuo, Danny Carvalho, Patrick Landeza, and of course, Uji Omaʻomaʻo.

Instruction Books

Learn to Play Hawaiian Slack Key Guitar by Keola Beamer and Mark Nelson (Mel Bay Publications, Inc.)

The first widely available slack key instruction manual. Includes 28 songs, detailed information on different tunings, duets and more. Covers material from beginning to advanced.

Guitar Playing Hawaiian Style by Ozzie Kotani (Mel Bay Publications, Inc.)

The perfect introduction to playing slack key.

Old Time Hawaiian Slack Key Guitar by Mark Kailana Nelson (Mel Bay Publications, Inc.)

Featuring 24 essential *kī hōʻalu* instrumentals every aspiring slack key player should know. The arrangements are all transcriptions from live recordings; many feature improvised intros, solos and codas. Best for intermediate to advanced guitarists.

Masters of the Hawaiian Slack Key Guitar by Mark Hanson (Music Sales)

A superb collection of transcriptions from recordings by Raymond Kane, Leonard Kwan, Sonny Chillingworth, Ledward Kaʻapana and Cyril Pahinui. Intermediate to advanced guitarists.

Keola Beamer Teaches Hawaiian Slack Key Guitar (Homespun)

Five songs arranged in Keola's unique style. Best for intermediate level guitarists.

Slack Key Guitar: The G Kilauea Tuning Daniel Ho (Daniel Ho Productions)

Six-time Grammy award-winner Daniel Ho shares the secrets of his personal slack key guitar tuning in this comprehensive study. Intermediate to advanced.

Hawaiian Slack Key: A Lifetime of Study. Vol 1: Methodology by Peter Medeiros (Kapahua, LLC)

Peter Madeiros, a university music educator and the heir to a long family musical tradition, brings rare insight into the hows and whys of slack key guitar. For all levels. Essential, no student of slack key should be without this book.

Mark is proud to endorse **Po Mahina ʻUkulele and Guitars**, made by Big Island luthier Dennis Lake.
www.PoMahina.com

Mark Kailana Nelson

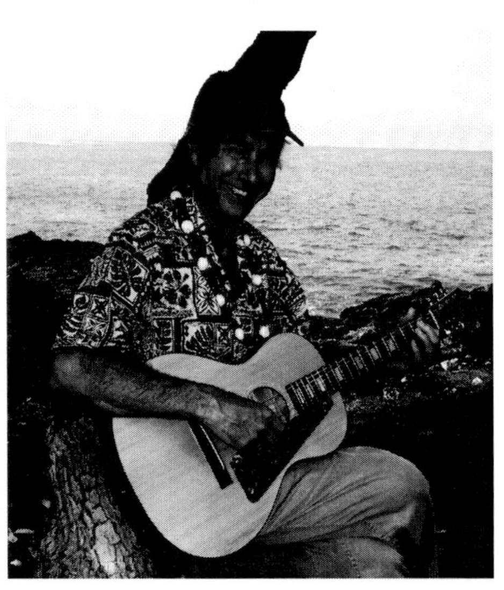

Multi-instrumentalist Mark Nelson has carved a unique niche for himself as an entertainer, musician and educator. His deep love and understanding of traditional music led him to the mastery of several different musical idioms, ranging from old time western music to Celtic to Hawaiian. In a career that began well before he was able to drive, he has performed everywhere from street corners to hay barns to festivals to the concert stage in the US, Europe and Canada. He once worked as a banjo playing gorilla in Dublin, but that's a different story.

Growing up near the beach in Southern California, Mark was surrounded by the music and culture of the Hawaiian Islands. His love of *kī hōʻalu*, slack key guitar, led him to travel to Hawaiʻi and study with some of the masters. Aunty Nona Beamer gave Mark his Hawaiian name, *Kailana* (Floating on the Sea).

Mark lives in Southern Oregon's Applegate Valley with his wife Annie and various furred and finned friends, where he divides his time between studio work, writing, and watching the trees grow.

Selected Discography

The Water Is Wide
Old Time Hawaiian Slack Key Guitar
Slack Key Style Ukulele
Aloha Hawaiian Slack Key Guitar (as "Uji Omaʻomaʻo." Allegro Records)
Ke Kukima Polinahe: Hawaiian and Polynesian Music for Appalachian Dulcimer
It Sounds So Sweet: Jug Band Music for Ukulele
Juke'n' the Uke: Blues, Ragtime & Hokum for Ukulele
Funtime Uke-A-Rama
Fiddle Tunes for Dulcimer: The Rights of Man
After the Morning
The Faery Hills
autumn...

Books

Learn to Play Hawaiian Slack Key Guitar
Old Time Hawaiian Slack Key Guitar
Ke Kukima Polinahe: Hawaiian and Polynesian Music for Appalachian Dulcimer
Learn to Play Slack Key Style Ukulele
It Sounds So Sweet: Jug Band Music for Ukulele
Juke'n' the Uke: Blues, Ragtime & Hokum for Ukulele
Mastering Ukulele Chord Inversions
Fingerstyle Duets for Ukulele
Favorite Old Time American Songs for Ukulele
Favorite Fingerstyle Solos for Ukulele
Learn to Play Fingerstyle Solos for Ukulele
The Complete Collection of Celtic Music for Appalachian Dulcimer
Favorite Old Time American Songs for Appalachian Dulcimer

Mark Nelson • Acme Arts
PO Box 967 • Jacksonville, OR 97530

www.Mark-o.com

Be sure to check out Mark's free on-line video lessons for dulcimer, ukulele and slack key guitar.